Praise for *Living the Life of Jewish Meditation*

"Rabbi Yoel Glick reveals the way *into* the inner sanctuary of your soul and avails you to learn to utilize your Divine Intuition and Wisdom; to dwell in the Home of the One. It is miraculous how the vastness of the Divine Wisdom can be funneled into 'light-bites' digestible to all. Rabbi Glick is such a miracle-maker!"

—**Reb Mimi Feigelson**, lecturer in Rabbinics and Chassidic Thought, American Jewish University

"Using the tools of meditation and the wisdom of ancient teachers, Rabbi Yoel Glick's written guidance enhanced my own meditation practice, deepening my inner life and further uplifting me toward the Divine."

—**Rabbi Elie Kaplan Spitz**, author, *Does the Soul Survive? A Jewish Journey to Belief in Afterlife, Past Lives & Living with Purpose*

"Despite all of the positive benefits of meditation, most of us struggle putting it into practice. Rabbi Glick offers the wise guidance you need to start or restart a regular meditation practice for a lifetime of spiritual mindfulness."

—**Edith Brotman, PhD, RYT-500**, yoga teacher and author, *Mussar Yoga: Blending an Ancient Jewish Spiritual Practice with Yoga to Transform Body and Soul*

"This is the most sensitive and complete book on Jewish meditation to date. Combining traditional Jewish sources with the wisdom of Indian teachers such as Ramakrishna and Ramana Maharshi, it shines a light on the similarities of meditation techniques and outcomes.... A wonderful book that is a necessity for every meditator's bookshelf."

—**Avram Davis**, founder and codirector, Chochmat HaLev; editor, *Meditation from the Heart of Judaism: Today's Teachers Share Their Practices, Techniques, and Faith*

"Rabbi Yoel Glick opens doors in our soul that connect us to the power and beauty of the Jewish tradition and the wider expanses and all-embracing love of a universal vision. His book offers clear practical guidance, profound experiential insights, and a whole range of inspiring practices to nurture the inner life of any spiritual seeker."

—**Rabbi Zalman Schachter-Shalomi** (*z"l*),
author, *Davening: A Guide to Meaningful Jewish Prayer*

"This book is an excellent guide for those who wish to more fully integrate meditation and spirituality into their lives. Grounded in the Jewish tradition, it includes understanding from other spiritual sources, making it an especially rich and wise resource for the seeker."

—**Nan Fink Gefen**, author,
Discovering Jewish Meditation: Instruction and Guidance for Learning an Ancient Spiritual Practice

"Theory, practice, example—it's all here. Rabbi Yoel Glick has woven various strands of meditation theory and practices into a tapestry we all can trace."

—**Swami Yogeshananda**, Trabuco Monastery;
former director of the Vedanta Center of Atlanta

"There are many wonderful books about meditation, but it is quite rare to find a book that understands meditation not merely as a practice we do to enhance our lives but also as a key to how we live the whole of our lives in connection with God and the holiness that is our true essence. [This book] dares to step out of the habits of insularity by drawing on Eastern wisdom to illuminate the mysteries hidden in traditional Jewish practice. Rabbi Glick has created a masterpiece of bold erudition and passion that is both beautiful and comprehensive."

—**Rabbi Shefa Gold**, author,
The Magic of Hebrew Chant: Healing the Spirit, Transforming the Mind, Deepening Love

"Savoring the beauty and clarity of each sentence in this book, one enters a spiritual space that deepens our awareness of God and transforms us into divine instruments. I recommend this gem of a book to readers of every religious background, who will be greatly enriched by the Jewish sources and meditation techniques not available elsewhere."

—**Dr. Maria Reis Habito**, Zen teacher,
Maria Kannon Zen Center;
international program director,
Taipei Museum of World Religions

"In this rich and detailed guide to meditation, Rabbi Yoel Glick offers the Jewish seeker—every seeker —instructions for building a life of meditation. On the way, he also invites us to meet our true selves, to nurture our souls and so ultimately live in service of the Holy One, our ultimate purpose on earth. How fortunate are we to have such a gentle, well versed and compelling guide."

—**Rabbi Jonathan P. Slater, DMin,** codirector of programs,
Institute for Jewish Spirituality; author,
*A Partner in Holiness: Deepening Mindfulness,
Practicing Compassion and Enriching Our Lives through the
Wisdom of R. Levi Yitzhak of Berdichev's* Kedushat Levi

"The goal of meditation is to control the thought waves of the mind and divert that one-pointed mind to God. Rabbi Yoel Glick explores various spiritual traditions along with his Jewish faith and points out that goal wonderfully."

—**Swami Chetanananda**, monk, Ramakrishna Order;
minister, Vedanta Society of St. Louis

"This is the best book I know of about meditation—Jewish or otherwise. Written with clarity and depth ... destined to become a classic."

—**Yossi Klein Halevi**, senior fellow,
Shalom Hartman Institute; author, *Like Dreamers*

Living the Life of Jewish Meditation

A Comprehensive Guide to Practice and Experience

Rabbi Yoel Glick

For People of All Faiths, All Backgrounds

JEWISH LIGHTS Publishing

Woodstock, Vermont

Living the Life of Jewish Meditation:
A Comprehensive Guide to Practice and Experience

2014 Quality Paperback Edition, First Printing

Library of Congress Cataloging-in-Publication Data
Glick, Yoel, 1954– author.
Living the life of Jewish meditation : a comprehensive guide to practice and experience / Rabbi Yoel Glick.
  pages cm
Includes bibliographical references and index.
ISBN 978-1-58023-802-1 (pbk.) — ISBN 978-1-58023-814-4 (ebook)
1. Meditation—Judaism. 2. Spiritual life—Judaism. I. Title.
BM723.G56 2014
296.7'2—dc23

2014020813

10 9 8 7 6 5 4 3 2 1

Manufactured in the United States of America
Interior design: Michael Myers
Cover art and design: Tim Holtz
Cover background image: © Janaka Dharmasena/ Shutterstock

For People of All Faiths, All Backgrounds
Jewish Lights Publishing
A Division of LongHill Partners, Inc.
Sunset Farm Offices, Route 4, P.O. Box 237
Woodstock, VT 05091
Tel: (802) 457-4000 Fax: (802) 457-4004
www.jewishlights.com

For Nomi—life partner, best friend,
and companion on the path

CONTENTS

PREFACE

My search for God began in my late teens, though my father would say that I always was a dreamer. It is true that the big questions of life have always interested me. However, it was not until I was nineteen that I began to see a connection between these inner questions and how we live our lives. That was an eye-opener for me! It never occurred to me that God, the soul, and our inner reality had anything to do with my everyday existence. When this insight dawned, it totally transformed my life.

This insight did not happen without a number of external factors coming into play. My search began in earnest at a time of crisis in my life. My mother was ill and dying. Our family structure and the reality I had known since childhood was falling apart.

At the same time, a powerful new presence entered into our family dynamic. The renowned singer, composer, and Hasidic master Rabbi Shlomo Carlebach married my father's youngest sister, Elaine, one of my favorite aunts. My mother's illness made me seek a new understanding and a stronger anchor to hold on to in my life. Reb Shlomo's teaching and music provided a powerful answer to my call.

In the world of the Carlebach *chevreh* (community) I found a spiritual home for my soul. His Hasidim were warm and open people. They were also searching for greater meaning and purpose in their lives. My Jewish day school education suddenly took on a whole other level of meaning and importance as I began to study the sacred texts of our tradition. The wisdom of the Talmud and the insights of the Hasidic rebbes filled me with excitement and exhilaration, fueling a new passion for learning and a commitment to practice.

Inspired by my new life, I decided to become a rabbi and went to Yeshiva University to study Talmud under the great Rabbi Joseph B. Soloveitchik and to earn my *semikhah*—rabbinic ordination. My relationship with Shlomo, who was now my guide and teacher, developed even further during this period of my life. Our bond became so strong that I asked him to also give me *semikhah* as a rabbi. Shlomo agreed, and I became the first student upon whom he bestowed ordination.

In 1981, my wife, Nomi, and I moved to the Old City of Jerusalem, where we started a center for Jewish studies called Hochmat Halev—the Wisdom of the Heart. The yeshiva provided religious education to both men and women and was revolutionary in its approach to learning and its emphasis on the spiritual life. I became the director of the center and taught classes in Talmud, *Chassidut* (Hasidic thought), and Jewish meditation. The center attracted a large following of students as well as a rich array of eclectic teachers as it grew and thrived.

In 1985–86, I began to question some of the premises of my life. I had many doubts about the path I was following and the teaching I was offering to others. In 1987, I decided that I needed to broaden my horizons and deepen my spiritual insight, to experience the truths that I was teaching on a different level. I closed the doors of Hochmat Halev, and in 1988, I moved to a little village in the south of France with Nomi and our two young sons, Adir and Navonel.

In France, I plunged into the exploration of the wisdom of other religions. I made contact with a number of spiritual communities, befriending monks, nuns, and other fellow seekers on the path. A swami whom I had become close to was my central guide and teacher during this phase of my journey. Under her guidance, I began to delve into my inner reality and learn the mysteries of the higher worlds. I also spent time in India, getting a firsthand taste of its spiritual dynamism and power. But more than anything else, I lived a contemplative life. I focused on my inner practice and worked to strengthen my understanding. I strove to intensify my experience of meditation and the process of inner awakening.

My life continued on in this fashion for twelve years. Then, on an autumn trip to Israel ten years ago, an old friend of mine asked if I would consider beginning to teach meditation again. I had led a meditation group as part of Hochmat Halev, but since then I had withdrawn from public life, working quietly with a few close students. My friend's words struck a chord inside me. The following year I formed a new meditation group in Jerusalem and began to fly back and forth to Israel three months of the year. I also started teaching and leading meditation workshops in North America.

My circle of students continued to grow and expand from year to year. Then on a recent trip to Israel, I was sitting in Jerusalem once again, discussing the tremendous rise of interest in meditation with another friend. As we spoke about the wonderful new books coming out on the subject, we realized that one book was still missing: a comprehensive guide to the *whole life* of meditation. This book would look at all the different stages of meditation and provide guidelines and techniques to follow for each phase. It would offer an in-depth analysis of the inner processes that occur during meditation. It would utilize the knowledge of the East to vitalize and illuminate traditional Jewish practices. It would present meditation as a path that connects us to the Higher Power—a spiritual practice that transforms our lives.

My friend urged me to write such a meditation manual. He felt that my own spiritual journey made me well suited for this task. He pointed out that I had a rich background and understanding of Judaism and Jewish sources, as well as a strong grasp of Eastern teaching and practice. I had studied the sources and lived the life. And I loved and appreciated both of these beautiful traditions.

The idea both inspired and frightened me. Who was I to write such a book? With some trepidation and a little awe, I set myself to the task.

In the end, working on *Living the Life of Jewish Meditation* has been both a gift and a blessing. It has lifted me beyond my own limitations and opened up new horizons in thought and experience. Now, I invite you to join me on this great adventure. Together we will explore the byways of the mind and the expanses of our consciousness. We will probe the secret worlds of our inner reality and climb the lofty heights of the spiritual realm. We will encounter the peace and stillness at the core of our being. We will learn how to live the life of Jewish meditation.

ACKNOWLEDGMENTS

*M*any people have helped bring this book to fruition. I am deeply grateful to all of them.

My father, Earl Glick, and my sister, Rani, have offered me their generous support. My wonderful sons, Adir and Navonel, have been an incredible source of help and encouragement throughout the process of writing this book. My dear friends Yossi and Sarah Halevi have shown their love and support in a whole host of ways. Reb Mimi Feigelson provided friendship and support and also helped with the translations. Rabbi Elie Spitz provided the great author photo for the book and the right words at an important time in the publishing process. Moriah Halevi contributed her beautiful drawing of the *sefirot*. Dov Elbaum provided the original impetus for this project. Dalia Landau convinced me to return to public teaching. Minna Amsel provided a home in Jerusalem for me to live in and work from. Sharon Laufer and Norman Enteen kept the fire burning through the years. Michelle Katz ran the workshops with me where many of the meditations in the book were first presented. Rabbi John Moscowitz offered space and support for the workshops at Holy Blossom Temple in Toronto. Dvora Mizrachi and Roxanne Bensaid read the manuscript and provided helpful insights and encouragement. Rabbi Yael Saidoff helped with the transliterations and offered her support, encouragement, and enthusiasm throughout the project.

Stuart M. Matlins believed in the book. He has been the best publisher an author could ask for. Emily Wichland and Rachel Shields have been terrific editors who have provided helpful guidance and suggestions all along the way. Barbara Heise, Kelly O'Neill, Leah Brewer, Tim Holtz, Amy Wilson, and all the rest of the friendly and professional staff at Jewish Lights have been a pleasure to work with.

My deep gratitude and reverence to Swami Chetanananda of the Vedanta Society of St. Louis, who has given me permission to use material from his books *How a Shepherd Boy Became a Saint*, *They Lived with God, God Lived with Them*, and *How to Live with God*.

Thanks to David Godman, for permission to use material from his books, *The Power of the Presence* series and *Be as You Are*.

Thanks to revered Swami Muktananda and Anandashram for permission to use the teachings of Swami Papa Ramdas and Mataji Krishnabai in *The Gospel of Swami Ramdas, Guru's Grace*, and *With the Divine Mother*.

And thanks to the Ramakrishna-Vivekananda Center of New York for permission to use quotations from *The Gospel of Sri Ramakrishna* as translated into the English by Swami Nikhilananda.

And finally, special thanks to my beloved wife, Nomi, who read every draft and worked on every word and chapter. Nomi contributed clarity, insight, and wisdom to the book, as well as many key passages and ideas. Without her help, love, and support, *Living the Life of Jewish Meditation* could never have been written.

The Path of Meditation

$\mathcal{M}$ editation is a marvelous and potent spiritual tool. It takes us on a voyage of spiritual discovery that leads us into our interior world. Meditation empowers us to transcend our material mind-set and touch That which is Infinite and Eternal. It brings us into the living presence of God.

Meditation aligns our heart and mind with our soul. It enables us to tap into the light, wisdom, and energy contained within us, so that it can flow freely into our consciousness. Meditation teaches us a higher perception and way of living. It creates a radical transformation in our awareness.

How Does Meditation Work?

Meditation achieves this goal through two major channels: the mind and the senses. Through the practice of meditation, sensation is transformed into intuition, and imagination is transformed into inspiration.

Our physical senses are like radar; they reach out to sense the world around us and then return to tell us what they have discovered. Their integrated input provides us with an impression of our external environment—its shape, color, feel, taste, and smell. From these impressions we determine what is pleasurable and what is unpleasant, what is desirable and what is not. Our senses are the means by which we assess the state of our reality.

Like our five senses, our spiritual intuition is an instrument that stretches out and touches the world around us. The intuition, however, uses the sensory apparatus of our soul to gather its information. This subtle faculty takes in the spiritual impressions that are emitted on higher levels and then creates a picture of the reality that the soul has revealed. It is this "soul reality" that we want to learn to feel and perceive.

Meditation teaches us how to move from our physical senses to our soul sense. It sensitizes us to the flow of subtle forces through our centers (see the explanation on pages xix–xx) and develops our awareness of our inner space. Meditation awakens us to the world of energies. It makes the spiritual realm come alive.

The mind is another channel through which meditation transforms our consciousness. There are two components to the mind—the lower mind and the higher mind. The lower mind is our logical reasoning mind. It is a finite instrument that categorizes, analyzes, and orders things into concrete forms. The higher mind is an expression of our divinity. It enables us to experience the inner reality. It enables us to tap into the Universal Mind of God.

The lower mind learns through experiment and observation of a material reality that is fleeting and always in flux; the higher mind gains wisdom by touching the timeless, boundless existence that lies behind all external forms. The lower mind is contracted and fixed; the higher mind is expansive and fluid. The lower mind sees in details and theoretical constructs; the higher mind perceives in patterns and the impressions of direct experience. The lower mind is about thinking; the higher mind is about being. The lower mind helps us to negotiate life on this earth; the higher mind enables us to travel into the heavens.

During meditation, we use the imaging power of the lower mind— our creative imagination—to create a space in which the higher mind can manifest. Through steady concentration, we gradually forge a link between the lower mind and the higher mind. Once we have learned how to contact our higher consciousness, then God takes over and transforms our mental imaginings into spiritual inspiration.

According to Rebbe Nachman of Breslov, the eighteenth-century Hasidic master who was known for his practice of constant conversation with God, the essence of the process of prayer is the movement from a narrow consciousness into an expanded consciousness—from the lower mind to the higher mind. This is also an excellent definition of meditation. Meditation is a process of infinite expansion that raises us into higher and higher states of awareness.[1]

A useful analogy for this process is Jacob's ladder from the Hebrew Bible (Genesis 28:10–17). In a dream, Jacob sees a ladder reaching from the earth to the heavens, with angels ascending and descending upon its rungs, and God looking down from above. Think of the ladder as the universe, stretching from the finite out to the Infinite. Each rung represents another state of consciousness along the continuum of being.

The medieval text *Olelot Efrayim* teaches that Jacob's vision is a paradigm for life on our physical plane of existence. This whole world is a ladder of ascension. Each life is an opportunity to take another step. We move from one incarnation to another, climbing from one rung to the next, until we reach the top of the ladder and enter into the glory of the divine embrace.[2]

Another viewpoint that helps to facilitate our understanding of the meditation process is to compare God's relationship with us to the relationship that we have with the cells in our body. There are trillions of cells in our body and a complex system of interrelated organisms that make up its parts. Yet we alone are the overriding consciousness that binds all these elements into a cohesive unity. We are the ones who direct the entire body and its actions.

Similarly, there is a great Divine Being who oversees our planet. Life and consciousness flow forth from this Great Being to infuse the earth. This life force courses through the hearts of all living creatures. This vast Mind encompasses the thoughts of everything that exists. We are all cells in the Body of God.

The same is true for the solar system, the galaxy, and the entire universe. Everything is overshadowed by God. Everything is imbued with Divine Consciousness. Everything is an expression of the One Life.

The principles of biofeedback teach us how to be aware of and interact with the living organisms that make up our body. Meditation teaches us how to link into the greater Body and Consciousness of which we are a part. The more we advance in our spiritual practice, the more refined our inner contacts will become, and the further we will penetrate into the mystery of the divine unity.

Through the power of meditation, we can transform emotion into intuition, and imagination into inspiration. We can lift our mind up into the limitless expanses of the spiritual realm.

What Are "Spiritual Centers"?

Besides implementing changes to our emotions and imagination, meditation performs one other important spiritual task. Meditation stimulates and refines our spiritual centers. According to the science of Yoga, a human being's physical body is underlain with a body of energy centers. These centers form a field of energy and light that infuse the physical body with life and consciousness. In Sanskrit these centers are called *chakras*.[3]

In the Kabbalah, the mystical teachings of Judaism, we find a similar description of a body of energy centers. Sometimes they are depicted as the limbs of a heavenly body, and sometimes they are portrayed as the trunk and branches of a celestial tree, *Etz haChayim*—the Tree of Life. In Hebrew, these energy centers are called *sefirot*, or spheres.[4]

These centers, or *sefirot*, have two major functions. First and foremost they are conduits for the passage of energy. Every living thing is composed of energy. There is a dynamic exchange of spiritual power flowing back and forth all the time. Everything is emanating and absorbing the life force at every single moment. Each *sefirah* is composed of a particular energy, and this energy is of a grosser or more refined nature depending on our state of evolution. Our goal in life is to develop our centers until they are composed of pure spiritual force. We then become effective conduits for the distribution of this refined energy into the greater world around us.

The second function of the centers, or *sefirot*, is to establish the nature of our consciousness. Each center has its own characteristic state of mind. Each *sefirah* is given a name that reflects the particular state that it embodies. There are many different gradients to the awareness that is evoked in each center. We determine the quality of the consciousness in our centers through the actions of our daily life and the intensity of our inner strivings.

Work on these centers is of an intricate and delicate nature. Think of each *sefirah* as a flower. The different petals of each *sefirah* need to be carefully opened for the harmony of our spiritual body to be maintained. The constant activity of ordinary life makes the adjustments and stimulation of our centers difficult. In meditation, the environment is calm, the body is still, and our mind is focused inward. Under these conditions, the subtle inner work can move ahead.

Meditation functions on many different levels. It stimulates our *sefirot*, or spiritual centers, aligns our personality with our soul, and builds a bridge between our lower and higher mind. Meditation enables us to transcend our physical consciousness and glimpse the Absolute. Different meditation techniques affect different aspects of these inner processes. All of the techniques empower us to shift our mind from the finite to the Infinite.

True meditation transforms the way we see reality. It changes the way we look at the world and at ourselves. Meditation generates an inner awakening that lifts us to a higher level of being. It touches the place inside us where a spark of the Eternal dwells. Meditation unites us with our true Self.

Why Jewish Meditation?

Just as no two people are the same, no two souls are identical. Souls come from diverse spiritual sources. In the *Ein Sof* (the Absolute) all is one, but outside of this higher reality, which is beyond all words and concepts, numerous levels of being exist.

The Kabbalah speaks of the "Holy Apple Field," a celestial garden where all the souls of humanity are planted. There are many different trees in this garden, and each tree represents a separate collection of souls.

In the Kabbalistic imagery, the tree is upside down, with its roots planted in the heavens and its trunk and branches dangling down through the worlds. Each individual tree is a supernal source, with many roots, branches, and leaves that extend from it. We all represent an individual element on one of these trees.

Just as each leaf and branch has its own particular character, so it is with the souls who make up the body of these celestial trees. Every soul has its unique quality and spiritual emanation. Every soul has its own special beauty. Every soul shines with radiant divine glory.

For those of us who are Jewish, the Tree of Israel is our natural abode. We are each a leaf or branch on the tree. Our individual coloring and shape are a reflection of the tree's character, a small expression of the atmosphere in our spiritual home.

It is easy for us to follow the line of our own soul root—to connect ourselves to the sacred tree from which we have come. If we are an oak leaf, there would be no point trying to attach ourselves to a palm tree. If we are a branch from a conifer tree, there would be no way that we could survive in the cactus's desert environment. It makes sense for us to follow our native soul path. That way we will receive the nutrients, soil, and shade that we need. We will obtain the right stimulus to blossom and grow.

When we pray or meditate using a Jewish practice or ritual, we connect ourselves to *Knesset Yisrael*, the Soul of Israel. This Soul is a vast collective that stretches way up into the higher worlds of the Kingdom of Heaven. The Soul of Israel is composed of all those who have incarnated over the millennia as part of the people of Israel: the Patriarchs and Matriarchs, the prophets, the holy rabbis and teachers throughout the generations, the souls who stood at Mount Sinai, and the six million who perished in the Holocaust. It includes all those who have shared in the mission and destiny of Israel.

This is the true Israel to which we belong. The Israel that we perceive in this physical reality is just a minute expression of this immense Soul. It is the outermost manifestation of its divine essence, the lowest vehicle for this mighty spiritual force.

When we link ourselves to the higher Israel, we harness the tremendous spiritual power of the exalted souls who live on the celestial planes. We draw on the strength and inspiration of their overshadowing presence. Enfolded in their loving embrace, we receive the energy and faith to overcome all obstacles and the wisdom to face any crisis. Joined to this majestic Soul, we can accomplish almost anything.

Each larger Soul has its own spiritual vibration. Each has its own energy and character. The Soul of Israel resonates with a specific rhythm. That inner rhythm is embodied in the teachings and traditions of the Jewish religion.

When we use the images and rituals of Judaism in our spiritual practice, we send out an energy signal that reverberates within the Soul of Israel. This spiritual pulsation merges into the stream of energy and consciousness at the heart of the Soul and ascends swiftly toward its Source.

The power of this energetic vibration draws our own being upward into the spiritual vortex of the Soul. It binds us to those who live on higher planes. It lifts us up onto their shoulders and carries us toward the Absolute.

When we follow the path of our own Soul, we swim with the current of the supernal river. We immerse ourselves in the upward flow of the heavenly waters. We align with the Soul's energy and consciousness. We become part of its divine purpose and mission.

At the same time, whenever we meditate, we carry with us our dual identities as members of the Jewish people and members of the human race. Judaism is the language that we use, the particular garment that we wear, but the goal is the same for every human being: we are all seeking God. We are searching for our higher home.

There is only one God with many names. All of humanity is part of the divine spiritual body. We all have a place in the Holy Apple Field—in God's celestial garden. We all have a role in God's Eternal Plan.

There are many planes in the cosmic vastness. The existence of separate religions ascends through planes well beyond our own. But in the higher reaches of the Kingdom of Heaven, all sense of distinction disappears, and the whole notion of separateness is transcended. In that sublime place, religion has no meaning at all.

This book will teach you how to meditate as a Jew. It will use the rituals, wisdom, and imagery of Judaism to take you toward the Holy One of Israel. But once you have arrived on the divine doorstep, then all the outer trappings fall away, and you become a simple human soul standing naked before the Indescribable and Unknowable Reality.

Silence and Words

"Silence is very beautiful, because in silence one can contemplate the greatness of God and bind oneself to God more than one can bind oneself through speech."

—Baal Shem Tov[5]

There is a path of silence and a path of words. Words are powerful and creative; but God is revealed in the silence, in the *kol demamah dakah*— the still, small voice.

Silence is a means of direct soul-to-soul contact that transcends the misunderstandings and arguments that arise out of verbal communication. Silence turns us inward. In silence, we remain in intimate contact with our surroundings and ourselves. We rest in a state of inner clarity, an alert witness to the actions and feelings of everyone and everything around us.

The Baal Shem Tov was an eighteenth-century Jewish mystic who is esteemed as the founder of Hasidism. He was known for his ecstatic prayer and innovative spiritual teachings. The Baal Shem offers a novel interpretation of the Rabbinic saying in Ethics of the Fathers (*Pirkei Avot*) 3:13, "A fence for wisdom is silence." When we are silent, he explains, we can reach beyond the world of speech and thought and join ourselves to the world of wisdom from which all thought originates. Through silence we know a thing not by analysis or formulation, but by direct contact with its essence in the Mind of God.

The path of silence is about creating a space where the Divine can enter. We remove the lower self and make a place for the higher Self. We empty ourselves of all speech, thought, and feeling and find the One True Existence in the stillness that remains.

Silence is central to meditation. It is only by learning to quiet the mind and enter the place of inner silence that our meditation will become potent and alive. The path of silence has tremendous power. Silence leads us to the Supreme Consciousness. In silence, we go straight back to the Source of our being and meet the living God that is there.

The Baal Shem saw prayer as a progression from words into silence: we move from words to sounds to thought, and finally to the silence of Nothingness. Though both the path of words and the path of silence will take us toward God, ultimately the Eternal One is found only in the stillness of interior silence. The Hebrew Bible makes this truth explicit for us in the story of Elijah's experience on Mount Horeb (1 Kings 19:1–12).

Elijah set out for Mount Horeb in search of the Almighty. Seating himself in a secluded cave, he plunged inward in meditation. It was not long before the images in his inner reality came alive. First, he experienced a howling wind that broke upon the mountain, then a powerful earthquake that shook the ground around him, and finally a raging fire that filled his cave. But, the *Tanakh* (Hebrew Bible) tells us, the Divine Spirit was not in the wind, nor in the earthquake, nor in the fire, but in the "still, small voice" that came afterward and resounded in the very depth of Elijah's being.

The story of Elijah's encounter with God on Mount Horeb makes clear that meditation and silence were once an integral part of our practice. Over the millennia, however, Judaism has become a religion of many words and sounds. Today, there is a renewed interest in meditation. A growing number of books and teachers are engaged in the flowering of Jewish meditation techniques. Meditation has the potential to again become an important catalyst in the development of Judaism. For this to happen, we need to once more forge a place for silence in our religion.

We accomplish this goal by shifting the Jewish community away from speech, argument, and social interaction to contemplation, reflection, and silence. We attune ourselves to stillness, learn to look inward instead of outward. We habituate ourselves to listen for the inner voice and look for the higher vision.

It is essential for our approach to meditation to be simple and direct. We want to focus our practice on inner experience rather than manipulations of the mind, to cultivate serenity and silence while we seek out the living presence of God.

There is a lot we can learn in this regard from the Eastern religions. The East has thousands of years of unbroken meditation practice. Inner silence is an integral part of their religious life. Hinduism and Buddhism have developed the art of meditation into a spiritual science. This science provides clear principles and disciplines that deepen and advance the practice of meditation.

Throughout this book, I will draw on Eastern sources and make parallels between the Hindu, Buddhist, and Jewish traditions. I will make use of the wisdom of the East to shed light on Jewish teaching and practices—to vitalize and illuminate them in whole new ways. Together, we will learn how to tap into the reservoir of divine silence contained within our tradition and unleash its spiritual power into our lives.

The Stages of Meditation

When we speak about entering the path of meditation, we mean more than just the act of sitting for thirty to forty-five minutes and looking inward. Meditation is a way of life. Learning how to live that life encompasses a whole range of issues and disciplines.

The path of meditation has five stages: preparation, intention, forging a connection, holding the link, and merging with our spiritual source. These five stages can be summarized as follows:

1. **Preparation:** We prepare for meditation on a number of different levels: the physical, emotional, mental, and spiritual or energetic levels. The different religious traditions supply us with a range of methods that facilitate our preparation.

2. **Intention:** Intention plays a vital role in our meditation. The intention with which we sit down to meditate is the spiritual force that drives our practice. Our intention transforms this spiritual discipline from a dry mental exercise into a living evocation of God.

3. **Forge:** The central purpose of meditation is to forge a living connection with God, our soul—our true Self. There are five main categories of technique that we use in this process: stilling the mind, visualization, concentration, mantra chanting, and contemplation. Each of these techniques is a different form of meditation. Each method adds another melody to our spiritual repertoire.

4. **Hold:** Many people who practice meditation for an extended period of time have some kind of meaningful inner experience. However, the experience in itself is not enough. The challenge is to learn how to hold on to that which we have received—both inside and outside of the meditation room.

5. **Merge:** What occurs when we reach the level of union with God? And what are the indicators that tell us we have established a strong and lasting connection with our soul? This section will explain the spiritual dynamics of union and outline the signs that reveal that we have attained the ultimate goal.

As mentioned in the preface, this book provides a complete guide to the meditative life. It outlines the challenges that you will face at each stage and suggests practical advice on how to surmount those challenges. It highlights the spiritual opportunities that meditation places before you and offers guidance on how to make the most of those openings. It shows you how to protect yourself from danger as you enter into your inner reality.

To effectively accomplish this goal, the book has been divided into four parts. Part 1 deals with the fundamentals of daily meditation. This section lays the foundation for your practice. It is upon the rock of your day-to-day sittings that your spiritual life will either flourish or flounder. A solid routine will vitalize the whole of your existence and make your inner reality come alive. This crucial work involves the first three stages of the meditation process: preparation, intention, and forging a connection.

Part 2 gets down to the concrete business of meditation. It explores the nature of each of the five major types of meditation techniques—stilling the mind, visualization, concentration, mantra recitation, and contemplation—and explains the different aspects of their implementation. Most importantly, this section offers specific practices for the various types of meditation. Each practice is described in great detail, with step-by-step instructions. In total, there are nineteen different meditations in this second part. To facilitate easy access to the meditations, there is a full index of practices at the end of the book. In addition, audio recordings of all the meditations are available through the website ww.daatelyon.org.

Part 3 looks at the larger picture. It delves into the question of how we deepen our spiritual commitment and learn to live in constant communion with God. This noble endeavor involves the final two stages of the meditation process: holding the link and merging with our spiritual source. These decisive stages transform our meditation from a formal discipline into a way of life. They enable us to transcend the limitations of physical consciousness and enter into the expanses of the higher reality.

The first three parts focus on the five stages of the meditation process. They form the heart of the book. Part 4 investigates some of the broader issues that are not addressed elsewhere: the personal and impersonal approach to God, the inner dynamics of meditation, the dangers of psychic phenomena and powers, the advantages and disadvantages of individual and group meditation, and the relationship between personal and collective evolution.

The four parts, taken together, supply all of the information that you need to meditate. There are different ways to use this information. You can begin at the beginning and go through all of the stages from preparation to merging. However, if this seems daunting, you can simply go to the techniques section of the book (part 2) and start to meditate. You can then refer to the other sections afterward as you progress with your daily routine, or you can dip into them from time to time. You will gain from the book using either approach.

The life of meditation is a multifaceted and complex enterprise. Discovering the right balance among the various elements is an ongoing challenge. Each one of us has our own particular combination of spiritual disciplines that will make up our routine. The secret is to establish a regular practice but to be open to changing circumstances and evolving needs—and, as we meditate, to constantly ask God to bestow abundant blessing upon our voyage of the spirit.

A NOTE ON LANGUAGE

*W*riting a book that incorporates quotations and translations from a variety of different periods, cultures, and religions presents many challenges to the author. A whole range of questions and decisions need to be made about how to use these different sources and styles. Sometimes, opposing imperatives need to be carefully balanced. I tried my best to perform this writer's "juggling act" with wisdom, sensitivity, and poise. In the end, I believe that I have delivered a prose that is clear, relevant, and meaningful, without sacrificing the accuracy or authenticity of the teaching. Here are some of the decisions that I made along the way.

All the translations of the Hasidic, Kabbalistic, and Rabbinic texts are my own, unless otherwise indicated. All biblical quotations, unless otherwise indicated, are adapted from the 1917 version of the JPS Hebrew Bible. Although I love the poetry and nobility of the 1917 translation, I have adapted certain parts of the archaic language to make the passages more accessible to the modern reader.

In order to present each thinker with integrity, I have retained the original male gender bias in all of my translations and quotations, including the biblical passages. My own writing follows a gender-free style, except when specifically indicated by the subject matter.

In terms of the transliteration of the Hebrew, I have followed the *Encyclopaedia Judaica* general transliteration guidelines. However, for technical reasons, I have used *ch* for the letter *chet* instead of *h* with a subdot, and *tz* for the letter *tzadi*, instead of *z* with a subdot. Also, I have diverged from the *Encyclopaedia Judaica* guidelines in cases where a different form is in common usage, such as "Hasid," "Sephardic," and "*Knesset Yisrael.*" In these cases, I have used the common spelling instead. I believe this approach provides a greater ease of reading.

A simplified guide to pronounciation of the Hebrew transliteration can be found at the end of the book. Though helpful for Hebrew terms throughout the book, the guide is primarily meant for use in conjunction with chanting the mantras in the techniques section.

In Sanskrit terms, I have used the spelling or transliteration as it appeared in the Hindu sources that I used. I apologize to my more knowledgeable readers for any inaccuracies that might have occurred in this regard.

PART ONE

The Fundamentals of Daily Practice

*T*he center point of the meditative life is our daily meditation practice. In this first part of the book, we explore the first three stages of the meditation process: preparation, intention, and forging a connection. These three stages form the basis for our encounter with God. They enable us to contact our true Self and become aware of the living presence of the Divine that dwells within each of us. Mastering these three fundamentals is the key to serious spiritual progress.

The manner in which we begin our practice sets the tone for the whole endeavor, so it is essential to prepare well for meditation. Once we have prepared, we need to focus our mind in the right direction. We accomplish this task by forming a clear intention of our goals. Prepared and focused, we then concentrate our energies on building an inner connection. Following a technique that suits our temperament and skills, we sit down and enter into our inner reality.

Let us begin our journey into the wondrous world of meditation.

CHAPTER ONE

PREPARATION

Readying the Body, Heart, and Mind for Meditation

> "And the Lord said to Moses: 'Speak to Aaron your brother, that he come not at all times into the holy place within the veil, before the ark-cover that is upon the Ark; that he die not; for I appear in the cloud upon the ark-cover. Thus shall Aaron come into the holy place.... He shall put on the holy linen tunic, and he shall have the linen breeches upon his flesh, and shall be girded with the linen girdle, and with the linen miter shall he be attired; they are sacred garments; and he shall bathe his body in water, and put them on.'"
>
> —Leviticus 16:2–4

*H*ow do we prepare to approach God? How do we ready ourselves to contact the Higher Power?

There are two levels to this process. On one level, we prepare to approach God during every moment of our lives. As Rebbe Elimelekh of Lizhensk, one of the great early leaders of the Hasidic movement, teaches:

> If a person guards himself every day from negative matters—from flattery, lies, laziness, anger, pride, hate, competitiveness, and all other matters that undermine his devotions—and occupies himself with Torah study, good deeds (*gemilut chasadim*), and

3

> spiritually positive acts (mitzvot), then when he comes to pray, all
> the different aspects of the mitzvot that he has done will bestow
> upon him a "lovely fragrance" during his prayers, like the spices
> that give a good fragrance to a cooked dish.[1]

We prime ourselves for our divine encounter by walking mindfully through our day, by working on ourselves, by striving to transform our character, by practicing the constant remembrance of God. This is the first level of readying ourselves.

The second level of preparation consists of the specific actions that we undertake before we begin to meditate. These various methods put us into the proper frame of mind. They move us out of our mundane physical existence and enable us to approach the Creator of all life. This second level of preparation will be the focus of this first chapter of the book.

An Appointment with Our Beloved

The mind-set in which we approach our meditation is of the utmost importance. Our daily meditation is an appointment with our Beloved. We meet each other at the same time and in the same place for a few minutes of precious intimacy every day.

Our Beloved, of course, is God. Our meditation is an appointment with God. We can be sure that the One Who Is Pure Love will always be there. We should not leave our Beloved waiting. And most certainly we should never miss our divine date. We use whatever aids will help us to get ready for our sacred appointment.

The Jewish sources on prayer have a lot to offer us in this regard. Traditionally, Jews have an obligation to pray three times a day—morning, afternoon, and evening. Learning how to prepare for prayer is a very important part of Jewish devotion. The Talmud tells us that the *chasidim rishonim*—the pious individuals in Talmudic times—would wait for an hour (*shoheh*) before they began their prayers. What this *shoheh* was is not exactly clear; it might have been a period of meditation or self-reflection, or maybe they simply sat in silence. Whatever form this period took, it was certainly a time of spiritual preparation.

An hour of preparation is a very serious commitment. It emphasizes the fact that setting the groundwork for spiritual practice is as important as the practice itself. This is a key principle in approaching God. We cannot expect our spiritual practice to be fruitful if we jump directly from involvement in mundane activities into prayer or meditation. We need to ready ourselves. We need to build a bridge between our outer life and our inner life.

This bridge is composed out of a number of elements. There are physical, emotional, mental, and spiritual components to this work. All the different dimensions of our being need to be aligned before we come before God. Without proper labor on all these levels, our meditation is unlikely to bear fruit. Let us take a look at each of these areas individually.

Physical Preparation

Preparing ourselves physically has two components: cleanliness of the body and the manner in which we dress.

Bathing: Cleansing the Body

Physical cleanliness is important for a few reasons. Cleanliness is a sign of respect and humility before God. In addition, it washes away our negative energy and emotions and helps to clear the mind.

We can wash ourselves in the shower, or we can undergo a ritual immersion. In Judaism, Hasidim and Kabbalists immerse themselves in a ritual bath called a mikvah. A mikvah must have a natural source of water, either a body of flowing water or water that has been gathered from rainfall. Special prayers are said as the seekers immerse themselves in the mikvah.

One practice is to immerse in the water seven times. During the first three immersions, we focus on the purification of our body, mind, and heart, respectively.

While completing the last four immersions, we concentrate on each of the four letters of the Divine Name: *Yud Heh Vav Heh* יהוה.[2]

Ritual immersion is a common practice in Hinduism as well. A traditional Hindu would never think of entering a temple before bathing. Cleansing the body also plays a role in Islam. Traditional Muslims wash their face, hands, arms, and feet before each of the five daily prayers.[3] And in Christianity, immersion in water is regarded as a symbol of spiritual rebirth.

Ritual immersion adds a higher dimension to the physical act of cleansing. It raises the act from the mundane to the sacred. Yet at the same time it serves the practical purpose of cleansing the body and wipes away any negative thoughts and energy.

Even if we cannot bathe our whole body before meditation, we should at least wash our hands and face. Washing the face clears the mind and eliminates some of the energetic residue of our outer life. It is also a symbolic expression of our desire to purify ourselves before beginning our spiritual practice.

Dress: How Should We Appear Before God?

The manner in which we dress when we approach God can transform our practice. On one level, it is a matter of showing respect. If we were going to meet the president or prime minister, would we not make an effort to look our best? How much more so when we are about to meet the Sovereign of sovereigns! On another level, it is a way of raising our consciousness.

In many religions, there are special garments that are worn during worship or prayer. In the ancient Temple in Jerusalem, the priests dressed in elaborate garments before they began the worship. Christian priests have continued this practice, wearing a series of vestments that parallel the clothing of the Temple priests.

In traditional Judaism, we cover our heads when praying. During morning prayers, we wear a tallit (prayer shawl) and put on tefillin (phylacteries)—little black boxes with leather straps containing parchments with sacred prayers that are bound on the arm and head. The head covering, or *kippah*, is a sign of humility before the Creator of all life. It also represents *keter,* the crown center, and the energy of the will of God. The prayer shawl signifies that we are surrounded during prayer by divine light and protection. The tefillin remind us to keep our heart and mind on the Most High at all times.

Over time these ritual garments become spiritually charged. The very act of putting them on lifts our mind and gives us a boost of energy. The garments help to shift our mental space into a state of holiness. They act to set aside the time of prayer and meditation as something that is precious and sacred.

Yet how we dress during our practice is a matter of individual choice. Some people like to wear special clothes for meditation. They find that the change of clothing helps them move into a more spiritual space. Other people feel that formal garments interfere with their connection. They prefer to dress comfortably and focus on what is happening in their hearts. Neither approach is superior. Any way of dressing during meditation is acceptable. It all depends on what works for us.

Whichever way we dress, however, our clothes should always be clean and comfortable. This enables us to concentrate our attention on the inner work. Clean clothes allow the energy to flow freely, while dirty clothes carry the energy of the world of outer activity. Their vibration impedes our entrance into a higher state of awareness.

Exercise: A Limber Body Enables Us to Concentrate on the Soul

Another aspect of physical preparation is the condition of the body itself. This is particularly so with respect to meditation. We want to feel comfortable and at ease while meditating. Therefore, many people do some form of exercise before practice. This exercise can take the form of stretching or yoga postures. It can also be a quiet walk in the woods. The purpose of the physical activity is to limber up the body before sitting. This makes sure that it is flowing and relaxed during meditation. It prepares the body for the time of stillness that lies ahead.

Posture: What Is the Right Position for Meditation?

There are a number of different positions we can assume for meditation. The full or half lotus yoga posture is ideal. This posture provides our body with solid balance and facilitates the flow of energy in our spiritual centers. Simply sitting in a cross-legged position is also acceptable. Alternatively, we can use the Zen posture of sitting with the legs bent at the knees and tucked under us. Many Westerners, however, find these Eastern positions difficult to sustain for an extended period of time. If this is the case, we can also sit on a straight-backed chair. The most important issues are to keep our back relatively straight and to find a comfortable position that we can maintain for the whole meditation.

Emotional Preparation: Balancing Calmness and Devotion as We Approach God

The next level of preparation is the work of aligning our emotions. We want our emotional self to be calm and clear. Too much turbulence will break the spiritual connection, much as static interrupts the clear reception of sound from a radio. Like our body, our mind and heart need to be free of any impediment.

Rebbe Elimelekh of Lizhensk teaches:

> Before praying, a person needs to purify his thoughts to make sure they are without anything that is repulsive or disgusting, and examine his actions. And if he has sinned, he needs to do wholehearted *teshuvah* (repentance), so that his prayers will be able to ascend without any separating barrier or veil, just clear and pure, without any blemish whatsoever.[4]

The Hasidic text *Ma'ayan haChokhmah* provides us with the reason for this act of *teshuvah*. Each of the Hebrew letters in the prayers, the text explains, possesses an inner divine "livingness." When we think negative thoughts, use base language, or do evil deeds, it affects the power or energy of the letters. As a result, instead of becoming exalted words that lift us to God, these letters form into impure or distracting thoughts that disturb our prayers.[5] Therefore, Rebbe Elimelekh recommends that we undergo a process of *teshuvah* or self-examination before we begin our practice. This introspection will wipe our hearts clean, so that we can approach our prayers with a refined state of being. The same principle can be applied to the images that we visualize in meditation. If our mind has a lower vibration, it will interfere with our image-making faculty. The images will lack spiritual power and will quickly lose their form.

Teshuvah is one way of cleansing our emotions. The sixteenth-century Kabbalist Rabbi Yitzchak Luria, who was the central figure of the Safed circle of mystics and who is commonly known as the Ari, offers a totally different approach to this spiritual task. He suggests that before beginning our prayers, we first take upon ourselves the commandment to "love your neighbor as yourself" (Leviticus 19:18). Focusing on this commandment will open our heart wide with love for others. This love, in turn, will wash away any negative emotional residue that remains inside us.[6]

In a similar fashion, Rebbe Nachman of Breslov instructed his Hasidim to donate a small sum to charity before prayers. Giving charity is another way to unlock the heart. It awakens the innate compassion within us and opens the door for God's light to shine in.[7]

A third option is to recite a few words of prayer asking for God's help in calming and steadying our emotions before we begin our practice. Here is an example of such a prayer composed by the Hasidic rebbe Avraham of Trisk:

> Master of the World, it is revealed and known before You that I want to serve You in truth, but what can I do, since You have imposed upon me a huge evil inclination that confuses my mind and heart and prevents me from serving You. Therefore, have compassion upon my soul and help me to overcome it [my evil inclination], and speak words of truth before You.[8]

This prayer is an appeal to God to sweep away the confusion in our hearts created by all the worries and desires of the ego. It is a plea for divine help in rising above our lower self during meditation.

Mental Preparation: Creating a Mind That Is Clear and Focused

As was mentioned at the beginning of this section, the *chasidim rishonim* would prepare for an hour before starting their prayers. Rebbe Elimelekh of Lizhensk asserts, "Their intention was to refine and purify their thoughts and bind themselves to the supernal worlds until they were close to transcending body consciousness."[9]

Transcending body consciousness is the highest form of meditation experience. The key to achieving this experience is purifying the mind. All forms of preparation are meant to aid us in quieting the mind and focusing it inward. Only in this way can we transcend physical awareness and enter into the reality of the supernal realm. How do we achieve this mental calm and clarity?

Rebbe Nachman of Breslov suggests that we can silence the mind by evoking a sense of awe, or *yirah*. *Yirah* is expressed by resting in God and accepting that the All-Encompassing One is in control of everything. This attitude gives us peace of mind and allows us to pray with full intention. Through the experience of awe, we create harmony between soul and body, between heart and mind. This inner serenity enables us to pray with full awareness and intention. It arouses a feeling of peace and well-being. It fosters a strong spiritual connection with the higher worlds.[10] A sense of awe helps us to concentrate.

When we experience God's living presence, we immediately become intensely focused. Nothing can disturb or distract our mind. Total concentration leads us to inner stillness. It is the gateway to a pure and serene consciousness.

Study is another way we can ready our minds for spiritual practice. Reading a spiritual book for a few minutes before meditation will raise our spiritual vibration. Resonating with a higher state of awareness, we will be able to plunge inward with greater ease. Rebbe Natan of Nemirov, the premier disciple of Rebbe Nachman of Breslov, suggests that we rise before first light and spend some time in Torah study. Study in the early hours illuminates our mind and brings it alive with God's living presence. From this place of heightened awareness, our prayers will be more real.[11]

Another form of training is to take some time before and after practice to reflect on our present spiritual state—to look at where our mind is right now and where we want it to be. Rebbe Levi Yitzchak of Berditchev, another great teacher of the early Hasidic movement who was known for his love of God and the Jewish people, speaks poignantly on this subject:

> It is fitting that every person should consider before each prayer how many angels, *ofanim* and *chayot* there are, and they all are calling out to each other, "Where is the place of His glory, etc.?" And [by contrast] let your ears hear what is coming out of your [own] mouth. And they [the angels] "are all filled with love etc., and all do the will of their Maker in fear and awe." And it would be fitting for him to tremble in all of his limbs when he stands before such a great King as this. And also after prayers, he should reflect upon how he allows his heart to speak about worthless things, and to [even] enjoy them, when just a moment before, "I was speaking before a great and awesome King," and, in particular, that he will soon be speaking before Him again in the future. And the glory of the Holy One, blessed be He, fills the whole world.[12]

Whether we engage in any of these mental exercises or not, it is essential that we banish the concerns of ordinary life before we sit down to meditate. If we cannot eradicate them completely from our minds, we can at least attempt to place our worries on a mental "shelf" for the period of our meditation. We mentally give them over to God's care for the time being and then begin to meditate.

Routines: The Habits of a Meditative Life

Preparation work is not only the domain of the novice meditator. Priming ourselves for practice is as much a concern of the longtime meditator as it is for the beginner. There is always a need to refresh and reestablish our spiritual habits. The better we lay the groundwork, the more easily we will enter into meditation.

It is not necessary to do all of the different routines described above. We can pick those disciplines that work for us and be consistent in performing them, or we can use all the various practices at different times. We can change our preparations, depending on how we feel and on the time and circumstances available to us. The crucial issue is to create a routine that awakens our inner awareness and facilitates our entry into a meditative state.

Space: Creating a Divine Sanctuary

"Make me a sanctuary and I will dwell therein."

—Exodus 25:8

We each have a divine call to prepare a place for God in our lives. In one aspect, this "place for God" is built in our hearts and minds. Success in meditation requires steady practice on a daily basis. The more we sit, the more easily we will be able to enter into a meditative state. Every sitting is another brick added to the temple. If we lay a brick every day, our temple will gradually take form.

In another aspect, this divine sanctuary is a physical space where we seek our innermost being. The space we use for meditation will powerfully impact our practice. When we meditate, we need a spot that is clean and clear of clutter. We need a place that is quiet and serene—a separate room or a partitioned section of a room. There needs to be a minimum of distractions in a meditation room—no one entering or leaving, no one engaged in any other activities. Meditation demands silence and stillness. Movement and activity will break our focused ascent and block the proper flow of energy. The only activity that should be taking place in this space is the inner work of meditation.

Daily meditation in the same place builds up a strong spiritual atmosphere. A reservoir of energy infuses the spot, a sense of familiarity and "at homeness" greets us whenever we enter our sacred space. We feel a resonance and ease in our room. We are not entering into a strange house but arriving home. At home, everything is welcoming. Everything feels right and in its place. Our sacred space becomes a spiritual abode where every object is as we want it to be, where every component of the space prepares us for the encounter with our soul.

How do we create a sacred space? How does a spot become holy? When Moses meets God at the burning bush, the first thing that the Unknowable One tells him is, "Take off your sandals from your feet, for the place where you are standing is holy ground" (Exodus 3:5). The first principle in creating sacred space is to treat the physical site as holy. When a place is set apart and treated with reverence, this gives it honor and dignity and immediately changes our relationship to the space. We enter it with a different mind-set and a different emotion.

The halakhic (legal) sources are very vocal on this point. The *Shulchan Arukh*, the authoritative legal text for Orthodox Jews, declares that there should be no *kalut rosh*, no "light-headedness," in a synagogue: no joking or ridiculing or mocking, no frivolous talk, no conversation about mundane affairs, no eating and drinking, no grooming or adorning ourselves, no wandering around or loitering about, no engaging in business.[13] All of these principles can be applied to our private meditation area.

In a sacred space, not only is what we do and say important, but also what we *think* will affect the environment. Our meditation room is more than a simple gathering point for meditation; it is a place of profound contemplation, a location where we encounter God. Inappropriate thoughts will disturb the sacred atmosphere that permeates this holy space.

The Temple in ancient Jerusalem represents the ideal sacred space. One of the names for the Temple was *Sukkat Shalom* (Shelter of Peace). This was because the pilgrims who came to the Temple found peace from their worries within the shelter of its walls. The Temple was a place whose very atmosphere emanated peace. The Hebrew word for "peace," *shalom,* comes from the word *shalem*, "whole" or "complete." When there is peace, there is a sense of rightness to all the elements of life. Each piece fits perfectly into place. When there is balance and harmony in an environment, it naturally evokes the energy of peace.

In Zen Buddhism, the physical arrangement of the environment plays a central role in creating sacred space. In a Zen temple, the emphasis is on harmony. The placement of every object is carefully thought out. The balance of everything in the temple and in the surrounding courtyard and gardens is vital to the formation of this sacred space. Every rock, every tree, every piece of furniture is part of the creation of an overall feeling of peace and tranquility.

There is a plane in the higher worlds where all is harmony, where everything is at peace. In creating our own sacred space, we are striving to make our surroundings correspond, in as great a measure as possible, to the nature of this plane. The sacred space acts as a key to unlock the door to this heavenly realm. In that moment, we get a glimpse of the true reality that underlies this material existence. In that moment, our spiritual centers, or *chakras*, open up, and the energy of peace comes flooding in.

The Temple was a location that was simultaneously in this world and on a higher plane. When pilgrims entered the Temple, they lost their earthbound state of mind and were lifted up into the celestial reality. In that altered state of being, all of their troubles and cares suddenly dropped away, and a feeling of joy and great peace arose in their place. We want to create an atmosphere that will awaken a similar experience in our meditation room.

The book of the *Zohar*, the central text of Jewish mysticism, teaches:

> A synagogue should be a handsome structure, beautifully decorated, for it is an earthly copy of a heavenly prototype. The Temple below had its counterpart in the Temple above, and everything there, holy vessels and holy ministers, corresponded to something above. The same was true of the Tabernacle that Moses constructed in the desert. And a synagogue must have the same object: it must be a true house of prayer.[14]

The need for harmony does not mean that a sacred space has to be simple. It can also be highly decorated. In this case, the decoration is carefully chosen to raise our inner vibration. Infusing a sense of physical and spiritual beauty into our meditation room is an essential component of this process. Our mind should be uplifted when we enter the space and drawn to think of God and eternal questions. The energy of our dedicated area should dispel all thought of the outside world; it should calm our minds and soothe our hearts. A holy place provides us with a refuge that washes away the tensions of our physical reality and brings us a peace that is not of this world.

> Rabbi Chiyya bar Abba states in the name of Rabbi Yochanan, "It is forbidden to pray in a building devoid of windows." (Talmud, *Berakhot* 34b)

> A sanctuary must have windows, as Daniel had in his upper chamber where he prayed (Daniel 6:11), corresponding to the "windows" in heaven, as it is written: "My Beloved ... He looked forth at the windows, showing himself at the lattice" (Song of Songs 2:9). (*Zohar* 2:59b)[15]

Light and an expansive view help to create an environment that is warm and welcoming. They also bring in the positive influence of the natural kingdom. The presence of an expansive view raises the mind. The sound of birds during meditation can lift us clear up to the heavens. Some of the most wonderful places of prayer and meditation are set in the wonder of nature. Before there were synagogues and churches, people prayed in spots of exquisite natural beauty where they felt that God was near.

Specific rituals that are associated with entering into a holy place help to reinforce the sense of sacredness. In the *Shulchan Arukh*, we are told that the entrance to the synagogue should be opposite the *Aron Kodesh*—the Holy Ark—so that we can bow in its direction as we enter the house of prayer. We also are instructed to light candles in the synagogue as a symbol that the *Shekhinah*, the Divine Presence, dwells there. We can follow similar customs in our sacred space.[16]

Obstacles and Solutions in Preparing for Meditation

At each stage of the meditation process, there are numerous obstacles and difficulties that can appear. In this section, we will investigate some of the major issues that we face in preparing for meditation and offer some practical solutions.

Putting Too Much Energy into the Preparations

One of the difficulties that can arise in meditation work is putting massive effort into our preparations and then having nothing left for the practice itself. This is a common problem in traditional Judaism, where the spiritual disciplines often contain many steps and a multitude of details. In this regard, the Baal Shem Tov instructed his Hasidim to curtail their preparatory prayers and actions:

> One should not recite a lot of psalms before the daily prayers, so as not to weaken his body, and thereby become unable to say the essential part [of the morning service] … with great devotion (*devekut*), because he has lost all of his strength by [reciting] other things before the [main] prayers…. Also on Yom Kippur, before *Neilah* [the concluding service], he should recite the prayer book (*machzor*) with a small mind (*bekatnut*)—with minimal fervor, so that he will be able to pray afterward with [strong] devotion.[17]

If we focus too much on preparation, it is easy to lose track of the goal. We can forget that we have undertaken these exercises as preliminary actions to ready us for our practice. In general, there is always a danger that we will become too attached to our own specific routine.

We can become so accustomed to having certain circumstances in place before we pray or meditate that we are unable to function otherwise. We cannot meditate without our special pillow or the silence of our sacred space. We cannot pray except in our *makom kavua*—our usual spot. We are only able to enter into a contemplative state when our environment has no distractions and we have the right people and atmosphere around us. This, of course, defeats the whole purpose of building a preparatory routine. We do not want to be tied to our spiritual props. Our goal is to be able to meditate or pray anywhere and at any time. In fact, we are striving to be in a constant state of meditation. We want to be able to infuse every situation, no matter what it is, with divine spirit. Our spiritual practice is an attempt to transcend our environment and circumstances and dwell in an inner reality that is wholly in God.

Poor Preparation for Meditation

Though we can become overly involved in our preparations, the big problem for most people is the opposite one: a lack of care before beginning practice. We tend to go straight from our worldly activities into the meditation room. We fall into a kind of automatic pilot, where we run through the motions of the meditation without being truly present. As a result, we have a meditation where nothing really happens. Immersed in material consciousness, our mind whirls with countless thoughts and feelings as our centers shut down.

The solution to this dilemma is to build a solid routine. Our preparatory exercises create a firm foundation for our practice. They enable us to immediately dive inward in meditation. Our daily habits lay the groundwork for whatever blessings God wishes to bestow upon us.

Too Much Emphasis on Physical Preparations

The process of readying ourselves for meditation encompasses many practices and details. It is important to remember that of the different aspects of preparation, the physical dimension is the least important. Concrete aids facilitate the centering of our hearts and minds, but it is the inner training that is the focus of our work. We can meditate without special garments or even a sacred space. But we cannot meditate unless we have a clear mind and a pure and peaceful heart.

Grace: We Cannot Succeed without God's Help

There is one more step that we need to take as part of our preparations for meditation. Before we begin our practice, we need to ask for God's grace. Without divine grace all our other labors are useless. Our meditation will not come alive. As Sri Ramakrishna, the nineteenth-century Indian saint who was known for his blissful states and universal teachings, once remarked, "Nothing can be achieved—neither knowledge, nor devotion, nor direct spiritual experience—without God's grace."[18]

This truth is expressed in the Jewish tradition by a short prayer from Psalm 51:17 that we recite before the *Shemoneh Esrei*, the daily prayer of communion with the Eternal: "O Lord, open my lips, so that my mouth may declare Your praise." With these words, we are in effect saying to God, "Please bestow upon us the gift of Your infinite grace. We cannot say a word of prayer without Your benediction. Please bless our prayers." This is a wonderful way to get ready for spiritual practice. It is a beautiful mode in which to begin our appointment with the Source of All Being.

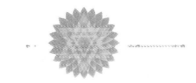

CHAPTER TWO

INTENTION

What Is Our Focus and Goal?

*T*he intention with which we sit down to meditate is the spiritual force that drives our practice. It expresses the goal to which we aspire. It arouses our heart and mind. This fervent conviction transforms our meditation from a dry mental exercise into a living invocation.

What Is the Role of Intention in Meditation?

Intention, or *kavanah*, is the second of five stages in the meditation process. During this stage we affirm our fundamental beliefs. This is like announcing our desired destination. A firm resolve is kindled to attain the goal of our practice. It is this stimulated willpower that fuels our journey toward the objective. By sending a mental message out to the universe, we are proclaiming the path that we will tread. We are calling out to those in the higher realm, asking for their aid in our quest.

The Jewish prayer cycle provides us with a paradigm for invoking our intention. During the morning and evening prayer service, the *Shema* acts as an affirmation of purpose before entering into silent communion with the Infinite.[1] In the *Shema*, we attest to our faith in the oneness of all of existence. We uphold the belief that everyone and everything is part of God. We abide in the truth that everything exists in the Omnipotent and Omniscient; everything comes from the same divine source. We declare our love for the Holy Blessed One and our commitment to express that love by the way in which we live.

The *Shema*, then, is an avowal of love and unity. Through the *Shema*, we dedicate ourselves to divine love and service. We express our desire to touch the sacred space at our very core. We reach beyond the limits of our finite physical awareness to the source of all life in the Absolute.

Our conviction empowers our meditation. It creates a spiritual force that arouses our heart, mind, and soul. It builds a dynamic vortex of energy to vitalize our practice. Like the foundation stone of the Temple, our intention is the rock upon which everything rests—the center from which all else evolves.

Kavanah can be expressed in different ways. It can be invoked with a time-honored prayer like the *Shema*. A traditional prayer has the advantage of being spiritually charged. Worshipers have recited the *Shema* for over three thousand years and voiced this supplication under all manner of circumstances. This has built up a potent reservoir of energy over the generations that we can tap into whenever we say the *Shema*. Uttering a long-established prayer, or *kavanah,* links us with all those who have spoken its words before us. It connects us to the souls upon the Jewish path in the upper worlds. It enables us to draw on their strength and spirit as we attempt to make contact with the Higher Power.

At the same time, traditional prayers have the disadvantage that they can appear stiff and awkward. Their outdated imagery and language make it difficult to relate to them. This, in turn, makes it hard for us to bring our innermost feelings to life.

For those of us who find the customary *kavanot* too formal and impersonal, there are more personal and individualistic declarations that we can make. We can simply assert, "I want to be one with God," or like the Vedantists we can exclaim, "*Om Tat Sat*—I Am That." I am That which is Timeless and Boundless. I am that Power that underlies all there is.

Alternatively, we can adopt a more devotional approach: "God please hear my prayer"; "I turn to *Yud Heh Vav Heh*, the Guardian of Israel, for help"; "I call on my true Self." All these pronouncements have the same purpose: to vitalize our practice and thrust us inward. Each is another way of propelling us toward the Essence of All Goodness. The approach we choose is a matter of personal preference and background. The secret is to pick a *kavanah* that is not only spiritually potent but also alive and meaningful to us.

The Three Steps: Forming, Vitalizing, and Invoking Our Intention

Let us take a closer look at the different steps of the process whereby we form, vitalize, and invoke our intention.

1. Forming the Intention

Creating words of intention is a spiritual adventure that takes us on an exploration of our soul. It leads us deep within to discover what we believe in. It forces us to articulate our truths.

This interior investigation requires much time and effort. The effort, however, is well worth our while. In the end, we will awaken to new levels of self-understanding and knowledge. We will clarify our ideals and concentrate our mind.

In this task, we are guided by three principles:

- **Be humble before God.** The Talmud, *Berakhot* 28b, cautions, "Know before whom you stand." It is an awe-inspiring thought to be standing before the Creator, Sustainer, and Destroyer of all the worlds. How can we dare to imagine that the Originator of all existence will turn the divine thought toward us? It is one of the great miracles of this life that we can call out to God. We have been given an extraordinary gift, the ability to reach across the barrier of this physical reality to touch the realm of the Infinite.

- **Be sincere when approaching God.** It is important not to invoke our intention frivolously, but to think of the meaning and implication of our words. The words we say can only be sincere if we take responsibility for what they mean. Each word we pronounce demands careful thought and reflection; it requires clarity of mind and a determination to take our practice seriously. We have to be completely honest with God. We cannot recite antiquated phrases just because others have repeated them for thousands of years. Many words that our ancestors spoke may feel inappropriate on our lips. Prayers that were profound and uplifting for them can seem false and primitive to us. If we want to use the traditional *kavanot*, we need to find a way to

express them with sincerity. Our words must be vibrant
and come from the heart.

- **Take the direct route in approaching God.** If we express
  our intention with sincerity and with humility, then there
  is no need for an abundance of words. The Torah (Numbers 12:13) records a prayer by Moses for his sister, Miriam;
  it consists of only five words: "O God, please heal her."
  Two minutes spoken with real feeling are worth more than
  hours said by rote. It is better to say nothing than too much.
  There is no place for philosophizing or clever formulations
  in a conversation with the All-Powerful. Just turn to God
  from the core of your being; then what emerges will pierce
  the barrier between heaven and earth and fly to the Throne
  of Glory.

In short, we need to develop *temimut*, or holy simplicity, as Rebbe Nachman of Breslov calls it, in our relationship with God. It is not a question
of being simpleminded or of acting with blind faith, but of being direct.

There is a story about an ordinary villager in England around whom
there occurred miraculous cures. When a journalist asked the villager if
he had any particular spiritual practices, he replied, "I go to church and
I sit and look at the Lord, and the Lord, He looks back at me." This is
simple and immediate communication.

Rebbe Nachman teaches that we attain this kind of holy simplicity by
stripping away all of our *chokhmot*—all of our cleverness, all of our carefully constructed rationales, all of our spiritual pride and vanity. Once
we have removed all of the preconceptions and expectations, then our
words will ascend straight to the One Who Hears All Prayers.[2]

2. Vitalizing the Intention

How do we empower our intention?

The Baal Shem Tov teaches that each mitzvah possesses an intrinsic
spiritual energy that is our task to actualize. However, just as the body
of a human being is only a physical vessel made of flesh and blood to
hold the infinite light of the soul, so the words of a prayer or the act that
constitutes a mitzvah is only its outer vessel or garment. Therefore, if we
want to draw upon the full power of a mitzvah, the physical fulfillment
of that mitzvah is not enough. In order to vitalize the mitzvah and bring it

to life, we need to infuse it with the spiritual power of the supernal *sefirot* and the divine light of the *Ein Sof* that animates them.[3]

According to Rebbe Dov Baer of Mezeritch, the Hasidic master who was the successor to the Baal Shem Tov, the most effective way for us to harness this sublime energy is to awaken the devotion that lies hidden in the depths of our heart.[4] Rebbe Nachman of Breslov provides us with ample guidance on this subject. Each of his teachings is a living instruction about how to evoke a heightened spiritual mood during our practice.

In one teaching, Rebbe Nachman tells us that when we begin our devotions, we should imagine that we are standing in the royal palace. During our practice, we need to forget everything else that exists, even ourselves, to see nothing but the royal presence before whom we stand.[5]

For Rebbe Nachman, lukewarm devotion is not an option. When we pray, we should pray with all of our heart until we feel the words in our very bones, like King David, who bursts forth in Psalm 35:10, "All my bones shall say: Lord, who is like unto You!"[6]

Nor is our practice intended to be a somber affair. It is important for us to have joy in our practice. We need to meditate and pray with joyfulness. If necessary, Rebbe Nachman believes, we should begin with a forced sense of elation and continue on in this fashion until it becomes real.[7]

Swami Chidananda, the twentieth-century Indian teacher who was the president of the Divine Life Society and was known for his humility and inner radiance, also spoke about joy in the spiritual life. He too felt that it is vital to walk the path with joy:

> We have mentioned the thrill, the joy of the spiritual adventure, this journey to reach the great destination. We have mentioned that the joy, the thrill is not so much in reaching the destination but in the effort itself, in the onward and upward progress towards the goal. It is in the journey itself that the joy is there.[8]

This sense of joy will infuse our intention with light. It will stir our heart and energize our meditation.

On a deeper level, we are not just vitalizing our thoughts and emotions. We are attempting to galvanize our will. How do we accomplish this aspect of the work? How do we vivify our will?

We begin by asserting our profound belief that our goals are attainable. The spiritual life is about living with optimism; it is about living with hope and faith. The act of meditation should be empowering. Through our spiritual disciplines, we join ourselves with our higher nature and become filled with the power of the Creator of All Life. Swami Brahmananda, a direct disciple of Sri Ramakrishna and the first president of the Ramakrishna Order, used to tell the novice monks, "You must have conviction that if you realize God and receive his grace, all the problems of your life will be solved, the purpose of your coming to the world will be accomplished, and that by tasting the bliss of the eternal Brahman, you will be immortal."[9]

This requires not just positive thinking but also intense determination to reach our destination. When the sixth-century-BCE Indian prince Gautama left the royal palace in search of enlightenment, he engaged in a life of severe penance. After six years, he realized the futility of severe asceticism. Deciding that it was better to follow a path of moderation and build up his body's strength, Gautama took some simple food and then sat under the bodhi tree to meditate. As he began his practice, Gautama declared, "I will not leave this spot until I find an end to suffering." The whole of that night passed in inner combat. By the following morning, he arose from meditation, transformed into the Buddha.

The rousing of our will is founded upon a tangible awareness of the truth of our innate divinity. As Swami Chidananda exclaimed to a gathering of Western devotees:

> To be like God is the natural ability of every individual soul. The ability to shine as God—sublime and radiant—is the natural heritage of one and all....
>
> What you really want to become, you can be. This is the absolute, unchanging truth. This great law will stand by you, and through this law, what you are determined to become, that you will become.[10]

Finally, Rebbe Nachman reminds us, when we undertake our practice, we do not approach God alone. He told his Hasidim that when they pray, they should connect their soul with the souls of *kol shokhnei afari,* "all those who dwell upon this earth." Spiritual practice is part of a universal yearning for union, an eons-long journey back to our home.[11] This teaching is especially important during the third part of the work. In this phase, we draw all aspects of our being together and intone the actual words of *kavanah.*

3. Invoking the Intention

There exists a tremendous gulf between God and us. How can we, insignificant creatures who exist for the blink of an eye, approach the Timeless All-Encompassing One? How can our finite material minds traverse the abyss that leads to the *Ein Sof*? How can such imperfect beings bind themselves to the One who is absolute perfection?

In trying to bridge the gulf between the grandeur of the Supreme Power and the reality of our numerous human imperfections, the Baal Shem Tov offers the following advice: whenever we begin our spiritual practice, we should attach ourselves to the great souls of Israel. In this manner, he explains, we will draw on their celestial support in accomplishing our spiritual goals. We will harness the energy of the whole of the Soul of Israel to bring our work to fruition.

The Soul of Israel is a divine mission that was created thirty-five hundred years ago to inspire the ancient world of the Middle East with the ideals of divine justice and the unity of God. This Soul contains all those who have incarnated as part of the people of Israel over the centuries. It embraces everyone who has taken up this spiritual task. It includes all those who have shared in the destiny of Israel. This Soul is a great vortex of energy and consciousness, a vast assembly that stretches way up into the higher worlds of the Kingdom of Heaven.

All of the souls in *Knesset Yisrael* (the Assembly of Israel) are working to support, guide, and strengthen us. They all are ready to pour their love, light, and energy into us if we but turn in their direction.

This is the reason, the Baal Shem explains, why the Kabbalistic *kavanah* that is recited before performing a mitzvah ends with the phrase *beshem kol Yisrael*, "in the name of all of Israel." It is also the reason behind the Ari's instruction to recite the phrase "I fulfill the mitzvah of loving your neighbor as yourself" before we begin to pray. If we want our prayers to be truly effective, the Ari is informing us, we need to bind ourselves to the Soul of Israel through the attribute of divine love.[12]

Meditation is the place where we most powerfully link with the Soul of Israel. According to the Baal Shem, there is a correlation between *menuchah* (rest), stillness, and unity. On the outside, he explains, all of Israel appears to be many. On the inside, however, all of Israel is one. When does this interior reality manifest itself in the outer world? When the people of Israel cease their separate worldly activities, join together as one heart, and strive to bind themselves to God. In response to this one-pointed aspiration, God binds Himself to Israel. In this moment of interconnectedness, all of Israel becomes still and one.[13]

This is the heart of the meditation experience. In the external world, we are separate individuals. But when we enter into the inner reality, the innate divinity of every human being is revealed. In this place of holiness, all of Israel—in fact, all of humanity—is one.

This urge toward unification with the Soul of Israel and all of humankind is part of a larger movement toward union that envelops every level of the manifest universe. The yearning for oneness is a cosmic force that lies at the center of creation. In the Kabbalah, the different aspects of the heavenly Godhead are ever striving toward unity. This striving is embodied in the Kabbalistic concept of *yichud,* or union, between the male and female dimensions of Divinity called the Holy One, blessed be He, and the *Shekhinah*. Their union is the inner focus for many of the practices of the Kabbalists and Hasidim. It is considered the supreme intention that will awaken a great spiritual transformation within the practitioner. Rebbe Elimelekh of Lizhensk captures the fervor of this ideal in the following passage from his writings:

> And in all the matters of this world, be it study, be it prayer, be it
> positive spiritual acts (mitzvot), he should habituate himself to say
> these words: "I am doing this for the sake of the unification of the
> Holy One, blessed be He, and the *Shekhinah*, in order to bring
> pleasure to God." And he should habituate himself to recite this
> in the inner depth of his heart, and with time, he will experience
> a great illumination with this recitation.[14]

Sometimes, the power of thought alone is not enough to vitalize our *kavanah*. The integration of sound and gesture into an invocation can be helpful in energizing our intention. An example of the use of these elements in prayer is the halakhic instructions for reciting the *Shema*. According to the tradition, when we recite the first line of the *Shema*, we are supposed to cover our eyes and extend the last word of the phrase—*Echad*, "One." The *Shulchan Arukh* provides us with clear guidelines in this regard:

> You should extend the *chet* [the middle letter] of [the word] *Echad*
> (One), in order to proclaim God King in heaven and on earth …
> and extend the *dalet* [the last letter] of *Echad* (One) long enough

so that you can think that there is only one God in the world and
that He rules over the four corners of the earth.[15]

Here sound, visualization, and *kavanah* combine together to create a
powerful invocation of oneness. As the sound of the letters reverberates in our mind, our thoughts expand out toward the four corners of
the world and reach upward to the heavens. Such an invocation creates an energetic gateway that leads us directly into the supernal seat
of Unity.

Obstacles and Solutions in Forming Our Intention

Getting our intention right is essential for our practice. Doing so is more
complicated than it would first appear. There are many impediments that
can hinder our attempts to formulate a strong intention. This section outlines the key areas that we need to address.

An Undefined Intention

The first problem that most of us face is dealing with goals that are vague
and undefined. How can we clarify our goals? How do we evoke a
focused contemplative mind-set?

The tradition provides us with various ways to sharpen our objectives. One such instruction comes from the writings of Rebbe Natan of
Nemirov. Rebbe Natan teaches that each of us has a spark of truth inside
us that animates our whole existence. If we can tap into this spark of
truth, he explains, our purpose will soon become clear. We accomplish
this task by continually asking ourselves what we believe in until we
arrive at the core truths on which we base our life. Once we have discovered these core beliefs, then we have found our spark of truth.[16]

A Lack of Conviction

Another common issue for many of us is a lack of dynamic belief. We
follow the technique, but without conviction. Meditation without conviction is unlikely to produce positive results. If there is no will or heart
invested in our practice, then our meditation will not come alive.

An Overly Elaborate Intention

Another problem is getting too elaborate with the formulation of our
kavanah. This is a major issue in some religions. Traditional Judaism, for

example, tends to have elaborate and lengthy *kavanot* for contemplating the prayers and performing the mitzvot.

The Baal Shem Tov battled against these complex formulations. He attempted to simplify the many Kabbalistic intentions. He also put less emphasis on proper formulation and gave more weight to the intention of the heart. He believed that even if we don't know the *kavanot*, a pure heart will take us to God.

> The individual who focuses during prayer on all the ritualistic formulations of intention (*kavanot*) that are known to him can only formulate those intentions that he knows. However, if he says each word with great attachment [to God], all the *kavanot* will, by themselves, automatically become included in each word, since each and every word is a whole world. And when he recites the word with great attachment, those higher worlds will most certainly be aroused, so that he thereby creates great [spiritual] activities. Therefore, a person should see to it that he prays with attachment and great fervor, and then he thereby will definitely create great [spiritual] activities in the higher worlds, because each letter arouses [the worlds] on high.[17]

Our generation, which is much less connected to the intricate minutiae of the tradition, certainly needs a simpler approach. Creating a clear-cut and direct *kavanah* is crucial for our practice. By following the three principles outlined in the section on the formulation of intention, we will avoid this methodological entanglement.

Wrong Intention

There are many challenges to building our *kavanah*. There are also a number of real dangers. One of the greatest dangers in spiritual practice is wrong intention. Inappropriate objectives can distort our inner experience. A desire for occult powers or a wish for fame and glory can undermine our whole spiritual life.

The story of the eleventh-century Tibetan Buddhist saint Milarepa is a poignant example of the negative effects of wrong intention. Milarepa was born into a happy, prosperous family. He had a blissful childhood until the age of seven, when his father suddenly died. Before Milarepa's father's death, he entrusted all of his wealth and business affairs into the hands of his brother and sister-in-law. He instructed them to take care of his wife and two children until Milarepa reached the age of manhood and could assume responsibility for the family. However, Milarepa's uncle and aunt betrayed his trust. They stole the family's wealth and property, leaving Milarepa, his mother, and his sister in abject poverty, and then forced the family to be their servants.

When Milarepa grew to manhood, his mother commanded him to go study black magic with a sorcerer so that they might take revenge on her husband's brother and his family. Being a loyal and obedient son, Milarepa followed his mother's advice and went to seek a teacher. After learning the black arts from his teacher, Milarepa returned to his native village and brought forth storms and earthquakes to destroy his uncle and aunt and their home and property. In the ensuing calamity, thirty-five people were killed and the harvest of all the villagers was destroyed.

When Milarepa saw the tremendous loss of life and the great suffering that he had brought about by his magic, he felt profound remorse. Tormented by the horrendous consequences of his actions, he set out on a long quest for personal redemption. Milarepa spent many painful years going through much trial, tribulation, and penance to wipe away the karmic debt that he had created with his black work of destruction.[18]

What, Then, Is Right Intention?

The tradition provides us with a clear understanding of what is right intention. A desire for selfless service, a yearning to know and love God, a wish to purify our imperfections—these are all examples of the goals that we hope to achieve with our spiritual quest.

A clear intent gives depth to our practice. It reminds us why we are meditating or praying. It links our spiritual discipline to the rest of life.

A coherent purpose keeps us from being distracted during meditation. It harnesses the forces of our heart and mind. A well-formed *kavanah* propels us toward the One True Reality. It produces an invocative cry that rises up through the heavens and calls forth a potent divine response.

A Living Process

Intention is not just a preparatory stage that is separate from our central practice. Meditation is a living process. Our intention is in constant dialogue with our meditation technique. The different stages all interact with each other and weave together. We draw on the power of our conviction to reinforce our practice. We use our *kavanah* to focus and stimulate our will. Our aspiration keeps us aware of the purpose of our meditation. It continually reorients our awareness toward That which is without Beginning or End.

CHAPTER THREE
FORGING A CONNECTION

How Do We Touch Pure Spirit?

*N*ow we come to the heart of the work: forging a connection. In this stage, we invest all of our energies into building an inner link between ourselves and our soul, between ourselves and God. When looked at objectively, this work seems like an impossible task. How can a physical mind grasp something that has no tangible qualities?

Before we begin to talk about the specifics of practice, we need to understand what our meditation is meant to achieve.

Methods: How Do We Bridge the Gap between God and Us?

The fundamental goal of the meditation process is to lift our consciousness from the finite to the Infinite. Meditation bridges the gap between the higher and lower worlds, between our soul and us. In meditation, we utilize the power of the mind to go beyond the mind. The Hindus compare this to using one thorn to remove another thorn embedded in our flesh. This transformation in consciousness is accomplished through four main methods. These four methods form the basis for all meditation techniques. Some of the techniques focus on images while others concentrate on specific sounds. All of the techniques, however, are constructed to set into motion one of these methods of transcending the limits of our physical mind.

Building a Meeting Place in the Mind

We are in the physical plane, and God is in the higher planes. The mental plane is the place where we can meet. We create a special compartment on the mental plane that we and the Holy One enter. There we can encounter the unknown and touch the intangible.

Expanding Our Interior Space

There is a place in our mind where we think and imagine. Normally we are unconscious of this inner space. During the process of meditation, we become aware of its existence. We learn how to recognize its dimensions and expand its boundaries until we can reach out into the Absolute.

Creating a Focused Spiritual Vibration

Vibration is the hallmark of energy. In meditation, we strive to create a concentrated vibration of mind energy to which God can send a corresponding pulsation of divine force. These two vibrations then converge and pulsate together until there is perfect harmony between them. This resonance results in an overlapping of consciousness between our soul and ourselves.

Emptying the Mind

Our finite, separate consciousness is contained within the boundaries of our mind. Through the process of inner reflection, we can learn to empty our mind of all thoughts. When thoughts stop, our finite consciousness dissolves, and infinite awareness spontaneously arises in its place.

The Dynamics of Forging a Connection

There is a distinct dynamic to the process of forging an inner connection. Building a spiritual link does not follow a simple linear progression. It alternates between several different types of actions. Each action has its specific counterpart that complements and facilitates its work. The two actions together make that aspect of the work complete. There are three such pairs during this phase of the meditation process. The balance between the different parts shifts as we enter different periods in our practice. The three dynamic pairs are forging and energizing, striving and resting, and holding and receiving.

Forge and Energize

Forging a connection is the central work of this stage and of the whole meditation process. The purpose of all the practices in this book is to create a conscious link between God and us, between ourselves and our soul. The various techniques are built on a science of energies and consciousness. They utilize symbols and images that resonate with the Jewish path. Each of these approaches enables us to go toward God as a Jew and to link up with the Soul of Israel and the Kingdom of Heaven.

Learning a practice properly is crucial if we are to be effective in our inner work. We need to proceed slowly and make sure that we are clear about each step in the meditation. Taking the time to prepare and engaging in regular practice are the keys to achieving a good meditation technique.

We are striving to master the mind. Like any other skill, this takes time and effort. Just as we would not expect to have full control of a car the first time we sit in the driver's seat, we should not expect to master our thoughts when we first begin to meditate. The technique is our vehicle for ascending into the higher worlds. We need to learn how to operate our vehicle and negotiate our way along the road if we want to successfully arrive at our destination.

The more we drive, the better drivers we will become. The more we get to know our vehicle and learn the rules of the road, the more quickly and safely we will reach our goal.

A careful study of the technique as we begin our routine will build a strong foundation for our meditation. Giving our full attention to each section of the meditation will solidify our relationship with our technique, especially during the early stages of training.

At the same time, a technique is only a methodology for practice. It is like a body without a soul. Without the power of our heart, mind, and will to energize it, the technique is an empty vessel that will not take us on high.

Going through the steps of the exercise on a daily basis will have a definite effect on our mind. The components of the meditation are constructed to change our state of consciousness. However, for the meditation to penetrate our heart and soul and draw the presence of God toward us, we need to infuse our practice with love, will, and devotion.

The interplay between these two elements is the first dialectic of our practice. As we meditate, we constantly move back and forth between going through the steps of the technique and vitalizing our meditation with strength and yearning. One part of this work is strictly an effort of the mind; the other draws on the whole of our being.

Our intention plays an important role here. It helps us to keep focused and to energize our practice. Yet intention is not identical with the work of this stage. Our *kavanah* expresses our fundamental goals and objectives. The ideal embodied in our intention underlies all of our meditation work. The vitalizing of our technique requires a more nuanced use of our energies.

The use of heart, mind, and soul power during this stage of practice is directed along a particular path in accordance with the needs of each aspect of our meditation technique. Some parts of the approach will require a strong focus on the energy of the mind. Others parts will demand an awakening of the love in our heart or the willpower at the core of our being. A careful balancing of these different aspects is needed during our practice. Our intention, on the other hand, underpins the entire meditation process. It acts to keep our vehicle headed in the right direction.

Strive and Rest

There is a second dynamic that takes place during the practice of our technique. On one hand, this stage of the meditation focuses on doing the particular approach that we have chosen (or that has been chosen for us). We put our full effort into setting the different steps of the meditation into action. Leaving all else aside, we strive single-mindedly, or "one-pointedly" toward our goal.

On the other hand, the reality of meditating for twenty minutes, half an hour, or even an hour or more is that we cannot invest our full effort continuously for that whole period. We need to take a break from our intense concentration on the technique from time to time. Therefore, as part of any approach, there is a need to withdraw from striving and let the mind relax for a few minutes. However, we do not simply stop practicing; rather, we place our mind on an aspect of the technique that is less strenuous, a thought or an image that enables us to hold on to a higher state of awareness as we rest. Any good practice will have such meditative pauses. Specific elements will be incorporated into the technique to be used in this way.

The Baal Shem Tov speaks of the need to rest the mind in his instructions to his Hasidim about ascending through the higher worlds:

> And he needs to descend below a number of times during the day in order to rest his mind a little, and there will be times when he can only serve God with a contracted consciousness, where he is not able to ascend to the higher world....[1]
>
> And he shall descend in order to ascend, because from the power of the descent that he descends, afterwards when he ascends, he will ascend to a very high place.[2]

Our meditation practice moves back and forth between these two poles. We throw all of our energy into actualizing the technique. We work to still the mind, visualize the image, and concentrate one-pointedly on God. But when we feel our attention slipping, when our mind cannot keep the image or focus any longer, we withdraw from our striving and rest quietly in God, using the thought or practice that has been given for that purpose. Once we feel recharged and vitalized, then we return to the practice with our full energy. And we move back and forth between striving and resting as often as we need to throughout the period of meditation.

Learning to judge the balance between these two modes is one of the keys to effective spiritual practice. Some of us burn ourselves out in a flurry of mental activity that exhausts our mind after the first few minutes of meditation, while others become too laid-back and just remain in a superficially contemplative state. We need to engage fully with both aspects of our practice. A proper equilibrium in our approach will enable us to meditate for hours at a time.

Hold and Receive

The main focus of the forging stage of the meditation process is to create an inner contact through the medium of our technique. Establishing an inner link requires a great deal of effort and a large measure of purity and grace. Building this spiritual connection, however, is only part of the process. Once we have created a link, we need to keep that line open for the duration of the meditation.

Holding on to our link means more than simply maintaining a state of mental tension. We have made contact with a part of the larger collective soul that we belong to on higher planes. This inner link represents a line of communication between that soul and us. The firmer we can hold that connection, the stronger the bond between us will become, and the broader the spectrum of spiritual experiences that can be initiated through the contact.

A solid connection allows the presence of the soul to powerfully overshadow our consciousness and bless us with its love, light, and peace. Part of the meditation process, then, is for us to stop focusing on the technique in order to receive the divine gifts that God is bestowing on us. We need to simultaneously hold on to our inner contact and turn to receive the blessings of the One who has come.

As we go through the different steps of the meditation technique, we strengthen and deepen our connection. Each step has the potential to bring another new contact, to open our mind to hitherto undiscovered realms. We solidify these inner impressions through the combined efforts of clinging to and receiving from our higher source. In this manner, we establish a lasting soul presence in our consciousness.

These are the three dynamic pairs that characterize this phase of meditation: forge and energize, strive and rest, hold and receive. We work our way through the steps of the technique while vitalizing its different components with our will and devotion. We move between actively implementing the technique and resting in God's presence. We bind ourselves to our inner contact, while simultaneously absorbing the life, energy, and inspiration emanating from its supernal source.

Obstacles and Solutions in Forging a Link

The twentieth-century Indian sage Sri Ramana Maharshi was known for his complete identification with the Self of All Being and the profound inner peace that people experienced in his presence. He used to tell a story about the Tamil saint and poet Tattvaraya, who lived in the 1500s. Tattvaraya composed a *bharani* (a kind of poetic composition) in honor of his guru. When the *bharani* was completed, he gathered together a group of *pandits* (scholars) and asked them to assess its worth.

> The *pandits* raised the objection that a "bharani" was only composed in honour of great heroes capable of killing a thousand elephants, and that it was not in order to compose such a work in honour of an ascetic. Thereupon the author said, "Let us all go to my Guru and we shall have this matter settled there."

They went to the Guru and, after all had taken their seats, the author told his Guru the purpose of their coming there. The Guru sat silent and all the others also remained in *mauna* [silence]. The whole day passed, night came, and some more days and nights, and yet all sat there silently, no thought at all occurring to any of them and nobody asked why they had come there.

After three or four days like this, the Guru moved his mind a bit, and thereupon the assembly regained their thought activity. They then declared, "Conquering a thousand elephants is nothing compared to the Guru's power to conquer the rutting elephants of all our egos put together. So certainly he deserves the 'bharani' in his honour!"[3]

In order to really succeed with our practice, we need to realize that meditation takes tremendous work. Restraining the mind is like reining in a herd of wild elephants. Forging a connection is a battle to control our thoughts, for, as the Baal Shem Tov wisely observed, "you are where your thoughts are."[4] The mind is our instrument for communing with God. If we can master our mental processes, the doors to the inner realm will swing open for us.

Steadiness: The Importance of Regular Practice

There is a great value to putting one foot in front of the other in the spiritual life. Constant effort and perseverance will overcome all obstacles along our path. The story of Rabbi Akiva, perhaps the greatest of all the Rabbinic sages, beautifully illustrates this truth.

Rabbi Akiva was an illiterate shepherd who fell in love with the daughter of a rich man. She refused to marry him unless he became a learned scholar. Rabbi Akiva was forty years old at the time, and he despaired of ever reaching such a lofty goal. In the throes of despondency, Rabbi Akiva went to the town of Lod and sat by the local well. By the side of the well, he noticed a rock with a large convex indentation. He asked one of the people sitting nearby, "Who has carved out this rock?" "It has been carved out by the water that has fallen on it drop by drop over many years," was the reply. Rabbi Akiva thought for a moment and then declared, "Is my heart harder than stone? If water can cut through the surface of a rock, then surely I can learn the teachings of the Torah."[5]

Many times in the spiritual life, it is not the people with the greatest spiritual talents who succeed in reaching God, but rather the individuals who have the strongest determination to keep plodding on. Sticking to our spiritual routine is crucial to the path of meditation. We cannot reach God by merely dropping in from time to time. The importance of daily practice cannot be stressed strongly enough.

In her diary the sixteenth-century Christian saint and mystic Teresa of Avila makes clear that one of the greatest mistakes she made in the early part of her spiritual journey was to give up mental prayer (another way of saying meditation) because she thought that she was unworthy of it.[6] Swami Chidananda of the Divine Life Society also echoes her words: "He who neglects mental prayer does not need a devil to carry him to hell. He takes himself there by his own hand."[7]

Achieving regularity in our practice is a question of forming good spiritual habits. As Swami Ashokananda, the head of the Vedanta Society of San Francisco for over thirty years, explains, "Regularity in life is like the structure of a building. The hidden arches and supports of a building are the most important thing. A regular life, building up of good habits, is the foundation of spirituality."[8]

If we want to build a firm foundation for our practice, then we need to make it an integral part of our daily existence. This is done by disciplining ourselves to keep to a regular schedule, by habituating our minds and bodies to repeat the same actions over and over again until they become a natural part of our life. In a similar vein, the Talmud (*Chagigah* 9b) exhorts the spiritual aspirant to learn a text 101 times— to go through the text 100 times, and then still once more. Through these multiple repetitions, the habit of study becomes ingrained in our bones.

There is also a deeper logic to this constant repetition.

Across Asia, one can see whole communities of migrant workers who labor all day long breaking rocks with hammers to make gravel for construction. The twentieth-century Buddhist teacher Anagarika Munindra, who introduced insight meditation to the West, used an analogy from the lives of the rock breakers to explain the nature of the process involved: "If the rock-breaker strikes the stone ninety-nine times and it doesn't break, yet it breaks on the hundredth strike, were the first ninety-nine wasted? Perhaps all ninety-nine strikes were needed before the stone would break, but at the ninety-ninth strike you may feel like you are making no progress at all."[9]

Each meditation is another blow from God's hammer on the rock of our ego mind. We need to persevere with our practice, even when nothing seems to be happening, as we can never know which hammer stroke will break the rock of our "I." In fact, Rebbe Nachman of Breslov taught that if we strengthen ourselves to pray even when there is no flow of energy or devotion, then when our prayers begin to flow again, the prayers that were blocked and uninspired will be lifted up by those that are vibrant and alive.[10]

Meditating on a regular basis maintains our inner connection with God. With each meditation, we build up our store of energy and solidify our spiritual link. Through this daily work, we prepare a vessel to receive the great influx of consciousness and energy when the presence of God finally descends. In this sense, all of our earlier sittings are indeed lifted up by the final one.

Steadiness is crucial in the early stages of practice and at every other point along the path. The nineteenth-century Hasidic rebbe Yitzchak Ya'acov of Biala teaches that every step onto a higher spiritual level takes effort and struggle. We are trying to break through into a new level of being, and that is difficult for us to achieve because our innate materiality constantly gets in the way.[11]

There is an intrinsic resistance within our concrete material mind to the further expansion of our consciousness. There is an instinctual opposition in the body to the assimilation of new and more refined energies. Therefore, each time we attempt to ascend onto a higher level, it is like beginning anew. On each progressive level, we must break through a barrier within ourselves and then plod on with patience and perseverance until the internal obstacles are overcome and energy begins to flow.

A Steady Mind: It Is All in the Mind

The key to achieving a sound practice is, first and foremost, a steady mind. Sri Ramakrishna would tell his devotees, "Unless the mind becomes steady there cannot be yoga [union with God]. It is the wind of worldliness that always disturbs the mind, which may be likened to a candle-flame. If that flame doesn't move at all, then one is said to have attained yoga."[12]

Sri Ramakrishna also compares the struggle with the mind to the sailor's struggle to control his boat in turbulent waters:

The helmsman stands up and clutches the rudder firmly as long as the boat is passing through waves, storms, high wind, or around the curves of a river; but he relaxes after steering through them. As soon as the boat passes the curves and the helmsman feels a favourable wind, he sits comfortably and just touches the rudder.[13]

To steady the mind requires great willpower. Harnessing our willpower enables us to overcome the various caprices and sensitivities of our mind and body. A disciple of Swami Ashokananda once asked him if she could stuff cotton in her ears during meditation to block out the exterior noise. His response was, "Use willpower. Do you know willpower?" "No," the disciple sheepishly retorted. "Become acquainted with it," the Swami snapped back. "Balanced strength is the true strength. It is like the serene surface of a calm lake. It goes deep, deep. One feels one can give oneself to it and be held securely. If necessary, serene strength can raise waves mountain high."[14]

Steadiness Means Constant Care and Attention

Steadiness means more than mindless regularity. It also means giving constant care and attention to our spiritual practice. The Baal Shem Tov tells a parable to illustrate this point about two friends who had each planted a field of wheat, one a large field and the other a smaller one.

The owner of the large field went about his business enjoying life, eating and drinking and going to the tavern, because he felt secure in the large amount of wheat that he had planted and the great harvest that he would reap. The owner of the little field was concerned at every moment for his tiny crop. Therefore, he went down to his field every day, hour after hour, to check on the plants, pull out weeds, and do anything else that might aid its growth.

In the end, the large field's crop came up poorly and sickly, its stone fence was broken down, and passersby came and took the wheat, while the plants in the small field flourished and produced a rich and healthy crop.[15]

If we take care to nurture and water our practice, then it will flourish. If we do the necessary preparations to quiet our heart and clear our mind, then we will have fruitful meditations and harvest an abundant crop of spiritual inspiration and awakening.

Steadiness Brings a Sense of Joy, Freedom, and Peace

At the same time, we should not think that such diligence means resigning ourselves to a daily grind. Slow and steady work also has its benefits and pleasures. There is a great joy in this kind of approach to practice, a wonderful sense of freedom and peace. We do not have to face the stress and tensions of the quest for "the incredible inner experience." There are no great choices that we have to make, no do-or-die meditations to face, no fantastic revelations to receive, no fear of disappointments that will knock us down; all we have to do is put one foot in front of the other, something that each one of us is capable of doing every single day.

It is a bit like jogging. In the beginning, it is hard to get going, but once we are on the move, we fall into a rhythm and continue on almost effortlessly until the destination is reached. So it is with our meditation practice. If we can set out on the path and keep on moving, eventually we will shift into another state of consciousness, where the contemplative life comes with ease, and meditation becomes our natural way of being.

Let Go (Nonattachment) ...

The first step is to learn how to still the emotions, to shrug off the moments of depression and despair, and to let go of the moments of euphoria and excitement. This is achieved by living with the awareness that whatever heights we have reached, there are still higher mountains for us to climb. And it is maintained by knowing in our hearts that even if we do not reach the goal in this life, nothing is lost, nothing is in vain.

The next step is to pay no attention to either success or failure—for today's success may become tomorrow's catastrophe, and yesterday's disappointment may become today's triumph. Whatever happens, we take all experiences in stride.

We accomplish these goals by remaining ever conscious of the fact that the real "gold" in the spiritual life is not our inner experiences or the development of psychic powers, but our constant efforts to align every thought, word, and deed with the will of God.

Another aid in this process is to establish reasonable expectations for ourselves. If we are just beginning to meditate, we should not try to meditate for hours. We can start with a short period of reflection and then progress from there.

Rebbe Nachman of Breslov would tell his Hasidim to start out by doing a small portion of the prayers with total *kavanah* and then add new portions over time. In this way, they would gradually build up their capacity to pray with concentration and devotion.[16]

... But Hold On (Tenacity)

On the other hand, we must not forget the importance of tenacity in meditation. The Torah declares, "*Naaseh venishma*—We shall do and we shall understand" (Exodus 24:7). Practice itself will lead to understanding, and then to more practice. We need to start modestly but stick to our routine. We need to have firm determination. As Swami Brahmananda told his disciples, "The new-born calf tries to stand up, but it falls down many times. Still it never gives up; finally, after repeated efforts, it is not only able to stand, but it learns to run also."[17]

Rebbe Natan of Nemirov echoes his call for inner resolve. Whatever happens in our lives, whatever obstacles or difficulties come our way, we need to just keep on going toward God.[18] Obstacles and difficulties, he explains, are a fundamental part of the spiritual life. This is how we gain wisdom and experience. This is how we develop love and compassion. This is how we grow and evolve. Therefore, we should not fear the difficulties but welcome them.[19]

Swami Ashokananda also saw struggle as a necessary ingredient in a serious spiritual life. He believed that the strength to face profound inner struggles and overcome great personal obstacles was an essential characteristic for a spiritual seeker:

> To work for the Lord is never easy; there is always struggle. Always! There is no other way. It is good to have the spirit of struggle. Out of that, growth comes.... Always struggle—the struggle of a hero, not of a coward—a conquering struggle, without even a thought [that] there could be defeat in that struggle.... Outside troubles may come; inside troubles may come—but rise up and be a conquering hero. There is no other way.[20]

In the late 1700s, the Hasidic master Mordekhai of Chernobyl was known as the rebbe in charge of the hidden righteous ones of his generation. He exhorted his Hasidim to be diligent and resolute in their inner work. Rebbe Mordekhai brought the Rabbinic teaching "Even if a snake is wound around his heel, he should not break off [from prayer]"

(Talmud, *Berakhot* 33a) as proof of the importance of spiritual steadiness. We need to strengthen our spiritual disciplines, he declared, until we can still keep up our practice no matter what is happening around us.[21]

Faith and Grace: Meditation Is More Than a Mental Exercise

Rebbe Mordekhai's father, Nachum of Chernobyl, saw faith as a key component in achieving regular habits and spiritual steadiness. The Kabbalists, he explained, consider the last *sefirah* of *malkhut*, or kingship, as the gateway through which the divine energies flow into the lower worlds. *Malkhut* is also identified with the attribute of *emunah*, or faith. Therefore, faith is the gateway to God, the door that will lead us to the higher realms.[22]

We need to have a great deal of faith to succeed in meditation: faith in ourselves, faith that God exists, faith that the One who is always awake will arouse us to Self-realization. As Swami Brahmananda used to tell the young novices of the Ramakrishna Order, "Doubts will come until you have realized God; therefore you must hold fast to God and pray. Think to yourself: 'God *is*! But because of the impurities of my mind I cannot see him. When my heart and mind have become purified, then, through his grace, I shall surely see him!'"[23]

More than anything else, to be steady in our practice we need the grace of God. Without grace, all our efforts will come to naught. As Sri Ramana Maharshi affirmed, "Grace is both the beginning and the end. Introversion is due to Grace; Perseverance is Grace; and Realisation is Grace."[24]

According to Avraham of Avritch, a Hasidic teacher who was a disciple of Rebbe Nachum and Rebbe Mordekhai, we receive God's grace by recognizing that all of our accomplishments are achieved by the divine power working through us and not by our own individual efforts. This recognition of our fundamental dependence on the One who is the Bestower of All Blessing opens up the door to the heavenly storehouse and calls forth an outpouring of supernal abundance and mercy.[25]

To attain God's grace demands love and devotion. Our practice needs to have the life-giving waters of yearning for God. This thirst for the Eternal One supports and sustains us in our meditation. It links us with the infinite love of the Divine Heart.

Part Two

Techniques

*T*he heart of our practice is the specific meditation that we use to approach God each day. There are a wide variety of different techniques available to us. These techniques can be grouped into five main categories:

1. **Stilling the Mind:** The central purpose here is to quiet and calm the mind. These meditations can range from breathing to prayer to listening to music. Stilling the mind is an essential part of any practice.

2. **Visualization:** In visualization meditation, we create a spiritually charged image in our mind. This mental picture serves as a focus for our love and devotion and builds a link between God and us.

3. **Concentration:** We work at developing one-pointed concentration on a single object or idea to the exclusion of all else. Our mind then becomes a focused beam of spiritual energy that resonates in harmony with the vibration of our soul.

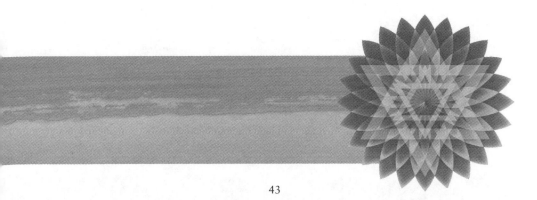

4. **Contemplation:** Contemplation is meditation on sublime ideas, images, or concepts. Through inner reflection, our consciousness penetrates the Universal Mind of God.

5. **Mantra:** We repeat potently energized phrases that awaken a tremendous spiritual force and lift our mind beyond this physical plane of existence into the higher realms.

In part 2, we explore these five categories of meditation techniques in depth. For each of the techniques, a number of different practices are presented for use in daily meditation.

Now let us dive into the world of our inner reality and take a swim in the boundless ocean of light and consciousness.

Chapter Four
Stilling the Mind I

How Do We Quiet Our Restless Mind?

*I*n the Kabbalah, there are three pathways that run through the Tree of Life. The left-hand path is called the path of *din* (judgment), and the right-hand path is called the path of *chesed* (mercy). The middle path is the path of harmony and balance, where the left- and right-hand sides are attuned and aligned to each other, joining together to form a single whole.

The middle path is also the path of the *Shekhinah*, because the Divine Presence only dwells where there is harmony and balance, where there is unity, wholeness, and peace. God's presence overshadows us when we are inwardly tranquil, like the perfect mirror of a rippleless lake. If there is any emotional or mental turmoil, our mind will reflect a disturbed and distorted picture and we will receive an incoherent image of the divine thoughtform in our consciousness.

Most of us think that we are quiet when we are not speaking. It is only when we start to meditate that we begin to hear all the "noise" that is generated by our busy minds. There is a never-ending stream of thoughts moving under the surface. The purpose of meditation is to still that flow and bring it to a halt.

Our minds are like wild horses, always running out of control. Meditation teaches us how to grab the reins, master our thoughts, and silence the mental uproar racing through our heads. Meditation transforms our thought processes. It clears away the mental clutter, so that we have a serene inner space.

Breathing: The Rhythm of Life

The first goal of meditation is to still the mind. There are many different approaches to achieving this state, but breathing is one of the most common techniques. By concentrating on the breath, the mind is drawn away from its ceaseless creation of thoughts. It centers on the rhythmic pattern of the breath and settles there.

Psalm 150:6 declares, "Let everything that breathes praise the Lord." The Midrash gives this phrase an alternative interpretation: "For every breath a person breathes, he should praise the Creator."[1] The great Hasidic teacher Dov Baer of Mezeritch, also known as the Maggid of Mezeritch, expands on this interpretation. The life force, he explains, goes in and out through the breath. It descends into the body and then out and up into the higher worlds. When we inhale, the divine breath comes into the world. When we exhale, it rises into the higher worlds again.[2]

The Hebrew word for "breath," *neshimah*, is very close to the Hebrew word for "soul," *neshamah*. The breath carries the energy of divine livingness. "And He breathed into his nostrils the breath of life" (Genesis 2:7). There is a higher breath and a lower breath; there is the breath of God and the breath of a human being. In meditation, these two breaths mingle and become one.

The Hebrew letter *heh* is pronounced like an "h." It is the sound we make when we exhale. The *heh* looks like a doorway: ה. It is the doorway of our breath. As we inhale, the *heh* swings one way. As we exhale, it swings in the other direction. As we focus on our breath, we ourselves become the letter *heh*. We become a swinging door through which divine livingness flows in and out.

The letter *heh* is often used as a short form for the name of God. As we focus on our breath, everything else slowly fades away until we become one with the breath—one with all that is. Then we touch the place of the *heh* inside us—the place of calm, harmony, and stillness where God dwells.

Meditation on the *Chakras* or *Sefirot*

For many of us, focusing on the breath alone is not sufficient. Our minds are too active and unruly. When we try to focus on the breath, our thoughts wander in all directions. Jumping straight to inner stillness is beyond our present capacity. We need some other point of attention to quell the mental waves.

Not all thoughts are the same. Some of the thoughts that run through our mind are clearly negative and harmful to our practice and consciousness. Other thoughts are of a more positive and spiritual nature; they encourage and strengthen our practice. And then there are thoughts that are more or less neutral—mental noise that does not so much harm as distract our meditation. And finally, there is the state beyond thought that we are striving toward—an inner stillness, silence, and peace.

For those of us with busy minds, it is useful to have an additional focus during meditation. Contemplating spiritual ideas while we breathe will help calm the mind and raise its vibration. This added focal point provides us with an intermediary step along the path to thought-less-ness. One such alternative practice is to concentrate on the different Kabbalisitic *sefirot* as we do our breathing. This brings in the positive energy of the attribute associated with each *sefirah*.

As was mentioned in the introduction, according to the Kabbalistic tradition, there is a subtle spiritual body that underlies our outer physical frame. This body is composed of vibrant centers of spiritual force called *sefirot*, or spheres. Each of these *sefirot* has its own particular energy and character. These energy centers run along the spinal column, from the base of the spine to the crown of the head. They are interconnected with each other through a network of energy pathways that flow between them. The whole subtle body of energy centers and pathways is called the *Etz haChayim*—the Tree of Life.

The Tree of Life is the medium through which energy and consciousness pour into our heart, mind, and body and then emanate out from us into the world. In Yoga, there are seven major centers, or *chakras*. The Kabbalah speaks not of seven centers but of ten (the *sefirot*). The reason for this discrepancy is that each of the centers has a left-hand and a right-hand component to its makeup. In three of the centers, the difference between the left- and right-hand side is so marked that the Kabbalah considers each side of the center as a separate *sefirah* in itself. Yogic teaching, on the other hand, continues to think of the left- and right-hand elements of these three *chakras* as two halves of a single whole. This accounts for the addition of three extra centers in the Kabbalah.

We will use a seven-center Yogic and Kabbalistic framework, where the *sefirot* are associated with the different *chakras* (see the diagram below). These are names for the *sefirot* as expressed within this seven-center framework:

Keter—crown: the crown center at the top of the head

Chokhmah/binah—wisdom and understanding: the center between the eyebrows and slightly above, what is called the third eye

Chesed/gevurah—mercy and power: the throat center

Tiferet—beauty: the heart center

Netzach/hod—eternity and splendor: the solar plexus center

Yesod—foundation: the sacral or genital center

Malkhut—kingship: the center at the base of the spine

Yogic / Kabbalistic *Sefirot*

crown	keter
wisdom/understanding	chokhmah/binah
mercy/power	chesed/gevurah
beauty	tiferet
eternity/splendor	netzach/hod
foundation	yesod
kingship	malkhut

Illustration: Moriah Halevi

The breath plays an important role in the work of meditation. The breath carries the supernal energies and is the link between our physical and spiritual bodies. Normally the centers are relatively dormant and inactive. When we focus on the centers while breathing, we awaken the *sefirot* into vibrant activity. When a center becomes aroused, its energy flows into our consciousness, lifting us up into a higher state of awareness.

Let's now make these concepts more concrete and tangible, by actually doing a meditation together with focused breathing on the *sefirot*.

Breathing Meditation on the Sefirot

Close your eyes and let go of all tension in your body. Relax every part of you; start with your neck and shoulders, and then move down through your body all the way to your toes.

Begin to breathe in and out in a normal fashion, focusing your mind on the intake and outflow of your breath.

Remember the doorway of the *heh* ה. Let the *heh* swing in one direction as you inhale and in the other direction as you exhale.

Shut out all of the outside noise. For this one moment, let nothing else exist but the movement of your breath. Become one with the *heh*. Become the doorway.

Now we will begin to focus our breathing on three of the seven centers or *sefirot*.

We start with the solar plexus center, the *sefirah* of *netzach/hod*—eternity and splendor. This *chakra* is located in the region of the navel and is the center of emotions. All of your emotional energy is concentrated in this *sefirah*. As you experience various feelings during the day, they build up a powerful vibration in *netzach/hod*. You can use your meditation on this center to channel pure, positive energy into your spiritual body and to clear away all the negative energy that has gathered there.

Breathe in and out, while focusing your mind on the solar plexus center—*netzach/hod*. With each inhalation, draw in pure, positive energy; with each exhalation, clear the negative feelings that have built up during the night or day.

Breathe in joy, hope, and contentment. Exhale out anger, fear, and despair. Feel the negativity pour out of your being and dissipate away. Feel a strong stream of positive energy enter into your consciousness and spread throughout your body, heart, and mind.

Now move the focus of your attention to the heart center—*tiferet*, or beauty. This is the *sefirah* where the beauty of each person's soul is revealed. The heart *chakra* is the focus of the energy of divine love—the spiritual life force of the universe.

Begin breathing in and out while focusing your mind on this center. With each inhalation, draw in the energy of boundless, unconditional love. With each exhalation, emanate that love back into the world once again. With each inhalation, open your heart wider to receive more love. With each exhalation, send more and more love out into the universe.

Next, slowly shift your focus to the head center—the *sefirah* of *chokhmah/binah*—wisdom and understanding, what is often referred to as the third eye. This is a spot between your eyebrows and just slightly above.

As you focus your mind on this *sefirah*, imagine that the energy of peace is flowing in and out of this center, filling your consciousness with peace, calm, and tranquility. With each inhalation, feel peace come flowing into your mind and consciousness. With each exhalation, send that peace back out into your surroundings. With each inhalation, feel calm, quiet, and still. With each exhalation, let the energy of peace stream forth into the wider world.

Return, once more, to the heart center—*tiferet*—beauty. This time, as you focus on this center, hold each breath for five seconds. As you hold the breath, send the energy throughout the whole of your physical and subtle body. Feel it course through the pathways and clear away all blockages and obstructions, so that you have a free-flowing and harmonious spiritual vehicle that can receive the divine energies.

Just as the heart is the organ that circulates blood and oxygen throughout the physical body, the heart center is the *sefirah* that pours life, love, and energy throughout the rest of the *Etz haChayim*.

Relax your breathing, and inhale and exhale in a normal fashion.

As you breathe, let your mind rest quietly in the stillness and silence.

Finally, slowly open up your eyes.

When we do a breathing technique, we are clearing the body of any spiritual blockages and filling it with divine light. When the breathing is done properly, we breathe through our subtle body and not just our physical one. Energy is then drawn into the body to infuse it with life and vitality. The flow of breath circulates throughout the *Etz haChayim* to clear the passageways and to establish an internal harmony. This inner process transforms us into a clear, calm, and focused vessel that is fit to receive God's indwelling presence.

Prayer and Mantra Recitation: Using Spiritually Potent Words to Focus the Mind and Open the Heart

Not everyone is comfortable with the use of breathing to still the mind. Some of us find it hard to focus on the breath, even while concentrating on the *sefirot*. The whole practice takes place too much in the head. In such cases, there is a different route that we can follow, where the centerpoint of the practice is not thought but sound.

One possibility is to use the sound of the traditional prayers as a tool to still the mind. Many Orthodox Jews have the habit of reciting psalms throughout the day, going through the whole of the book of Psalms each week. The recitation of the prayers creates a current of thought toward God. It taps into a higher spiritual vibration and links the mind there. As a result, all outside thoughts drop away, and a feeling of inner peace prevails.

The Baal Shem Tov saw prayer as a gradual progression from words to silence. Using the intention in our heart, we join together each letter, word, and phrase to create a single unified stream of praise and yearning that flows toward heaven.[3] Rebbe Nachman of Breslov compares this method of prayer to a person picking flowers as he walks through a field, gathering them together into beautiful bouquet to offer to his beloved.[4] This is a lovely metaphor for the practice of meditation.

Despite the beauty of this approach, there are many of us who find the traditional prayers hard to say; their archaic style and language turn us off. Those of us with this difficulty can employ another way of using sound: the recitation of a mantra.

A mantra is a spiritually empowered phrase that is repeated for a given period of time. By reciting the phrase over and over again, our mind becomes completely absorbed in the sound of the mantra and the spiritual thought that it evokes. The constant repetition of the mantra keeps the mind occupied so that no distracting thoughts can enter. It acts as an energetic field that blocks out all intruding thoughts. Like breathing, the sound of the mantra serves as a clearing agent to quiet and soothe our consciousness.

In a practice that closely resembles the use of a mantra, Jews of the Sephardic tradition communally chant all of the prayers during the service. When recited with feeling, the power of this chant is tangibly evident to anyone who is present. For Sephardic worshipers, the connection between sound, chant, and prayer is self-evident.

There is a great deal more to say about Jewish mantras. It is a concept that opens up all kinds of new possibilities for practice. We will explore the topic of mantras in greater depth in chapter 8.

Music: Using the Power of Voice and Instruments to Uplift Our Consciousness

The use of sound to still the mind can be taken yet another level further through the introduction of elevating music. Music raises the consciousness and gives the mind a powerful outside focus. When we are immersed in a beautiful piece of music, our other thoughts become still. As long as the music continues to play, all our cares and worries disappear.

The Hebrew Bible provides us with a rich storehouse of stories that illustrate the spiritual power of music. The book of Samuel tells us that after the throne was taken away from the descendants of King Saul, the king would periodically fall into fits of mental torment. Whenever Saul fell into these moods, he would call upon the young David to play the harp for him. David's music and his peaceful presence would quiet the king's troubled spirit.

King David also used music to elevate his own awareness. The Talmud (*Pesachim* 117a) tells us that the introductory words of each psalm indicate the spiritual mode in which it was composed. When David played his harp until a sublime mood overtook him, and only then composed a psalm, the psalm begins with the words *mizmor leDavid*, "a song by David." But when the Divine Presence first overshadowed David, so that he picked up his harp and music poured forth from him, the psalm begins with the words *leDavid mizmor*, "by David a song."

In the Hebrew Bible, music is used not only to achieve a sense of inner peace and stillness but also as a vehicle to enter into a transcendental state of consciousness. In another example, from earlier on in the book of Samuel, King Saul is brought to a state of prophetic ecstasy by a passing band of prophets playing musical instruments.

> Then Samuel took the vial of oil, and poured it upon his head,
> and kissed him, and said, "Has not the Lord anointed you to be

prince over His inheritance? When you depart from me today, then you will find two men by the tomb of Rachel, in the border of Benjamin at Zelzah; and they will say to you, 'The asses that you seek are found'; and, behold, your father has left the matter of the asses and has become anxious about you, saying, 'What shall I do about my son?' Then you shall go forward from there, and you shall come to the oak of Tabor, and there you shall meet three men going up to God to Bethel, one carrying three kids, and another carrying three loaves of bread, and another carrying a bottle of wine. And they will greet you and give you two cakes of bread, which you shall receive from their hands. After that, you shall come to the hill of God, where the garrison of the Philistines is; and it shall come to pass that when you come to the city there, you will meet a band of prophets coming down from the high place with a lute, and a timbrel, and a pipe, and a harp, before them; and they will be prophesying. And the spirit of the Lord will come mightily upon you, and you will prophesy with them and shall be turned into another man. And let it be, when these signs are come to you, that you do as occasion serves you; for God is with you." (1 Samuel 10:1–7)

Music and Meditation in Eastern Traditions

The literature of the Eastern traditions is also filled with stories of spiritual practices and experiences involving music. There are many tales of spiritual figures who went into a superconscious state by singing or listening to music. The sixteenth-century Indian saint Chaitanya Mahaprabhu traveled throughout the length and breadth of India chanting the name of the Lord Krishna. Large parties of kirtanists (people singing and chanting the Lord's Name) would follow him wherever he went. Chaitanya would fall into a rapturous state when he chanted God's Name and lose all sense of body consciousness. Sometimes, he would lead the crowds in chanting for two or three days without a break. Everyone was lifted to a level of awareness where they did not need to rest or sleep.

Sri Ramakrishna was also known for the power of his ecstatic chanting and singing. While he was singing and dancing, Ramakrishna would fall into such a profound spiritual mood that he would enter into *samadhi* (a superconscious state). In that state, his major bodily functions would stop, and his mind would become completely still. Some of these extraordinary experiences have been described by his devotee "M," in *The Gospel of Sri Ramakrishna*:

> Sri Ramakrishna had been invited to the great religious festival at Panihati, near Calcutta.... Thousands of the followers of Sri Chaitanya participate in it. Its chief feature is the singing of the names and glories of God, and the dancing of the devotees in religious fervour....
>
> He joined the kirtan party of Navadvip Goswami ... and danced, totally forgetting the world. Every now and then he stood still in samadhi, carefully supported by Navadvip Goswami for fear he might fall to the ground. Thousands of devotees were gathered together for the festival. Wherever one looked there was a forest of human heads. The crowd seemed to become infected by the Master's divine fervour and swayed to and fro, chanting the name of God, until the very air seemed to reverberate with it. Drums, cymbals, and other instruments produced melodious sounds. The atmosphere became intense with spiritual fervour. The devotees felt that Gauranga [Chaitanya] himself was being manifested in the person of Sri Ramakrishna. Flowers were showered from all sides on his feet and head. The shouting of the name of Hari [a name of the Lord Vishnu] was heard even at a distance, like the rumbling of the ocean.
>
> Sri Ramakrishna entered by turn into all the moods of ecstasy. In deep samadhi he stood still, his face radiating a divine glow. In the state of partial consciousness he danced, sometimes gently and sometimes with the vigour of a lion. Again, regaining consciousness of the world, he sang, himself leading the chorus....
>
> The crowd, with the Master in the centre, surged toward the temple of Radha-Krishna. Only a small number could enter. The rest stood outside the portal and jostled with one another to have a look at Sri Ramakrishna. In a mood of intoxication he began to dance in the courtyard of the shrine. Every now and then his body stood transfixed in deep samadhi. Hundreds of people around him shouted the name of God, and thousands outside caught the strain and raised the cry with full-throated voices. The echo

travelled over the Ganges, striking a note in the hearts of people in the boats on the holy river, and they too chanted the name of God.[5]

In India there is an entire science that deals with the appropriate music for meditation. There is specific music for each of the different parts of the day. And there are particular musical patterns that are considered conducive to each meditative state. This music is a type of meditation experience of its own, and there are whole schools dedicated to it.

Music and Meditation in Jewish Tradition

There is also an understanding of the spiritual science of music in Judaism. One exponent of this science was Rebbe Nachman of Breslov. In one of his teachings, Rebbe Nachman speaks about the ten types of *nigun, or melody*.[6] In this way, he links each type of melody to one of the ten *sefirot* in the *Etz haChayim*, the body of spiritual centers.

What is a melody? A melody is harmonic sound. And what is sound, but a wave or oscillating vibration in the air? Vibration is the fundamental characteristic of all life, from the vibration of an atom to the pulsating vibration of the universe itself. So we can say that sound is a key element of everything that exists.

We also know that there are seven major notes in the traditional musical scale. This connects Rebbe Nachman's teaching about *nigun* with the seven *chakras*. So each note will stimulate a specific center in our spiritual body. And each piece of music will vitalize a number of different *sefirot*. We can learn how to use a *nigun*—a wordless tune—or a piece of instrumental music to arouse a particular vibration of energy and bring in a certain spiritual influence. We can choose the music that we play or listen to according to the state of consciousness that it will induce.

We see this power brought to a high level of expertise in the life of the Hasidic master Yisrael of Modzitz. Rebbe Yisrael was famous for his *nigunim*. During his lifetime, Rebbe Yisrael composed over two hundred melodies. In 1913, Rebbe Yisrael traveled to Berlin for medical treatment. The doctors told him that the only way to save his life was to amputate his leg. Rebbe Yisrael agreed to undergo the operation on the condition that no anesthesia be used during the procedure. When the operation began, Rebbe Yisrael withdrew deep within himself and started to compose a new melody. In this way, he went through the whole of the operation in a fully conscious state. The majestic *nigun* that he composed is made up of thirty-six sections and takes over half an hour to sing.[7]

The capacity to still the mind in this manner takes an extremely evolved level of mental control. In such a state, the mind is detached from the body and enters into a different realm. In the highest form of stilling the mind, the lower mind is not just detached but completely extinguished. One then enters into the boundless consciousness of the higher mind, the mind of pure consciousness—the awareness of the Self. In this state, there is literally no thought. The silence and stillness are complete.

CHAPTER FIVE

STILLING THE MIND II

Bitul: Self-Nullification or Surrender

*T*here are many levels of stilling the mind. The highest level is when the mind is totally quiet and there is no thought at all. This thought-free state is both the final stage and the goal of meditation. In this condition of pure emptiness, the individual mind merges into the Universal Mind, and the meditator merges into the *Ein Sof*.

There are specific meditation practices that strive to take the practitioner directly into this state beyond thought. One classic method is the Hasidic practice of *bitul*, the annihilation of the ego, or self-surrender. The Baal Shem Tov uses a famous saying of Rabbi Hillel in the Ethics of the Fathers to explain this unique approach:

> "If I am not for myself, who will be? And if I am only for myself, then what am I? [And if not now, when?]" (*Pirkei Avot* 1:14).
>
> "Because in prayer," the Baal Shem explains, "one needs to transcend physical consciousness. And this is what it says: 'if I am not for myself'—that is to say: at the moment when I have transcended physical consciousness, and I do not experience my existence in this [physical] world—that is to say: when I arrive at the level where I do not know or feel at all whether I am in this [physical] world or not; then I will definitely have no fear of negative or distracting thoughts, because what negative thought can come close to me when I have transcended this [physical] world.

And this is, 'who will be for me'—that is: what negative thought will come to me?

"But when 'I am for myself'—that is to say: when I think of myself as something having a reality in this world; then, on the contrary, I am thought of as nothing. And this is what it says: 'what am I'—that is to say: of what importance is my service and what I think before God? Because under these conditions, negative thoughts will confuse me, and therefore, I am as one not in this world; because the central reason for the creation of humanity in this world is for divine service, and I cannot serve God [properly], because of the negative thoughts that are disturbing me."[1]

Rebbe Menachem Mendel of Vitebsk, one of the leading disciples of the Maggid of Mezeritch, expands further on the Baal Shem's teaching. What prevents us from experiencing the presence of God, he elaborates, is the multitude of thoughts and desires that clutter our hearts and minds. If we can push aside all this "somethingness" for even a moment, Rebbe Mendel asserts, we will discover that there is a vibrant Nothingness that remains: an emptiness that is full of God. By making ourselves into nothing (ayin), we create space for the divinity within us to be revealed.[2]

This whole manner of thinking resembles the teaching of the Indian sage Sri Ramana Maharshi on the Self, as evidenced by the following story:

[A devotee once asked Sri Ramana:] "You say that I am in the Self, but where exactly is that Self?"

"If you abide in the heart [the core of one's being] and search patiently you will find it," was the reply.

The questioner still seemed unsatisfied, and made the rather curious observation that there was no room in his heart for him to stay in it.

Bhagavan [Sri Ramana] turned to one of the devotees sitting there and said smiling ...

"To say that there is no room in the heart after filling it with unnecessary vasanas [tendencies or impressions left on the mind by past actions] is like grumbling that there is no room to sit down in a house as big as [Sri] Lanka. If all the junk is thrown out, won't there be room?

"The body itself is junk. These people are like a man who fills all the rooms of his house chokeful of unnecessary junk and then complains that there is no room for keeping his body in it.

"In the same way they fill the mind with all sorts of impressions and then say there is no room for the Self in it. If all the false ideas and impressions are swept away and thrown out what remains is a feeling of plenty and that is the Self itself. Then there will be no such thing as a separate 'I'; it will be a state of egolessness."[3]

The Maharshi's meditation technique of Self-enquiry is a form of practice that shows us how to achieve this spiritual goal. This is how he describes the path to thought-less-ness:

When other thoughts arise, one should not pursue them, but should inquire: "To whom do they arise?" It does not matter how many thoughts arise. As each thought arises, one should inquire with diligence, "To whom has this thought arisen?"

The answer that would emerge would be "to me." Thereupon if one inquires "Who am I?" the mind will go back to its source; and the thought that arose will become quiescent. With repeated practice in this manner, the mind will develop the skill to stay in its source....

Not letting the mind go out, but retaining it in the Heart [the core of one's being] is what is called "inwardness" (*antar-mukha*). ... When the mind stays in the Heart, the "I" which is the source of all thoughts will go, and the Self which ever exists will shine....

As long as there are impressions of objects in the mind, so long the inquiry "Who am I?" is required. As thoughts arise they should be destroyed then and there in the very place of their origin, through inquiry. If one resorts to contemplation of the Self unintermittently, until the Self is gained, that alone would do. As long as there are enemies within the fortress, they will continue to sally forth; if they are destroyed as they emerge, the fortress will fall into our hands.[4]

Rebbe Nachman of Breslov teaches a similar approach to eradicating negative thoughts that intrude on the mind. It is instructive to look at his teaching in light of the approach of Sri Ramana Maharshi.

Thought is in the hands of a person to direct to the place that he desires ... and even if sometimes his thoughts arise and wander off into strange or negative ideas, it is in the hands of a person to forcibly turn his mind and bring it back to the right direction of thinking that is appropriate. Just as when a horse turns from the path and strays onto another road, you grab its reins and forcibly pull it back to the right path, in exactly the same manner, as soon as you see the mind stray from the path, you need to forcibly grab ahold of it, and bring it back to the right path.[5]

Rebbe Nachman's disciple Natan of Nemirov provides further elaboration of his master's teaching.

And when holy thoughts overcome the opposite [negative thoughts] it is on the level of the rider [the meditator] overruling the horse [the mind]. And in this way, all the enemies and forces of the Other Side will fall away by themselves. In this manner the central victory of the battle [against the mind] is achieved.[6]

In the next teaching, Rebbe Nachman moves even closer to the Maharshi's approach. In this section, he advocates the total annihilation of oneself before God as a method of counteracting negative thoughts:

When the negative side strongly overwhelms a person and really confuses his mind with many kinds of negative thoughts and confusing ideas, so that it is very hard to vanquish them, he needs to annihilate himself completely before God. Because every person has the capacity to temporarily annihilate himself completely, that is, to shut his mouth and eyes and remove his mind completely, as if he has no mind or ability to think at all, just total surrender of the self before God.[7]

Here is the Maharshi's own response when asked by one of his devotees about how to achieve Self-realization:

There are two ways; one is looking into the source of "I" and merging into that source. The other is feeling "I am helpless by myself, God alone is all-powerful and except throwing myself completely on him, there is no other means of safety for me." ... Both methods lead to the same goal. Complete surrender is another name for *jnana* [knowledge of God] or liberation.[8]

"Be still and know that I am God" [Psalm 46:1]. Here stillness is total surrender without a vestige of individuality. Stillness will prevail and there will be no agitation of mind.[9]

Interestingly, this teaching of Rebbe Nachman about self-nullification is also reminiscent of the Maharshi's description of the "death experience" that brought about his spiritual awakening:

> I was sitting alone in a room on the first floor of my uncle's house. I seldom had any sickness, and on that day there was nothing wrong with my health, but a sudden violent fear of death overtook me....
>
> The shock of the fear of death drove my mind inwards and I said to myself mentally, without actually framing the words: "Now death has come; what does it mean? What is it that is dying? This body dies." And I at once dramatised the occurrence of death. I lay with my limbs stretched out stiff as though *rigor mortis* had set in and imitated a corpse so as to give greater reality to the enquiry. I held my breath and kept my lips tightly closed so that no sound could escape.[10]

We can see that the methods of Rebbe Nachman and Sri Ramana Maharshi closely parallel each other. What is missing from Rebbe Nachman's teaching, however, is an empowering phrase or idea like "Who am I?" to push the mind inward. But we do find such an empowering phrase in one of the teachings of his disciple Rebbe Natan.

The first commandment that the Almighty gives to Abraham is *"Lekh lekha me'artzekha, umimoladtekha, umibeit avikha el ha'aretz asher areka*—Go out of your country, and from your kindred, and from your father's house, to the land that I will show you" (Genesis 12:1). In this phrase, the Hebrew word *lekh* is the command form of the second person singular of the verb "to go," that is, "you go." The word *lekha*, then, which means "to yourself," is a superfluous addition. Fully translated, the phrase is actually "go to yourself." Rebbe Natan interprets this verse as a command by God to Abraham, and every other spiritual seeker, to go to "your Self"—*to the essence of who you are.* Wherever you are going, and whatever you are doing, go toward your soul—dive deep into the source of your being.[11]

If we invoke this powerful spiritual exhortation as a response to whatever thoughts arise within us, we have a potent tool for meditation. If we combine this empowering phrase *Lekh lekha*, "Go to your Self," together with the teachings from Rebbe Nachman, we have an effective technique of Self-enquiry based on Jewish sources.

❦

Lekh Lekha—Go to Your Self

Close your eyes and let go of all tension in your body.

Begin to breathe in and out in a normal fashion, focusing your mind on the intake and outflow of your breath.

Now turn your mind inward. Whenever a thought arises, say "*Lekh lekha*" to yourself. Plunge deep inside your being, beyond emotion or intellect; reach to your very core.

This dive into your spiritual interior will set in motion a process of dynamic self-investigation into your true source. Your mind will be naturally drawn back to the spiritual heart, and whatever thought has arisen will be wiped away.

Whenever an image or a thought arises upon the screen of your mind, do not engage it, do not fight with it; simply repeat the phrase *Lekh lekha*.

No matter how often a thought arises, respond with your affirmation "*Lekh lekha*." Continue to react in this way, directing your awareness inward until the flow of thoughts slows down and then finally stops and only silence prevails.

❦

This practice is a powerful method of stilling the mind. For many people, however, it is a discipline that is hard to sustain for a long period of time. What works well for days, weeks, or months can suddenly feel stale and lifeless. In this vacuum of motivation, the mind begins to run riot.

This is the moment to take out our secret weapon of self-nullification. We fall flat on our face before the Controller of Destiny and surrender our very life. This act of *bitul* clears the decks of the ego and reinvigorates our Self-enquiry/*lekh lekha* practice. In this manner, the switch to a period of devotional I–Thou duality serves as a springboard for a plunge into the formless spaces of unity once more. Used as two arrows in our spiritual quiver, these two practices will ensure that we are always centered on the changeless and ever-present Reality.

For both Rebbe Nachman and Sri Ramana Maharshi, it is the mind itself that stands in the way of realizing our true nature. In order to realize God, or the Self, we need to still the constant stream of thoughts in the mind. Once we have achieved the state of freedom from thought, then, as a matter of course, the boundless peace and vibrant stillness of the Self will stand revealed.

CHAPTER SIX
VISUALIZATION
Using Our Creative Imagination

*T*he human mind is an amazing instrument. It has a multitude of different abilities. It can analyze data, order facts, construct thoughts, and store information. However, it is the capacity to form mental images that has the greatest effect on our meditation life.

Using this image-making power, our thoughts lead us on flights of fantasy all the time. For the most part, these fantasies are based on the fulfillment of our desires. These unconscious and unrestrained reveries begin with input arising from our surroundings. Our mind then amplifies the original input a thousandfold.

In meditation, we take this unique mental ability and turn it to a higher purpose. Rather than allow a random collection of thoughtforms to run through the brain, we direct our inner gaze to a particular image that has spiritual potency. We then sharpen and vitalize that image. The clearer a picture we can form in our consciousness, the more potent its effect will be.

The process of constructing a spiritually charged image, or "thoughtform," is an arduous and extended task. At first, we may not be able to create an image at all. Later we may be able to form a mental picture, but with contours that remain vague. And we may only be able to hold the image for a few fleeting seconds.

For most of us, it takes many long hours of practice to achieve a steady and vibrant image. And some people seem to lack a sense of inner vision.

They can never get the picture clear. Yet they are able to sense its presence on an intuitive level. It is as if they can build the thoughtform, but only on some higher, imperceptible plane.

Creating Mental Space for Spiritual Images

Once we have learned how to still our thoughts, we will discover that there is an internal space where the mind naturally centers itself. This is where we visualize our image. This space is the gateway to our inner world. We let go of the outer perception and concentrate the whole of our being there. By focusing in this way, the image will become increasingly alive and immediate, until it blocks out all sensory input from the external world.

The spot where we focus our mind is important. One common place of concentration is the area between the eyebrows and above the bridge of the nose—what is referred to in esoteric literature as the third eye. When the third eye is opened, a whole new world of perception is revealed to us.

An alternative area of focus is the heart center. We visualize our meditation ideal sitting in our heart and feel its presence there. With practice, both the form and the feeling of a living presence inside us will grow to become a tangible reality.

At first, the picture we fashion will be the simple creation of our imaginative faculty. Over time, however, spiritual intuition will begin to supplant the imagination. In this stage, we will start to receive impressions from the Universal Mind and touch the deeper reality they embody. Then our image will take on a life of its own and guide us toward the One who is worthy of adoration.

Calling Out to God through Visualization

The images in our visualization are an invocation directed toward the heavens. We are calling out to the aspect of God that is linked to the form we have created. When our thoughtform is invested with love and clarity of mind, there will be a responding evocation from its supernal root. We then merge into the divine source by a kind of spiritual osmosis and become absorbed into its consciousness.

This process of identification and absorption plays a key role in the spiritual life. It is the power of our higher Self that infuses our visualization. To whatever extent we have purified ourselves, in the same measure we will be able to merge with our soul. If we have only traveled a short distance along the path, then we will be able to touch only the outer rim of the supernal realm. And if we have advanced further in our evolution, then we will be able to reach up into the higher regions of the Kingdom of Heaven.

God is imageless and nameless, but we need to use form in order to concentrate our mind and awaken our aspiration. Be it a Deity, or the letters of a Divine Name, or a particular scene in the life of a Great One, a visualization is a vehicle to draw our awareness upward. These devices facilitate spiritual experience. They provide a form through which the Overarching Presence can come close and overshadow us.

We can think of the image that we create as a bridge in mental matter. We are in the physical world, and God is in the Kingdom of Heaven. The realm of the mind is the "place" where we meet. Our visualization creates a transcendent space composed of consciousness. In this sacred space, we can touch the intangible and encounter the eternal.

The work of visualization requires a still mind to be effective. Therefore, some technique to quiet the mental waves needs to be employed before visualization can begin. Once our thoughts have settled, we can focus our attention on creating and vitalizing our spiritual image. Then, with devotion in our heart and longing in our soul, we invite the Blessed Holy One to come and dwell therein.

In the next section of this chapter, we will go through four visualization meditations together. We will begin by picturing a single image and then gradually progress to more elaborate visualizations.

Meditation on the Name I: The Power of a Name

The first technique that we will do is a meditation on the Divine Name *Yud Heh Vav Heh*. Meditating on God's Name has a long tradition in Judaism. Psalm 16:8 states, "*Shiviti Yud Heh Vav Heh lenegdi tamid*—I have set the Lord *Yud Heh Vah Heh* always before me." The Baal Shem Tov took this injunction literally. He told his Hasidim to continually visualize the Divine Name throughout the day. According to the Ari, when God created the universe, the first realm created was the world of *Ta'amim*, mystical sounds, whose spiritual potencies were embodied within sacred Divine Names.

When we intone a sacred Name in prayer or meditation, we are drawing on this great reservoir of spiritual energy. It is just like someone calling out our name. If we are walking down the street and hear someone loudly shout our name, we will immediately turn around and run toward the source of that outcry. But if we simply hear our name softly spoken, with no intensity or sense of urgency, then we will pay little or no attention to the summons. Perhaps we'll pause for a moment and look around.

The same is true with respect to God. If we cry out with all of our heart, mind, and soul, then the All-Compassionate One will come flooding into our consciousness. But if we just mechanically repeat a holy Name, we are unlikely to experience anything. Our sincerity and the depth of our yearning are what determine the divine response.

Let us now meditate upon the Divine Name.

Begin by making yourself comfortable. Close your eyes and relax every part of your body. Start with your head and shoulders, and move all the way down to your toes.

Now breathe in and out in a normal fashion, focusing your mind on the intake and outflow of your breath.

The Hebrew letter *heh* is pronounced like an "h." It is the sound we make when we exhale. The *heh* looks like a doorway ה. It is the doorway of our breath. As we inhale, the *heh* swings one way. As we exhale, it swings in the other direction. As we focus on our breath, we ourselves become the letter *heh*. We become a swinging door through which divine livingness flows in and out.

Inhale, and let the *heh* swing in one direction; exhale, and let it swing the opposite way.

Shut out all of the outside noise. For this one moment, let nothing else exist but the movement of your breath. Become one with the *heh*. Become the doorway.

Now visualize the Divine Name *Yud Heh Vav Heh* ה ו ה י on your forehead or just in front of your forehead. Imagine the Name in any form that you wish: as the delicate black script in a Torah scroll, as radiant letters made out of light, as great stone pillars that form a gateway, or as a splash of rainbow colors across your mind.

No matter which way you visualize the Name, the key thought is to know in your heart that the Bestower of Every Goodness is truly present in the Name.

Experience the glorious light, love, and power emanating from the Name and entering into the core of your being. Feel it inundate you with divine radiance.

Now focus once again on forming the letters of the Name on your forehead. Feel their vibrancy and luminosity. Know that God and the Name are One.

Let the letters dissolve and rest quietly in the silence.

Finally, slowly open up your eyes.

❦

Deuteronomy 28:10 exclaims, "And all the peoples of the earth shall see that the name of the Lord is called upon you; and they shall be in awe of you." May we all be filled with the majesty and splendor of God's Ineffable Name. May that celestial brilliance emanate out from us to all beings. Let us walk in this world with awe—awe of the Divine Architect and the wonder of creation.

Additional stages to the Name meditation will be presented in the next chapter, on concentration.

Visualizing the Name takes a great deal of effort. If you cannot see the image in your inner eye, then simply think about the letters. The Name is a code, a secret language that you are utilizing to approach God. Use that code in whatever manner you are able. Actual visualization of the letters is best, but many people find this hard to accomplish. Until you can see the letters, try to feel the presence of the Name. Feel the weight of the letters on your forehead. Think about the grandeur and beauty of the Name. As you continue on with the practice, the letters will slowly start to take form in your mind.

Exercise for Visualization

You can also try various exercises that will help you learn how to create a mental picture. Here is an example of an exercise that will strengthen your ability to visualize the Divine Name.

Take a period of time each day, and concentrate on a picture of the Divine Name *Yud Heh Vav Heh* י ה ו ה. As you gaze at the image, carefully follow the contours of the different letters of the Name, noticing their shape and dimensions. Then close your eyes and try to visualize the Name in your mind, one letter at a time. Next, open your eyes again and study the letters, paying particular attention to the details that you had trouble visualizing in your mind's eye. Then close your eyes again, and try to form the four letters of the Name. Continue going back and forth between the outer and inner images in this fashion for approximately five to ten minutes. Over time, your capacity to visualize will gradually improve.

Divine Spark Meditation

We now move on to the next level of visualization. This meditation is based on several images related to the concept of the divine spark within us. Though this meditation demands a greater level of image-making ability, some people may find they have less difficulty with this imagery than with the Divine Name. There are no set rules for which technique will come easily to us. Each person is different. Each mind has its strengths and weaknesses. Meditation is a process of discovery. We learn what works best for us through trial and error and steady practice.

According to the teachings of the Kabbalah, there is a divine spark concealed in every living creature. Everything is a vibrant manifestation of God's living presence. We all contain one fragment of infinity.

This divine spark lies at the core of our being. It can be reached by delving inward in prayer or meditation. These spiritual disciplines connect us to the eternal part of our nature. They enable us to transcend our own finite consciousness and touch That which is without Beginning or End.

Let us now enter together into our inner space. Let us reach toward the divine spark within us—toward the place where everything is unity and light.

Begin by making yourself comfortable. Close your eyes and relax every part of your body. Start with your head and shoulders, and move all the way down to your toes.

Breathe in and out in a normal fashion, focusing your mind on the intake and outflow of your breath.

Visualize the doorway of the *heh* ה. Let the *heh* swing in one direction as you inhale and in the other direction as you exhale.

Shut out all of the outside noise. For this one moment, let nothing else exist but the movement of your breath. Become one with the *heh*. Become the doorway.

Now picture the divine spark inside you. See it installed at the core of your being. Feel its vibrancy and its beauty. Let its energy permeate your mind.

Next, visualize the spark inside you awakening to greater activity and illumination. Imagine that from your individual ember, new sparks are shooting out in every direction. Feel the single glimmer inside you start to grow. Feel it get larger and larger, engulfing the other sparks and transforming into a mighty flame.

Let the flame spread out from your spiritual center, expanding beyond the boundaries of your individual body. It has now become a blazing sacred fire, encompassing all around you—enveloping everything in its warmth and light.

Now imagine that your inner fire has transmuted into a great column of light. Visualize the column rising up from where you are sitting, all the way to the higher worlds. Visualize its light penetrating through one plane after another and merging into the *Ein Sof*.

Let go of all images and rest quietly in the silence.

Finally, open up your eyes.

When our divine spark becomes a tangible reality for us, we will tap into the awesome power at the heart of the universe. We will bring the boundless light of the supernal wellsprings down into our earthbound reality.

Tekhelet Meditation

We live in a material world and are locked into a physical state of aware-ness. We see and understand but a tiny fraction of the greater reality that underlies the outer facade that we can see, hear, and touch. The purpose of all spiritual practices is to lift us out of the confines of our narrow mind-set. They force us to expand our horizons and attune us with ideas and perspectives that are beyond the normal realm of thought.

The expansion of our consciousness changes the way in which we experience the world around us. This, in turn, transforms the way in which we view ourselves. Through these shifts in perspective, we break down unproductive patterns of behavior and thinking. Through the energy of the will of God embodied in these heightened mind states, we find the courage to set out on new and uncharted directions in our life.

There are many tools in the Jewish tradition that can help us to expand our consciousness. One such tool is the tzitzit (ritual fringes). In the Hebrew Bible, God commands the Children of Israel to place ritual fringes on each of the four corners of their garments (Numbers 15:37–41). Each tzitzit had three white threads and one special blue thread. This thread had to be a specific blue called *tekhelet*.

We are told in the Talmud (*Chulin* 89a) that the blue of *tekhelet* resembles "the color of the sea, and the sea is like the deep sky, which resembles the color of the sapphire stone, which resembles the color of the Throne of Glory."

When we look at the *tekhelet*, our mind is lifted through a series of images that stretch our awareness out toward the Infinite. This ever-broadening point of view widens the boundaries of our mind and alters the manner in which we experience our daily existence.

We will now enter together into a meditation constructed around the color blue from the tzitzit and the passage cited from the Talmud. As we move through the different steps of the imagery, the thoughtforms become progressively more expansive and complex. If you have a tzitzit with *tekhelet*, then you can use this color in the meditation. If not, just visualize a beautiful blue.

Begin by making yourself comfortable. Close your eyes and relax every part of your body. Start with your head and shoulders, and move all the way down to your toes.

Breathe in and out in a normal fashion, focusing your mind on the intake and outflow of your breath.

Visualize the doorway of the *heh* הּ. Let the *heh* swing in one direction as you inhale and in the other direction as you exhale.

Shut out all of the outside noise. For this one moment, let nothing else exist but the movement of your breath. Become one with the *heh*. Become the doorway.

Now visualize a beautiful hue of blue in your mind. Feel its calm and peaceful energy. Let the thought of this tranquil color wash away all of the strain and tension in your mind. Be quiet, be peaceful, be still.

Next, picture the clear, blue waters of the sea. Let your thoughts take you there.

Hear the sound of the rolling waves. Stare out into the distant horizon.

Turn to the expanses of the heavens. Imagine the endless blue of the sky on a cloudless day. Let your mind stretch out in every direction. Feel the sense of openness and freedom in this inner space.

Move on to the image of a sapphire stone. Regarding the sapphire stone, we are told in the Hebrew Bible that not long after the revelation on Sinai, Moses returned to the mountain together with his brother Aaron and the seventy elders of Israel. Together, they climbed partway up the mountain, where they "beheld the God of Israel, and under His feet there was a paved work of sapphire stone" (Exodus 24:10).

This paved work of sapphire is a region of brilliant blue light that lies at the limit of our consciousness. It is the place where heaven meets earth. Visualize this great vastness of scintillating blue. Feel the exquisite clarity and the immense expanse that is there.

Finally, cross over the "wall of sapphire" and enter into the realm of heaven and the Throne of Glory. Hear the voices of the angels, as they sing the praises of the Creator: "*Kadosh, kadosh, kadosh Adonai tzevaot; melo kol ha'aretz kevodo*—Holy, holy, holy is the Lord of Hosts; the whole world is filled with His glory" (Isaiah 6:3).

Feel the incredible power and majesty of the Divine Presence. Experience the dazzling light and the tremendous outpouring of love that is radiating everywhere. Transcend all awareness of name and form and touch That which is Ageless and Everlasting.

Return to the image of the *tekhelet*, of a calm, relaxing blue, and center your consciousness there. Feel its vibrancy. Feel its beauty. Feel the peace.

Now let go of all images and rest quietly in the silence.

Open up your eyes, and end your meditation.

The continual expansion of our mental frontiers leads us to an awareness of the underlying unity of all religions and peoples. This understanding is not just intellectual knowledge. It is a glorious state of awareness that links us to a place in the Mind of God that is beyond all race and religion, a place where everything is one. May we all be worthy to experience this indescribable and wondrous state of being.

Holy Apple Field Meditation

In the final meditation in this chapter, we take our visualization abilities to the highest level, where we picture a series of intricate and detailed scenes in our mind. The technique that we will embark on is built around the Kabbalisitic concept of the Holy Apple Field and the presence of the *Shekhinah*, the feminine aspect of Divinity.

The *Zohar*, the central text of Jewish mysticism, states that there is a celestial apple field in the heavens. This field is the domain of the *Shekhinah*—the Divine Mother. Each human being is a tree planted in this field, as it states in Deuteronomy 20:19: "Man is the tree of the field."

According to the *Zohar*, dew descends every day from the place that is called heaven onto the Holy Apple Field. The place called heaven is the abode of the Lesser Countenance—the Holy One, blessed be He. This Great Being overshadows the Holy Apple Field. His Spirit falls upon this field like droplets of heavenly dew nourishing and soothing the thirsty trees.

We are all rooted in the Divine Mother—we all draw our life and vitality from Her sacred soil. By learning to center ourselves in this supernal source, we will draw new energies into our lives. We will experience true peace and contentment. We will find inner strength and solidity. Our existence will be permeated with the blessings of the Spirit.

Let us now enter into our inner space together and visit the Holy Apple Field.

Begin by making yourself comfortable. Close your eyes and relax every part of your body. Start with your head and shoulders, and move all the way down to your toes.

Breathe in and out in a normal fashion, focusing your mind on the intake and outflow of your breath.

Visualize the doorway of the *heh* ה. Let the *heh* swing in one direction as you inhale and in the other direction as you exhale.

Shut out all of the outside noise. For this one moment, let nothing else exist but the movement of your breath. Become one with the *heh*. Become the doorway.

Now imagine yourself as a tree in the Holy Apple Field. Visualize the Mother's loving presence surrounding you, permeating the whole of your being. Feel Her all-embracing aura spread out and cover the whole of the field.

Picture the other trees in the field. Feel them vibrating with the Mother's presence. Look at the celestial birds and other creatures that inhabit this spiritual domain. Hear their different sounds and calls as they fill the air. Feel the sunlight, the warmth, the rich, nurturing earth, and the cool, soothing breeze.

Experience your interconnectedness with all the other trees in the garden—the profound sense of intimate belonging. The same divine breath animates everything in the field.

Turn your mind up toward the heavens. Sense the overshadowing presence of the Holy One, blessed be He. Feel the power and majestic glory of His presence.

Visualize the divine dew as it falls from the heavens upon the field. Feel the tender caress of its drops, the rejuvenating effects of this life-giving energy as it is absorbed inside you.

Let the gentle descent of dew turn into a great downpour of supernal rain. Watch the heavenly waters pierce the ground all around you and soak deep into the soil. Feel it penetrate inside your being, saturating you with Divine Spirit.

Rest in the overshadowing presence of the transcendent Lord and the immanent presence of the Divine Mother.

Everything is right. Everything is as it should be. You are sheltered and vivified; rooted and unshakable. You feel overflowing joy. All is harmonious and tranquil as you stand tall, still, and firm.

Now let go of all images and rest in the silence.

And finally, slowly open up your eyes.

We are all planted in the Holy Apple Field. We all draw our life and vitality from its sacred soil. When we center ourselves in this celestial garden, we experience inner peace and contentment. We feel an immense sense of well-being. Our whole world becomes infused with blessing and light.

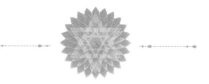

CHAPTER SEVEN

CONCENTRATION

Building Focused Spiritual Force

*U*p until this point in the book, the Hebrew word *kavanah* has been translated as "intention." *Kavanah* is the intention of heart, mind, and soul that we infuse into our spiritual practices. This aspect of *kavanah* or intention was the theme of the second chapter of the book.

In this chapter, we will explore another dimension of *kavanah*. A better translation for this aspect of *kavanah* is "concentration": the ability to be one-pointed in thought, word, and deed. When we do an act with this type of *kavanah,* it has a powerful effect on the results. The act is transformed from a simple physical action into a unit of focused spiritual energy.

Kavanah: Concentration of the Mind

The twentieth-century Indian spiritual teacher Swami Sivananda was the dynamic founder of the Divine Life Society. He was known for his universal teaching and his Yoga of Synthesis, which combines yogic postures, devotion, service, and meditation. In one of his many books, Swami Sivananda gives a wonderful explanation of the power of concentration:

> If you focus the rays of the sun through a lens, they can burn cotton or a piece of paper; but, the scattered rays cannot do this act. If you want to talk to a man at a distance, you make a funnel of your hand and speak. The sound-waves are collected at one point and then directed towards the man. He can hear your speech

very clearly. The water is converted into steam and the steam is concentrated at a point. The railway engine moves.

All these are instances of concentrated waves. Even so, if you collect the dissipated rays of the mind and focus them at a point, you will have wonderful concentration. The concentrated mind will serve as a potent searchlight to find out the treasures of the soul and attain the supreme wealth of Atman [the Self], eternal bliss, immortality and perennial joy.[1]

This type of *kavanah* plays an essential role in concentration meditation. Concentration meditation consists of single-minded focus on a particular object, idea, or image. The key to this form of practice is to engage all of our mind and willpower in keeping our attention on this one thing. Every thought that arises is swiftly repelled. Any other image that appears is cast aside, and we return to our focus. We are striving for total and complete concentration.

Silence and stillness are essential in concentration meditation. The slightest movement or distraction can break the mental bond that is being formed. Our entire reality becomes this one center of attention. Our body is forgotten as our awareness dwells on the mental plane. In this way, pure and true contact is achieved.

This is how the Baal Shem Tov instructed his Hasidim regarding contemplative prayer and the meditative ascent through the higher worlds:

> And he shall be careful not to fall from his very high thoughts in the supernal worlds to descend below; rather he must strengthen himself with all his might to remain on high in his thoughts.[2]

> And sometimes on high, he can speak without his body, just with his soul—placing himself apart from his body. And this is rising above body consciousness (*hitpashtut hagashmiyut*): that he does not sense his body at all or the appearance of this world, only the appearance of higher worlds ... and afterwards when he comes to the world of Emanation (*Atzilut*), he will feel nothing but the finest of the fine, that is, the emanation of the Lord.[3]

> And when he wants to bind himself [on high], there must be no other person in the house, because even the chirping of birds can cut him off [from the higher worlds], and also the thoughts of another [person] can cut him off [from the higher worlds].[4]

And sometimes, when a person is bound to God in the supernal world, he must guard not to make even the slightest movement with his body, so that his bond [with God] shall not be cut off.[5]

A One-Pointed Mind

The purpose of concentration meditation is to make our mind one-pointed. This then enables us to link with and be absorbed in God. As Rebbe Elimelekh of Lizhensk taught, "*Devekut* (binding oneself) is a matter of focusing the mind to eliminate all thoughts, so that all his senses and thoughts are only on the one thing that he is doing."[6]

Swami Sivananda defined meditation as a "regular flow of thought with regard to the object of concentration." He brought two analogies to elucidate this idea, likening meditation to "the flow of water in a river" and "the continuous flow of oil from one vessel to another."[7]

These sayings remind us of the teaching of the Baal Shem Tov that the first word of our prayer should be connected to the last word of our prayer[8] and of Rebbe Nachman's analogy that compares prayer to a person picking flowers in a field for his beloved, gathering them all together into a single beautiful bouquet.[9]

Sri Ramakrishna used a parable about a fisherman absorbed in the act of fishing to portray this one-pointed mind:

> A man was angling in a lake all by himself. After a long while the float began to move. Now and then its tip touched the water. The angler was holding the rod tight in his hands, ready to pull it up, when a passer-by stopped and said, "Sir, can you tell me where Mr. Bannerji lives?" There was no reply from the angler, who was just on the point of pulling up the rod.
>
> Again and again the stranger said to him in a loud voice, "Sir, can you tell me where Mr. Bannerji lives?" But the angler was unconscious of everything around him. His hands were trembling, his eyes fixed on the float. The stranger was annoyed and went on.
>
> When he had gone quite a way, the angler's float sank under water and with one pull of the rod he landed the fish. He wiped the sweat from his face with his towel and shouted after the stranger. "Hey!" he said. "Come here! Listen!" But the man would not turn his face.

After much shouting, however, he came back and said to the angler, "Why are you shouting at me?" "What did you ask me about?" said the angler. The stranger said, "I repeated the question so many times, and now you are asking me to repeat it once more!" The angler replied, "At that time my float was about to sink; so I didn't hear a word of what you said."[10]

When we are fully concentrated, we will have a continuous flow of thought toward the object of meditation. Beautiful bouquets of spiritual flowers will then be gathered to offer to the One to whom all praise is due. Effective spiritual fishermen, we will land the rare and incomparable catch of God Consciousness.

Maintaining One-Pointedness

"Despite our earnest requests, Maharaj [Swami Brahmananda] refused [meditation] initiation to some of us. When we approached him for it, he said: 'Clear your minds first, and then you will be granted it. What good would it be for me to sow seeds in a jungle? Clear your minds first. Then you will be able to reap the fruit of initiation.'"
—Swami Jnanatmananda, of the Ramakrishna Order[11]

These teachings by the Baal Shem Tov, Sri Ramakrishna, Rebbe Elimelekh, and Swami Sivananda enable us to clarify the nature of the goal for which we are striving. We want to be one-pointed and focused. We want to retain a single charged thought. How do we avoid the normal distractions that disturb us? How do we counter our wandering minds? How can we clear the undergrowth in our "jungle"?

Imagine that you are walking down the street on your way to an important job interview. You have left your home later than expected. Time is running out, and you need to move quickly or you will be late. As you walk along the street you see and hear all manner of activity: people passing by, cars with their horns blaring, radios blasting out music. There might be street vendors or sidewalk musicians, perhaps a work crew digging in a manhole. But you are in a hurry and can let nothing distract you. You turn your mind away from all of the action and continue on your way.

You pass the scene of an accident with bystanders, police, and first responders all milling about, but you don't stop to ask what is happening. You know that you need to stick to your purpose and head toward your encounter. You dash ahead to your meeting, carefully sidestepping all the obstacles along your path.

This is how we should approach our spiritual practice. We attend to our inner life with rigor and one-pointed determination. We apply the strength of our will toward reaching our destination.

This approach is reminiscent of the teaching of Rebbe Nachman of Breslov that was quoted in the section on stilling the mind. We treat our mind like a wild horse. We strive to keep it ever steady on the road. Whenever it wanders from the path, we forcibly pull on its reins and draw it back to the right course again.[12]

Another approach is to simply withdraw the attachment of the mind from all the mental activity that is taking place. We do not fight against the incoming thoughts. We think of the thoughts as fish swimming by in an aquarium—interesting creatures but of no account to us. We quietly observe their movements or even admire their beauty as they float by, but we do not attach the mind to them. We remain a witness, our attention fully focused on the object of our meditation. These thoughts are no longer an unsettling distraction. They are simply white noise, a pleasant background for our work.

A third approach is to use another meditation technique, such as a mantra recitation or visualization, to bolster our ability to focus. The sound of the mantra will provide an audio support to our work of concentration while simultaneously blocking out incoming thoughts. Mantra recitation guards against getting involved in mental chatter. Visualization complements the work of concentration by providing a spiritually potent thoughtform to counter other visual images that attempt to enter our mental space. A visualization image also offers a point of rest from the intensity of the concentration work while keeping us inwardly focused at a higher vibration.

Try these different techniques in your practice. Switch back and forth between them as you strive to focus and maintain your attention. Do not become discouraged by the many thoughts that enter your consciousness during meditation. Everyone has distracting thoughts that pop into his or her meditation. It is a perfectly normal occurrence. The key is not to get involved with these mental images, not to give them either attention or energy. In this way, the number of thoughts will naturally diminish, and you will gradually become the master of your mind.

Harnessing the Will

"Just as the cart driver controls the horses by holding the reins tight,
so does a meditator control his mind through the will."

—Swami Bhajanananda[13]

At the heart of concentration meditation is the power of the will. When we harness our will, we activate the power of the higher Self. The Baal Shem Tov spoke continually about the importance of employing our will-power in the practice of contemplative prayer. He told his Hasidim that the mere recital of the prayers is not enough. "One needs to put all of one's strength and will into the words."[14]

In another section, the Baal Shem describes each prayer as a *komah shelemah*—a complete person or form. If we do not put the whole of ourselves into our prayers, he warns, we will create a being with missing limbs.[15] If we are distracted or insincere when we pray, then our words will have no real spiritual power. They will not be charged with the necessary energy to create a *komah sheleimah*—a fully vitalized spiritual form.

The Baal Shem taught that "*kavanah* is the *neshamah* (the soul)."[16] When we act with *kavanah*, with a concentrated will, we are reaching into our innermost essence. We are touching the infinite power of our *neshamah*.

The power of the will is not accessed by stirring up the emotions or by galvanizing our feelings and resolve. It is a cool, clear light in which we work. The emotions, as well as the warmth they bring to meditation, are placed to one side. Yearning and devotion are not part of concentration meditation. We tap into this great divine power by diving deep within ourselves to the place of calm and stillness where the sacred presence resides. It is from this place of absolute quiet and tranquility that we awaken the power of Spirit, the power of the will of God.

The Dynamics of Concentration

The Midrash states that the souls of Israel are hewn from under the Throne of Glory. Rebbe Elimelekh of Lizhensk teaches that a spiritual cord connects each soul to this supernal source.[17] Regarding this cord, Ecclesiastes 12:6 declares, "Before the silver cord is snapped asunder, and the golden bowl is shattered, and the pitcher is broken at the spring, and the wheel falls shattered, into the pit."

When we are born, there is a thin line of consciousness, "a silver cord," which binds us with our soul. Our mind and personality, "the golden bowl," are the instruments that enable us to use this line of contact. When we die, the link between the body and the soul is severed, and the vessel of the individual personality and intellect is destroyed. The soul then goes on to greater adventures of the spirit, and the body is buried deep in the ground.

During our lifetime, the silver cord is the medium through which our soul can reach us. We, in turn, use the silver cord to communicate with our soul. We work to strengthen this inner link through contemplative prayer and meditation. Our goal is to transform the narrow cord into a broad bridge of spiritual connection.

Imagine that you are standing on one side of a great abyss and you want to get to the other side. There is someone who has tied a rope across the abyss, but it provides only a tenuous and fragile connection. You cannot transport anything heavy across the rope, nor would you dare to cross yourself. You can, however, make use of the cord to begin the process of building a bridge to the other side, first throwing additional lines of rope across the gap, and then gradually constructing a firmer structure. Eventually, you will have a solid bridge that allows you to transport yourself, as well as other people and materials, across the abyss—a reliable and safe passage from one side to the other.

This bridge is constructed through our efforts during meditation. In meditation, we are trying to traverse the gap in consciousness between God and ourselves. Our endeavor, however, is somewhat more complicated than in the above illustration. Most of us are unaware that a rope has been thrown across the gap. In fact, we cannot even see the other side of the abyss. So our work begins by looking for the person on the other side of the cliff and the line or silver cord that has been thrown across.

This task is fulfilled by creating an inner alignment between our personality and our soul. Concentration meditation is at the heart of this work. It creates an energetic resonance between the higher and the lower mind. In concentration meditation, we strive to set up a steady flow of conscious thought. This stabilized frequency allows our lower mind to attune itself with the spiritual vibration of our higher mind. This resonance in vibration enables an overlapping in consciousness to then occur. As a result, a direct contact is made between our soul and personality.

This process of alignment can be compared to receiving a radio transmission. Like a receiver in a radio, we learn to "tune in" to the divine frequency. This vibratory attunement allows God to come close and overshadow us.

The clarity of the communication depends on the mental makeup and equipment of the listener. If we want to get a clear signal, then it is essential to have a mind that is focused and free from all distracting thoughts. Otherwise, there will be static or interference on the line, and the incoming message will become garbled.

Once contact has been established, we can begin the process of transforming our fragile rope into a sturdy bridge. We do this by projecting our awareness toward the point of concentration. This action fills the spiritual gap between the personality and the soul, between the higher and lower planes, with the mental matter of our mind.

If our concentration is strong, then the alignment is strong. If our concentration is weak, then the alignment is weak. The stronger the alignment, the steadier the flow of thought will be, and the greater the amount of spiritual substance that is added to our inner bridge. The better the bridge, the better our contact becomes, and the more easily energy and guidance will flow across to us. When our bridge building comes to full fruition, a continuous stream of divine power and inspiration will pour into our mind. Our consciousness will merge into the awareness of our soul and unite with our supernal Source.

The practice of concentration meditation is a dynamic process. In most meditations, concentration is combined with other techniques, such as mantra recitation and visualization. Here are two meditations that blend one-pointed, focused thought with visualization of the Name. The first is a variation of the Name meditation in the previous chapter, taken to another level.

Meditation on the Name II: A Leap to Pure Being

Sri Ramakrishna was known for his state of divine intoxication. One day, he went with a devotee to a reservoir in a temple garden to teach him how to meditate on the formless God. The reservoir was filled with tame fish.

Later, the devotee recounted:

> Visitors threw puffed rice and other bits of food into the water, and the big fish came in swarms to eat the food. Fearlessly the fish swam in the water and sported there joyously.
>
> [As they sat by the reservoir together, Sri Ramakrishna exclaimed to the devotee:] "Look at the fish. Meditating on the formless God is like swimming joyfully like these fish, in the Ocean of Bliss and Consciousness."[18]

When the Almighty appeared to Moses at the burning bush, he asked God His name and was told, "I Am That I Am." I am that which *is*. I am Pure Being, Pure Consciousness.

The Name *Havayah*[19] is a bridge to the place of Pure Being. The four letters *Yud Heh Vav Heh* form the substance of that bridge. They provide us with a path to raise our consciousness to this place of pristine existence. They open up the passage into the Timeless Expanses of Infinity.

We will now return to our meditation on the Name. We will use the Name as a platform from which to lift ourselves up into the Absolute.

Begin by making yourself comfortable. Close your eyes and relax every part of your body. Start with your head and shoulders, and move all the way down to your toes.

Breathe in and out in a normal fashion, focusing your mind on the intake and outflow of your breath.

The Hebrew letter *heh* is pronounced like an "h." It is the sound we make when we exhale. The *heh* looks like a doorway ה. It is the doorway of our breath. As we inhale, the *heh* swings one way. As we exhale, it swings in the other direction. As we focus on our breath, we ourselves become the letter *heh*. We become a swinging door through which divine livingness flows in and out.

Inhale, and let the *heh* swing in one direction; exhale, and let it swing the opposite way.

Shut out all of the outside noise. For this one moment, let nothing else exist but the movement of your breath. Become one with the *heh*. Become the doorway.

Now visualize the Divine Name *Yud Heh Vav Heh* ה ו ה י on your forehead or just in front of your forehead. Imagine the Name in any form that you wish: as the delicate black script in a Torah scroll, as radiant letters made out of light, as great stone pillars that form a gateway, or as a splash of rainbow colors across your mind.

No matter which way you visualize the Name, the key thought is to know in your heart that the Bestower of Every Goodness is truly present in the Name.

Experience the glorious light, love, and power emanating from the Name and entering into your inner depths. Feel it inundate you with divine radiance.

Expand the Name outward and upward in every direction, as far as your mind can reach. Let the Name fill the whole of your mind—the whole of your consciousness. Feel that the entire universe has become the four letters *Yud Heh Vav Heh.*

Next, let go of your individual boundaries and merge yourself into this infinite space. Feel that you are swimming in a boundless ocean of light and consciousness, ascending ever higher toward the Absolute. Keep your mind fully focused on the Infinite. Let no other thoughts enter into your awareness. Forget all else and strive toward the *Ein Sof.*

Draw the Name back down in front of your forehead once again. Feel the immense power that now radiates from the Name. Feel the vibrancy and luminosity of the letters. Know that God and the Name are One.

Let the letters dissolve and rest quietly in the silence.

Slowly open up your eyes.

Psalm 99:6 refers to the prophet Samuel as one who "calls on the Name." May we all become callers of the Name. May the power of the Divine Name *Yud Heh Vav Heh* flow into our spiritual centers. May we become potent instruments to bring God's infinite compassion, mercy, and love into the world.

Meditation on the Name III: A Bridge to the Soul

Our second meditation will once again focus on the four-letter Name of God, *Yud Heh Vav Heh.* The Kabbalists understood the four letters as a symbolic representation of the spiritual pathway that links us with the Infinite. They saw the relationship between the different letters of the

Name as a reflection of the relationship between the different parts of our soul.

According to the Kabbalah, there are three parts to the soul: *nefesh*, *ruach*, and *neshamah*. The *nefesh* is the personality. It is the part of the soul that takes on physical awareness and infuses our body and mind with consciousness.

The *ruach* is our individual soul, what is often called our higher Self. It is the part of our individual identity that lives on after we die and that contains the essence of who we are. It is our *ruach* that goes from incarnation to incarnation, gaining knowledge and experience until it is finally liberated.

And lastly, there is the *neshamah*, the part of our soul that is a spark of the Infinite. The *neshamah* is our link to the Self of All Selves. The *neshamah* joins us to the place where everything is One.

According to the Kabbalah, *Vav* and *Heh*, the last two letters of the Name, represent the link between the *ruach* (our individual soul) and the *nefesh* (our personality). And the first two letters of the Name, *Yud* and *Heh*, represent the connection between the *neshamah* (our link with God in the Absolute) and the *ruach*.

The Kabbalists utilize these two groupings of the four letters of the Name as a meditation tool to contemplate the different aspects of our consciousness and to lift our awareness up to the loftiest heights.

We will now meditate using this Kabbalistic model, concentrating on the relationship between each letter and the different parts of our soul.

Begin by making yourself comfortable. Close your eyes and relax every part of your body. Start with your head and shoulders, and move all the way down to your toes.

Breathe in and out in a normal fashion, focusing your mind on the intake and outflow of your breath.

Visualize the doorway of the *heh*. Let the *heh* swing in one direction as you inhale and in the other direction as you exhale.

Shut out all of the outside noise. For this one moment, let nothing else exist but the movement of your breath. Become one with the *heh*. Become the doorway.

Now imagine the letter *Heh* ה imprinted upon your forehead.

Next, visualize the letter *Vav* ‎ו‎ extending upward above you, until it touches the living presence of your soul in the higher worlds.

Feel the power of your own soul shining down upon you from above in an unceasing stream of light and consciousness, with the *Vav* and the *Heh* forming a bridge between you and your soul.

Picture a second letter *Heh* ‎ה‎, or doorway, forming at the point where your soul shines down upon you. This second *Heh* opens up onto a completely different realm.

Imagine that at the furthest point your mind can reach, there resides the letter *Yud* ‎י‎.

Project your consciousness through the doorway of the second *Heh* out toward the *Yud*. Stretch your mind way up into the Infinite, where you, your soul, and God are One. Hold steady in that place as long as you are able.

Now visualize the four letters of the Name *Yud Heh Vav Heh* ‎ה ו ה י‎ upon your forehead. Feel the light of the Absolute flowing through the letters and spreading deep inside you, filling the whole of your being with peace and bliss.

Let go of all images and rest quietly in the silence.

Finally, slowly open up your eyes.

The more alive the Divine Name is inside us, the stronger the link with our soul will become. The stronger our connection is with our soul, the more expansive and elevated our consciousness will be. We will ascend further and further into the light of Divinity until we merge into the Awareness that is beyond time and space.

CHAPTER EIGHT

MANTRA RECITATION

Harnessing Spiritually Charged Sound

A mantra is an empowered phrase or sound that emanates a potent vibration that raises our consciousness. It might be a phrase from scripture, a sacred syllable, or one of the Names of God. By repeating the mantra continuously, we create a current of sound and energy that vitalizes our mind and spiritually charges our environment.

While mantras are very common in Hinduism and Buddhism, they are less common in Judaism today. However, in biblical times, they were used on a regular basis. We find one example of the chanting of a mantra in the spontaneous response of the people to Elijah's triumph over the prophets of Baal on Mount Carmel. In reaction to the fire that descends from heaven, the thousands who gathered to watch the confrontation fell on their faces and cried out, "*Adonai hu haElohim, Adonai hu haElohim!*—The Lord *Yud Heh Vav Heh* is God; the Lord *Yud Heh Vav Heh* is God!" (1 Kings 18:39).

The *Tanakh* does not recount how long the people's chanting went on, but it probably continued for some time. The power of this chanting has remained forever impressed upon the Soul of Israel. In fact, this phrase is one of the few chants that are still used in Judaism today. It is chanted seven times consecutively during the climactic moment at the end of the Yom Kippur prayer service. It creates a powerful spiritual vibration that fills the whole synagogue.

How Does a Mantra Work?

A mantra serves many different purposes. On the most basic level, it provides a continuous flow of sound that creates an audio barrier to block out other thoughts. In this manner, it acts as an effective tool for stilling the mind.

A mantra, however, does much more than quiet our mind. When we recite a mantra, we draw on the spiritual source of which this mantra is the seed. A mantra has an address in the Kingdom of Heaven. When we repeat the mantra, we send out a signal to that address, a type of spiritual beacon. When the signal arrives at its destination, the attention of the appropriate aspect of God is turned toward us. A stream of energy then flows in our direction. Once contact is made, our mind is raised to the state of awareness identified with the original seed thought.

For example, a Buddhist who repeats the prayer "*Om mani padme hum*" draws on the heavenly source associated with Avalokiteshvara, the Buddha of Compassion. As a result, a feeling of peace and compassion arises. The more the phrase is repeated with sincerity, the more intense that feeling becomes. A vision or an image of Avalokiteshvara may also appear to deepen the experience or impression that the all-pervading essence is close.

The Six Elements of a Mantra

According to the science of Yoga, there are six elements to a mantra.[1] In the description that follows, I have identified a corresponding Jewish counterpart for each of these six elements.

Inspired Master: *Baal Ruach Kodesh*

The *baal ruach kodesh* (*rishi* in Sanskrit) is the person who created the mantra. This is the one who forged the original link with the source on high.

The term *baal ruach kodesh* also refers to the spiritual guide imparting the mantra. He or she is the living representative of the original creator of the mantra through the chain of teachers linked over the generations. In Judaism, we find a similar conception, where the traditional chain of teachers is listed at the beginning of the Ethics of the Fathers: "Moses received the Torah from Sinai and gave it over to Joshua. Joshua gave it over to the Elders, the Elders to the Prophets, and the Prophets gave it over to the Men of the Great Assembly" (*Pirkei Avot* 1:1). The teacher is not simply a single individual. He or she is a representative of the whole lineage of the tradition.

Lastly, the *baal ruach kodesh* represents the connection we create with all the people who have chanted the mantra. Over the generations a great reservoir of power has been built up by their chanting. We tap into this reservoir of spiritual force whenever we intone the mantra.

The mantras in this book come from a number of different *baalei ruach kodesh*. Some are part of the tradition, with their source reaching far into the past. Others are mantras that I have learned from my teachers and there are also mantras that come from my own knowledge and inspiration.

Face of God: *Partzuf*

As explained earlier, each mantra has an address in the Kingdom of Heaven and is directed toward a particular spiritual source. Each particular *Partzuf* (*Devata* in Sanskrit) creates a focused beam of sound and energy. We can chant the mantra for *Yud Heh Vav Heh, El Shaddai,* or *Elohim*. Our chant creates a wave of vibration along the appropriate frequency.

There are countless planes and myriad beings in the spiritual realm. These celestial legions are extensively described in the Kabbalah. The *Partzufim*, or Divine Countenances, are Great Beings who embody a specific aspect of Divinity. Having a *Partzuf* makes sure our mantra reaches the proper destination. Otherwise, our mantra would be like a message in a bottle haphazardly blown across the waves of an ocean, arriving, if we are lucky, on a distant and random shore. Instead, the *Partzuf* ensures that our mantra is like a letter taken from our hand by the postman and passed on directly to the post office. We can be sure that it will go to the right place and the right person, because it has a name, an address, and a zip code.

Musical Intonation: *Nusach*

The *nusach* (*raga* in Sanskrit) is the intonation and musical sound of the mantra. It is the unique vibration of the mantra that creates a desired resonance in the person. In India, this is a highly developed science. They have a specific intonation and musical sound for each mantra. In

Judaism, we once had this knowledge, but it has been mostly forgotten. The detailed symbols and musical notes for chanting the Torah and the different *nusachs*, or cantoral styles, for the various prayer services during the year cycle are evidence of the once greater understanding that we had in the past. The chanting style of prayer in Sephardic synagogues more closely resembles the practice of mantra chanting than does the customary prayers of the Ashkenazi communities.

Seed: *Garin*

There is a seed syllable or word that is the spark that kindles the mantra and brings it to life. Like a seed, the *garin* (*bija* in Sanskrit) contains the spiritual essence of the mantra. This seed needs to be planted in our heart. Then the spiritual power contained within the mantra will sprout forth when we do our chanting.

All of the prayers in Judaism have a *garin*, or seed word, that vitalizes them. This *garin* is the spiritual heart of the prayer. An example of a *garin* in Judaism is the word *Echad* (One) in the *Shema*. According to the *Shulchan Arukh,* the central legal text for traditional Jews, when we recite the *Shema*, we need to "extend the *chet* of *Echad*, in order to proclaim God King in heaven and on earth ... and extend the *dalet* of *Echad* long enough so that you can think that there is only one God in the world and that He rules over the four corners of the earth."[2]

Divine Power: *Shefa*

The *shefa* (*shakti* in Sanskrit) represents the actual power behind the form of the mantra, the vibratory wave it sets in motion. This wave is carried from one person to the other and then emanated out into the world. The *shefa* converts the mantra into a dynamic force.

The *shefa* indicates which of the *sefirot* is stimulated by the mantra. It tells us the nature of the energy and consciousness we are arousing. It defines the vibration that will be transmitted through our words.

Driving Force: *Kavanah*

Kavanah (*kilaka* in Sanskrit) is the driving force behind the mantra. It represents the individual's contribution to the mantra chanting. *Kavanah* is the persistence and willpower that we infuse into our practice. A mantra said with *kavanah* becomes a living vibration inside us. Our *kavanah* draws all the six elements of the mantra together into a unified spiritual force.

Three Ways to Recite a Mantra

There are three ways in which we can recite a mantra. We can chant it out loud, repeat it quietly under our breath, or intone the mantra silently in our mind. Each manner of reciting a mantra has its strengths and weaknesses.

Chanting out loud is the easiest way to practice. The sound of the words keeps our mind focused and alert. Repeating the mantra quietly enables us to say our mantra even in the middle of a crowded room. Silently intoning the words makes it harder to concentrate our mind, but it permits us to dive deeply inward. As we go about our practice, we move back and forth between the three methods, doing whatever is needed to keep our chanting alive.

Though each type of chanting will be part of any practice, there is, in fact, a progression among the three methods. As our mantra chanting progresses, we move from spoken words to whispered words to words etched in silence. A passage from the Baal Shem Tov on the practice of contemplative prayer illustrates the evolution of this process:

> In prayer you must put all your strength into the [pronunciation] of the words. And you shall go from letter to letter until you forget your physicality. And you think that the letters are combining and joining one to the other, and this is a great joy. If also in the material this is a joy, how much more so in the Spirit. And this is the world of Formation (Yetzirah). And afterward you will come to the letters of thought and you will not hear what you are saying, and this is because you have come to the world of Creation (Briah). And then you come to the attribute of Nothingness (Ayin) that all your physical powers [senses] are annihilated, and this is the world of Emanation (Atzilut), the attribute of wisdom.[3]

For an explanation of the four worlds, see the Baal Shem's practice for ascending through the worlds in chapter 9.

Mantra chanting is a unique form of meditation. It forms a bridge between the path of meditation and the path of prayer. It combines words with silence. It joins outer action with inner thought. It uses sacred sounds to purify the mind.

Obstacles and Solutions When Reciting a Mantra

Chanting a mantra has its own particular challenges. There are many different questions that arise. Following are some of the main issues we face when choosing to use a mantra.

How Do We Decide Which Mantra Is Right for Us?

One of the first questions that we need to address is, which mantra is right for us? The best way to discover our mantra is to find a teacher who can guide us to the right choice. A spiritual mentor will be able to discern which mantra will resonate with our soul. In fact, the whole concept of taking initiation arises out of this relationship. The teacher selects a mantra according to our spiritual nature. He or she then transmits its spiritual power to us at the moment of initiation.

If we do not have a personal teacher, then we should try to receive our mantra from a reputable source. Energy can be transferred through voice and even through the written word. Therefore, the book, audio, or video from which we learn a mantra is very important. If we have no teacher and have to choose our mantra ourselves, we should look for a mantra to which we are drawn and then try it out. Gradually, we will discover the mantra that works for us—the one that comes alive with our chanting and that brings us closer to God.

Once we have chosen our mantra, we need to stick with our choice, no matter what happens. There will be periods when the mantra is vitalized and the energy flows abundantly. And there will be other times when nothing seems to work. But if we keep to our mantra, in due course we will see fruit from our practice.

How Do We Achieve the Proper Pronunciation and the Right Sound and Cadence?

There are two schools of thought on pronunciation and cadence. Some teachers are very particular about this matter. Swami Radha was a Western disciple of Swami Sivananda who founded an ashram in Canada. While in India, she spent many months studying mantra chanting from a swami who was an expert in this field. She learned the proper pronunciation, musical tone, and cadence for each mantra. As a result, she was very strict with her students about how they chanted a mantra.

Swami (Papa) Ramdas, on the other hand, put less emphasis on how his devotees recited a mantra. Papa Ramdas was another twentieth-century teacher known for his overflowing universal love. He was a great exponent of mantra chanting. Swami Ramdas felt that each of us finds the manner of chanting that is suitable for us. As we habituate ourselves to regular practice, the appropriate components will come together by themselves. The breath, voice, and rhythm will naturally fall into place.[4]

Despite her own insistence on the importance of the proper intonation, sound, and cadence, Swami Radha also admitted that getting all of these details right is not essential for effective mantra chanting. She compared this issue to what happened when people came to visit her teacher, Swami Sivananda. People came to see Swami Sivananda from all over India. They pronounced his name in all kinds of ways, some of them quite different than its proper pronunciation. Nonetheless, no matter how people pronounced his name, Swami Sivananda still responded to them.

The same principle, Swami Radha explained, can be applied to God and mantra chanting. Even when we get the pronunciation all wrong, if we chant our mantra with sincerity and devotion, God will answer us.[5]

How Do We Know When to Vary the Speed and Amplification of a Mantra?

The mind is easily bored; as a result, our attention strays. To counter this tendency, we need to vary the speed and amplification of the mantra. We start slowly and build speed as the intensity builds. We can slow down again if the intensity becomes too much or if we simply feel tired out by the pace. The key is to do whatever focuses the mind and comes naturally to us. These are practical details that get resolved with practice.

We can also change the part of the mantric phrase where we place our emphasis. This will help hold the mind alert and engaged. In mantra chanting, as well as other forms of meditation, there is a great need for our practice to always be fresh.

Lastly, we can vary our position while chanting. We can chant our mantra while sitting still in a comfortable position, or we can repeat it as we walk along the way. In this manner, we can keep up our chanting under all circumstances. We can carry our mantra with us throughout the day.

When Should We Sing a Mantra with a Melody, Instead of Simply Chanting the Words?

When we get tired of just chanting, then we sing the mantra with a melody, and we switch back and forth as often as we need. We use whatever form of chanting helps us to keep reciting the mantra and stay focused on God.

How Do We Develop Our Chanting Voice?

A good chanting voice is achieved through constant practice and purity of living. As our own energy vibration becomes more refined, our voice will automatically improve. In fact, according to Yogic tradition, an improved voice is one of the signs of progress in meditation.

How Do We Deepen Our Endurance in Repeating a Mantra?

The more we chant, the longer we will be able to chant. In addition to practice, working on our breathing helps. If we breathe properly, then the chanting will flow more easily. We start with a short period of chanting and keep to the same time limit every day for a week. The next week, we chant for a little longer until that time frame feels comfortable. Week to week, we build our endurance. If we get stuck on one particular length of time, we continue chanting that long for several weeks, until we feel that we are ready to add more time. Strong *kavanah* and a steady fluidity to the flow of the words are more important than the length of time that we chant.

An alternative approach is to gauge our chanting by the number of repetitions of the mantra that we have done, rather than by a given period of time. Those of us who like having the tangible goal of a specific number may find this way of pacing the chanting easier and more meaningful.

If we decide to chant according to this method, then we can try using a *japa mala,* or sacred string of beads. Counting the beads helps to keep track of the number of mantras we have recited. It also combats restlessness and builds mental focus. The *japa mala* itself develops an energy of its own, which helps to motivate our chanting. On the other hand, using a *japa mala* does make us more body conscious, and it can impede our going fully inward.

Whether we chant for a prescribed time period or do a set number of mantra recitations, these are only starting points for our practice. The goal that we are working toward is to have the mantra unceasingly on our lips. Ultimately, the mantra will sound by itself inside us. It will become the inner music that forms the background to our lives.

How Do We Keep Our Mantra Chanting from Becoming Just the Rote Repetition of Words?

We keep our mantra vibrant and vital by strengthening our *kavanah*. *Kavanah* is an essential part of any spiritual practice. Without it, our practice will quickly become a dry, mechanical exercise. The mantra is like a seed that we have planted. Our *kavanah* waters that seed and brings it to life.

We intensify our *kavanah* by remembering the mantra's *Partzuf* (supernal source) and *baal ruach kodesh* (original creator). When we direct our thoughts toward the source of the mantra, love and devotion awaken in our hearts. And when we center our mind on the *baal ruach kodesh*, his or her energy is drawn toward us. In this manner, we raise our consciousness and arouse a strong spiritual vibration inside us, thereby transforming our chanting into a vital inner experience.

Now that we have set out the basic principles of mantra chanting, let us now begin our practice. There are many kinds of mantras and various ways to go about them. We will begin with a simple mantra that has a long and rich history in our tradition. There is a guide to the pronunciation of the mantras on page 214.

Adonai Hu HaElohim

Our first mantra is the chant discussed at the beginning of this chapter: *Adonai hu haElohim*—"The Lord *Yud Heh Vav Heh* is God." As mentioned earlier, this mantra comes from the story of the prophet Elijah in the Hebrew Bible, in 1 Kings 18:20–39. During a time of great corruption and idol worship in the Kingdom of Israel, Elijah challenged the prophets of the cult of Baal to come to Mount Carmel for a showdown. Elijah stood alone against 450 prophets of Baal. Thousands of Israelites gathered on the mountaintop to witness the battle.

Elijah had two altars built on which sacrifices were placed—one altar for him and one for the prophets of Baal. Elijah then challenged the other prophets to pray to Baal to send a fire from heaven to consume the sacrifice, and he would pray to the God of Israel. Whichever prophet could bring down a heavenly fire, he declared, his was the real God.

The prophets of Baal agreed to the challenge, and the battle began. The prophets of Baal cried out from morning to night—banging on drums and gashing themselves with knives and spears—but no answer came.

Finally, as the day drew to a close and the time of the evening sacrifice was approaching, Elijah had the people pour bucket after bucket of water on his altar, until it filled the whole of the surrounding trench. Then he got down on his knees and prayed:

> Lord God of Abraham, Isaac, and of Israel, let it be known this day that You are God in Israel, and that I am your servant, and that I have done all these things at Your word. Hear me, O Lord, hear me, that this people may know that You are the Lord God, and that you have turned their heart back again. (1 Kings 18:36–37)[6]

As Elijah finished his prayer, a great fire fell from the heavens and consumed the sacrifice, the altar, and everything around it. When the people saw this miracle, they broke out in a spontaneous chant:

> *Adonai hu haElohim—Adonai hu haElohim*
> The Lord *Yud Heh Vav Heh* is God—the Lord
> *Yud Heh Vav Heh* is God.

Let us now follow in their footsteps.

Begin by making yourself comfortable. Close your eyes and relax every part of your body. Start with your head and shoulders, and move all the way down to your toes.

Breathe in and out in a normal fashion, focusing your mind on the intake and outflow of your breath.

The Hebrew letter *heh* is pronounced like an "h." It is the sound we make when we exhale. The *heh* looks like a doorway ה. It is the doorway of our breath. As we inhale, the *heh* swings one way. As we exhale, it swings in the other direction. As we focus on our breath, we ourselves become the letter *heh*. We become a swinging door through which divine livingness flows in and out.

Inhale, and let the *heh* swing in one direction; exhale, and let it swing the opposite way.

Shut out all of the outside noise. For this one moment, let nothing else exist but the movement of your breath. Become one with the *heh.* Become the doorway.

Begin to chant the mantra out loud. Say the words slowly and with feeling:

A-do-nai hu ha-Elo-him, A-do-nai hu ha-Elo-him,
A-do-nai hu ha-Elo-him, A-do-nai hu ha-Elo-him,
A-do-nai hu ha-Elo-him, A-do-nai hu ha-Elo-him …

As you chant these words, cast off all of the "idols" that you have been worshiping—all the false gods that you have allowed to take over your life—the search for self-gratification, the desire for fame, fortune, and power. Proclaim your desire to live a life of purpose and meaning. Affirm your commitment to live by high aspirations and divine ideals.

Now repeat the mantra quietly to yourself. Feel the words seeping inside you. Let them fill your heart and mind:

A-do-nai hu ha-Elo-him, A-do-nai hu ha-Elo-him,
A-do-nai hu ha-Elo-him, A-do-nai hu ha-Elo-him,
A-do-nai hu ha-Elo-him, A-do-nai hu ha-Elo-him …

Intone the mantra silently in your mind. Focus on the seed word: *haElohim*—only God is real. Only God is worthy of receiving your love and devotion. There is nothing else in which you should invest your energies and passion. Only God deserves the dedication of your life in service.

A-do-nai hu ha-Elo-him, A-do-nai hu ha-Elo-him,
A-do-nai hu ha-Elo-him, A-do-nai hu ha-Elo-him,
A-do-nai hu ha-Elo-him, A-do-nai hu ha-Elo-him,
A-do-nai hu ha-Elo-him, A-do-nai hu ha-Elo-him …

End your chanting and rest quietly in the silence.

Slowly open up your eyes.

Adonai hu haElohim is an affirmation of our loyalty to God—our unshakable living faith. It is a tool that aids us in rejecting the false pursuits that we have worshiped, the insubstantial and fleeting objects of this world that we grasp. Through the power of this mantra, we can break the veil of illusion that envelops us. We can rededicate ourselves as servants of the Most High.

Shema Mantra

Our next mantra is based on the *Shema*, the central prayer of Judaism. The *Shema* is a great affirmation of faith in the oneness of the Godhead. It is a declaration that everything is of God, in God, and from God.

The mantra that we will use focuses on the first line of the prayer: *Shema Yisrael, Adonai Eloheynu, Adonai Echad*—"Hear O Israel, the Lord *Yud Heh Vav Heh* is our God, the Lord *Yud Heh Vav Heh* is One."

This phrase can be broken down into three segments and used as a mantra: *Shema Yisrael*, "Hear O Israel"; *Adonai Eloheynu*, "the Lord *Yud Heh Vav Heh* is our God"; *Adonai Echad*, "the Lord *Yud Heh Vav Heh* is One." Each part of the phrase presents a separate focus for contemplation. Together they form a progression of spiritual ideas that increase in intensity, as we move from one to the other during our chanting. Let us look at each segment individually.

The first segment of the verse is *Shema Yisrael*. The word *shema* means "to hear." But *shema* is not just a physical hearing; it is a deep listening from the core of our being—a vibrant hearing in the very depth of who we are. *Shema* is God calling out and telling us to hear and receive the words of this prayer in the center of our heart. *Yisrael*, or Israel, tells us to whom God is speaking: to the part of us that belongs to *Yisrael*. Israel is a faith and a nation—but it is also a spiritual mission. It is a vast soul that is formed of all the people who are striving to reveal the Divine Presence upon earth—to fill the world with radiant light—to help all of humanity to live and act as one. It is from this place of high aspiration that we are to listen to this prayer.

The next segment of the verse is *Adonai Eloheynu*. *Adonai* means "Lord." However, in the Hebrew, what is written is the Ineffable Name *Yud Heh Vav Heh*. In the Kabbalah, this Name represents the aspect of Divinity that embodies compassion, the source of all compassion in the universe. *Adonai Eloheynu* then is "The Lord of Compassion is our God." This source of all-embracing love is not in some far-off heaven, but right here with us, walking beside us through life—sharing our joys and our sorrows, our triumphs and failures. We are never alone.

The last segment of the verse is *Adonai Echad*—"God is One." God is both immanent and also infinite and eternal. In the Absolute there is perfect unity—in the place of pure consciousness and being, in the place where all is peace, harmony, and bliss.

Let us now take these three segments from the first verse of the *Shema* and repeat them as a mantra.

Begin by making yourself comfortable. Close your eyes and relax every part of your body. Start with your head and shoulders, and move all the way down to your toes.

Breathe in and out in a normal fashion, focusing your mind on the intake and outflow of your breath.

Visualize the doorway of the *heh* ה. Let the *heh* swing in one direction as you inhale and in the other direction as you exhale.

Shut out all of the outside noise. For this one moment, let nothing else exist but the movement of your breath. Become one with the *heh*. Become the doorway.

Chant the whole of the verse out loud. As you chant the verse, focus your mind on the first two words: *Shema Yisrael*. As you do so, link up with the Soul of Israel and all those who are part of its mission.

> *She-ma Yis-ra-el, A-do-nai Elo-hey-nu, A-do-nai E-cha-d,*
> *She-ma Yis-ra-el, A-do-nai Elo-hey-nu, A-do-nai E-cha-d,*
> *She-ma Yis-ra-el, A-do-nai Elo-hey-nu, A-do-nai E-cha-d,*
> *She-ma Yis-ra-el, A-do-nai Elo-hey-nu, A-do-nai E-cha-d ...*

Repeat the verse quietly to yourself:

> *She-ma Yis-ra-el, A-do-nai Elo-hey-nu, A-do-nai E-cha-d,*
> *She-ma Yis-ra-el, A-do-nai Elo-hey-nu, A-do-nai E-cha-d,*
> *She-ma Yis-ra-el, A-do-nai Elo-hey-nu, A-do-nai E-cha-d,*
> *She-ma Yis-ra-el, A-do-nai Elo-hey-nu, A-do-nai E-cha-d ...*

Drop the mantra altogether, and silently reflect on the seed thought for the first part of this verse: listen from the core of your being, link with the Soul of Israel.

Next, let go of the first part of the verse, and repeat only the last two segments: *Adonai Eloheynu, Adonai Echad*. As you chant this part of the verse, link your mind with *Yud Heh Vav Heh*, the embodiment of compassion, a personal and immanent God, who is right here beside you as you meditate—watching over and protecting you; sharing your joys and your sorrows, your triumphs and failures.

Continue to chant this phrase while evoking the presence of the Guardian of Israel with all of your heart, soul, and might:

> *A-do-nai Elo-hey-nu, A-do-nai E-cha-d,*
> *A-do-nai Elo-hey-nu, A-do-nai E-cha-d,*
> *A-do-nai Elo-hey-nu, A-do-nai E-cha-d ...*

Repeat the mantra quietly to yourself:

> *A-do-nai Elo-hey-nu, A-do-nai E-cha-d,*
> *A-do-nai Elo-hey-nu, A-do-nai E-cha-d,*
> *A do nai Elo hey nu, A do nai E cha d ...*

Let go of the mantra altogether, and silently reflect on the seed thought of this segment. *Yud Heh Vav Heh*, the Lord of Compassion, is a personal and immanent God that is right beside you as you meditate.

Now drop the second portion of the verse as well, and just chant the third part. *Adonai Echad*—"The Lord *Yud Heh Vav Heh* is One." As you say these words, direct your mind toward the Supreme Awareness beyond personality, beyond time and space—beyond all perception and form.

> *A-do-nai E-cha-d, A-do-nai E-cha-d,*
> *A-do-nai E-cha-d, A-do-nai E-cha-d,*
> *A-do-nai E-cha-d, A-do-nai E-cha-d ...*

Quietly repeat the mantra to yourself:

> *A-do-nai E-cha-d, A-do-nai E-cha-d,*
> *A-do-nai E-cha-d, A-do-nai E-cha-d,*
> *A-do-nai E-cha-d, A-do-nai E-cha-d ...*

Now release the mantra altogether, and silently contemplate the seed thought for this segment: God is One in the Absolute; One in the place of pure consciousness and being.

Go back to chanting the whole verse, while focusing your mind on each of the three segments as you chant:

> *She-ma Yis-ra-el, A-do-nai Elo-hey-nu, A-do-nai E-cha-d,*
> *She-ma Yis-ra-el, A-do-nai Elo-hey-nu, A-do-nai E-cha-d,*
> *She-ma Yis-ra-el, A-do-nai Elo-hey-nu, A-do-nai E-cha-d,*
> *She-ma Yis-ra-el, A-do-nai Elo-hey-nu, A-do-nai E-cha-d ...*

End your chanting and sit quietly in the silence.

Slowly open up your eyes.

The essence of the *Shema* is a proclamation of the intrinsic unity of all Creation. Through this mantra, we link ourselves to the essence of who we are. We enter into the presence of our personal God. We stretch our minds and hearts to touch the *Ein Sof.*

Mantra of Compassion

Our next meditation combines mantra chanting with visualization and personal prayer. This meditation centers on the attribute of *rachamim*, or compassion.

There is so much suffering in the world. We see pain and sorrow everywhere we look. How can we ever relieve all this suffering? How can we ever help all those in need?

The Kabbalistic tradition speaks of the work of *tikun olam*, the labor of repairing and healing the world. According to the Ari, at the beginning of Creation, in an act reminiscent of the big bang, God sent an *or yashar*—a burst of light and energy—direct from the realm of the Infinite into the fragile vessel of the newly formed universe.

This fragile vessel could not withstand the tremendous force of the divine light, and a great shattering took place. As a result, our universe was left in a broken condition where sparks of divine light, *nitzotzot*, were fused with shards of concrete matter, *klipot*, and everything that existed became a mixture of light and darkness, good and evil, joy and sorrow, success and failure.[7]

As a result of this cosmic shattering, nothing in this universe can be perfect; nothing can be whole. Everything in this universe is in a state of essential brokenness. The suffering that we see all around us is a direct result of this fundamental universal condition.

If this were all that the tradition taught us, then life in this world would be a sorry affair indeed. But the teachings of the Ari do not end here; he also gives us a powerful message of hope. While it may be true that we live in a broken world, amid the brokenness there is the possibility of *tikun*—of fixing and of wholeness. Our brokenness is not irreparable. We can uplift ourselves out of our fallen state, by awakening the divine attributes that lie buried within us.

Leviticus 19:2 exhorts, "You shall be holy: for I, the Lord your God, am holy." The Rabbis tell us that we make ourselves holy by emulating the divine behavior. God is compassionate, so we should be compassionate.

God is generous, so we should be generous. In this way, we too will become holy.

When we act with compassion, we become extensions of divine compassion. When we move out of our self-centered reality and act to relieve the suffering of others, we are helping to uplift our physical reality. We are helping to repair the world.

There are many levels on which we can become part of this work of *tikun*, or repair. In our families, in our neighborhoods, and in the wider society, there are opportunities for us to serve others and express our caring concern. Our next mantra provides us with a vehicle for contributing to *tikun* on an inner level. It demonstrates how we can become an instrument of compassion through the practice of meditation.

The mantra is composed of two words: *Adonai,* "Lord," and *rachem,* "have compassion." We repeat these two words over and over again: *Adonai rachem, Adonai rachem.* This simple prayer is used to evoke the All Merciful's infinite compassion by all of the Abrahamic faiths.

Let us begin.

Make yourself comfortable. Close your eyes and relax every part of your body. Start with your head and shoulders, and move all the way down to your toes.

Breathe in and out in a normal fashion, focusing your mind on the intake and outflow of your breath.

Visualize the doorway of the *heh* ה. Let the *heh* swing in one direction as you inhale and in the other direction as you exhale.

Shut out all of the outside noise. For this one moment, let nothing else exist but the movement of your breath. Become one with the *heh*. Become the doorway.

Now, forget about your breathing, and picture the radiant light of your soul shining down upon you from above. Feel its power; feel the love and the beauty of its presence.

Think of all the people that you know who are suffering—all the people who are in need of compassion. Try to visualize their faces in your mind.

Standing in the clear light of your soul, look toward God, and with a sincere and open heart ask the Source of All Healing to relieve this terrible suffering.

As you turn toward the Higher Power, repeat the mantra: *A-do-nai ra-chem, A-do-nai ra-chem*—"Lord have compassion, Lord have compassion." As you recite this prayer, send the power of divine compassion to all those in need.

Chant the mantra out loud.

Repeat it quietly to yourself.

Silently intone the mantra in your mind.

> *A-do-nai ra-chem, A-do-nai ra-chem,*
> *A-do-nai ra-chem, A-do-nai ra-chem …*

Let go of the mantra, and focus on drawing the infinite compassion of the heavens down into your heart and mind.

Once more, imagine the light of your own soul shining down upon you from above.

Let go of all images and rest in the silence.

Slowly open up your eyes.

This mantra meditation enables us to harness the power of divine compassion in our inner work. It provides us with a vehicle to channel the mercy of the spiritual realm down into our physical plane of existence. Using this meditation, we can send light and energy to people all over the world. We can become effective instruments of compassion.

Hallelu-Yah Mantra

Yud Heh Vav Heh is called the Ineffable Name of God because we do not know how to pronounce it—that secret was hidden when the Temple in ancient Jerusalem was destroyed. However, this Divine Name can be broken down into two parts: *Yud Heh* and *Vav Heh*. We do not know how to pronounce the second part of the Name—*Vav Heh*. But we do know how to pronounce the first half of the Name. It is a Name that is used to address God in many places throughout the Hebrew Bible; that Name is *Yah*.

Chanting this Divine Name builds up a powerful spiritual vibration. When the Name *Yah* is combined with the Hebrew word *hallelu* (praise), then we have a wonderful mantra that is familiar to everyone: *hallelu-Yah*—"praise the One called *Yah*."

Hallelu-Yah is an exhortation to glorify God. It can be chanted, and it also can be sung to a melody. Our meditation will combine chanting and singing of the mantra with more focused chanting of the Name *Yah* on its own.

As we chant and sing *hallelu-Yah*, we lift our voices in praise of the Eternal One. As we chant *Yah*, we open our hearts to receive the awe-inspiring power of this sacred Name.

Let us begin our meditation.

Make yourself comfortable. Close your eyes and relax every part of your body. Start with your head and shoulders, and move all the way down to your toes.

Breathe in and out in a normal fashion, focusing your mind on the intake and outflow of your breath.

Visualize the doorway of the *heh* ה. Let the *heh* swing in one direction as you inhale and in the other direction as you exhale.

Shut out all of the outside noise. For this one moment, let nothing else exist but the movement of your breath. Become one with the *heh*. Become the doorway.

Sing to a slow, soulful melody (suggestion: Carlebach *nigun El Adon*):
> *Ha-lle-lu-Yah, ha-lle-lu-Yah,*
> *Ha-lle-lu-Yah, ha-lle-lu-Yah ...*

Now move into chanting:
> *Ha-lle-lu-Yah, ha-lle-lu-Yah,*
> *Ha-lle-lu-Yah, ha-lle-lu-Yah ...*

Repeat silently:
> *Ha-lle-lu-Yah, ha-lle-lu-Yah,*
> *Ha-lle-lu-Yah, ha-lle-lu-Yah ...*

Chant only the Name *Yah*:
> *Yah, Yah, Yah, Yah, Yah, Yah, Yah, Yah,*
> *Yah, Yah, Yah, Yah, Yah, Yah, Yah, Yah ...*

Intone the Name silently:
> *Yah, Yah, Yah, Yah, Yah, Yah, Yah, Yah,*
> *Yah, Yah, Yah, Yah, Yah, Yah, Yah, Yah ...*

Return to singing *Ha-lle-lu-Yah*:

> *Ha-lle-lu-Yah, ha-lle-lu-Yah,*
> *Ha-lle-lu-Yah, ha-lle-lu-Yah* ..

Shift once more into chanting:

> *Ha-lle-lu-Yah, ha-lle-lu-Yah,*
> *Ha-lle-lu-Yah, ha-lle-lu-Yah* ..

Chant just the Name:

> *Yah, Yah, Yah, Yah, Yah, Yah, Yah, Yah,*
> *Yah, Yah, Yah, Yah, Yah, Yah, Yah, Yah* ...

Now be still and silent.

> Slowly open up your eyes.

When we evoke the Name of God, we draw on the power of the Infinite. When we sing God's praises, we glorify the holy Name. Through our song and our chant, we bring the energy of *Yah* down into our material reality. We illuminate the world with the light of the eternal realm and infuse all of creation with the might of *Yah*.

Avraham Mantra

When the Guiding Force of the universe wants to introduce new ideas and energies into the consciousness of humanity, a plan is constructed to facilitate the revelation and growth of this fresh divine imperative on the earthly plane. Then, a *shoresh neshamah* (root soul) is formed to take up this spiritual mission and bring it to fruition in time and space.

Great souls from the higher reaches of the celestial planes are sent down to anchor the divine thoughtform in our world. The lives of these souls are filled with suffering and struggle, but they are lives where the Eternal Presence is real and tangible.

After these souls pass over, they form a spiritual nucleus in the higher realm. This nucleus becomes a new outpost of energy and consciousness in the Kingdom of Heaven. It acts as an intermediary link between those on the physical plane and their supernal source.

Avraham was the first Jew.[8] He provided the anchor for the Soul of Israel in this world. Avraham is the archetype of the father in Judaism. He is the father of the Jewish people and the father of the Jewish soul. This understanding is explicit in his original name *Avram*, which is composed of two words: *av*, "father," and *ram*, "high" or "esteemed." Together they form "high father"—the spiritual definition of his life and work.

As his life journey progresses, Avram receives a new name in a vision. He is blessed that he will become a father of many nations, and the Hebrew letter *heh* is added to his name. His name now becomes Avraham. The *heh* is one of the letters in the sacred Divine Name *Yud Heh Vav Heh*. By the addition of this letter to Avram's name, he is bound to God forever.

The addition of the *heh* to the name of *Avram* is also a symbol of the spiritual initiation Avraham underwent, whereby he was linked to a new, greater collective soul. This initiation transformed him into a soul "father of fathers"—*av*: father; *ra*: high father; *ham*: father of fathers. It led him another step in the journey to his Source.

Our next mantra meditation focuses on the patriarch Avraham. It is based on the spiritual significance of his two names: *Avram* and *Avraham*.

Let us begin.

Make yourself comfortable. Close your eyes and relax every part of your body. Start with your head and shoulders, and move all the way down to your toes.

Breathe in and out in a normal fashion, focusing your mind on the intake and outflow of your breath.

Visualize the doorway of the *heh* ה. Let the *heh* swing in one direction as you inhale and in the other direction as you exhale.

Shut out all of the outside noise. For this one moment, let nothing else exist but the movement of your breath. Become one with the *heh*. Become the doorway.

Take the original name of *Avram* and break it down into its two parts: *Av* and *Ram*.

Now chant the two parts of the name, one after the other, in a rhythmic fashion. Chant *Av* with each inhalation, and chant *Ram* with each exhalation:

Av-Ram, Av-Ram, Av-Ram, Av-Ram,
Av-Ram, Av-Ram, Av-Ram, Av-Ram …

While repeating this name, focus on Avram as the father of the nation and the Soul of Israel.

In the Kabbalah, each of the Patriarchs is associated with one of the *sefirot*. Avraham is identified with the *sefirah* of *chesed*—mercy or loving-kindness. As you chant the name of Avram quietly to yourself, draw down the energy of *chesed* into your consciousness:

> *Av-Ram, Av-Ram, Av-Ram, Av-Ram,*
> *Av-Ram, Av-Ram, Av-Ram, Av-Ram ...*

Next, take the full name of *Avraham*, and chant it out loud. With your first breath chant *Av*, with your next breath chant *Ra*, and with the third pronounce *Ham*, extending the sound of the *heh* with the breath as you exhale:

> *Av-Ra-Hhaaamm, Av-Ra-Hhaaamm,*
> *Av-Ra-Hhaaamm, Av-Ra-Hhaaamm,*
> *Av-Ra-Hhaaamm, Av-Ra-Hhaaamm ...*

While chanting the name, concentrate on reaching beyond the soul of Avraham to the touch the Supernal Source from which he has come—the "Father of all fathers."

Repeat the name of *Avraham* quietly to yourself. With your first inhalation, mentally chant *Av*; momentarily holding the breath, chant *Ra*; and as you exhale, chant *Ham*, extending the sound of the *heh*:

> *Av-Ra-Hhaaamm, Av-Ra-Hhaaamm,*
> *Av-Ra-Hhaaamm, Av-Ra-Hhaaamm,*
> *Av-Ra-Hhaaamm, Av-Ra-Hhaaamm ...*

As you repeat the name, feel the infinite loving-kindness of *Yud Heh Vav Heh* flow into your heart and mind. Feel that you are one with *Av-Ra-Ham*.

End your chanting and rest in the silence.

Slowly, open up your eyes.

❦

The *chesed* of Avraham was all-embracing. His tent was open on all four sides. He was ready to receive anyone who came to his dwelling. He was ready to receive everyone in the name of the Holy One of Israel.

At the same time, Avraham's self-renunciation was complete. He gave up everything for the Truth. He left his home and his country. He offered up his own son. Avraham walked through life holding on to God's out-stretched hand, with courage, willpower, and faith.

We are all the children of Avraham. May we learn to emulate his profound generosity and love. May we develop his remarkable openness to others. Like him, let us dedicate our lives to divine service.

Moshe Rabbeinu Mantra

In Hinduism, God manifests as three fundamental forces: the power to create, the power to preserve, and the power to destroy. In Judaism, the Supreme Power manifests through ten divine attributes, or *sefirot*. According to the Kabbalah, these ten *sefirot* are embodied by ten bibli-cal figures. The destructive aspect of Divinity expresses itself through several different *sefirot* and is associated with various figures.

One of the ways that the power of destruction manifests is through the *sefirah* of *netzach*. The root of the word *netzach* has two differ-ent meanings: *netzach*, "eternity," and *netzachon*, "victory." According to the eminent sixteenth-century Kabbalist Rabbi Yosef Gikatilla, the *sefirah* of *netzach* gives us the power to overcome our enemies—both internal and external. It enables us to vanquish evil, destroy ignorance, eradicate illness, and be victorious over our lower passions.[9]

In the Kabbalah, Moses embodies the energy of this *sefirah*. He wielded this destructive power in Egypt and in the desert to defeat the Egyptians.

Another attribute is also identified with Moses. The Baal Shem Tov teaches that Moses opened up the pathway to the attribute of *yirah*—the awe of God.[10] *Yirah* is another name for the *sefirah* of *gevurah*, or power. Through the manifestation of the great miracles of the ten plagues and the splitting of the Red Sea, Moses awakened in the people a profound sense of awe. This awakening culminated in the revelation at Sinai, where the Redeemer of Israel appeared to the Children of Israel as a great fire on the mountain, in the midst of thunder, lightning, and the sounding of the shofar (ram's horn).

Moses is also linked with a third *sefirah*, the sefirah of *daat,* or knowledge. Moses saw *Yud Heh Vav Heh* face-to-face. He was trusted throughout the heavenly "mansion." He experienced the intimate knowledge of the Ineffable One.

Moses is referred to in the tradition as *Moshe Rabbeinu,* "Moses our teacher." He was the great teacher of Israel who taught us how to subdue our lower self, how to overcome evil, and how to live in awe. Moses was the divine instrument who opened the door to higher knowledge.

Our next mantra centers on this epithet of Moses. Using this mantra, we connect to the different aspects of this great teacher and prophet.

Let us begin.

Make yourself comfortable. Close your eyes and relax every part of your body. Start with your head and shoulders, and move all the way down to your toes.

Breathe in and out in a normal fashion, focusing your mind on the intake and outflow of your breath.

Visualize the doorway of the *heh* ה. Let the *heh* swing in one direction as you inhale and in the other direction as you exhale.

Shut out all of the outside noise. For this one moment, let nothing else exist but the movement of your breath. Become one with the *heh.* Become the doorway.

Chant the mantra out loud:

> *Mo-she Ra-bbei-nu, Mo-she Ra-bbei-nu,*
> *Mo-she Ra-bbei-nu, Mo-she Ra-bbei-nu ...*

As you chant the mantra, link into the *sefirah* of *netzach* and its power to destroy your inner enemies: to vanquish anger, hatred, and fear; to eradicate ignorance, prejudice, and narrow-mindedness; to annihilate the desires of the ego and the lower self.

Repeat the mantra quietly to yourself:

> *Mo-she Ra-bbei-nu, Mo-she Ra-bbei-nu,*
> *Mo-she Ra-bbei-nu, Mo-she Ra-bbei-nu ...*

As you repeat the mantra, visualize the grandeur of Creation: the majesty of the great mountains, the splendor of the mighty seas, the vastness of the empty desert. Experience the raw divine power that flowed into Moses as the natural forces were channeled through him. Feel a profound awe awakening within your heart.

Intone the mantra silently in your mind:

> *Mo-she Ra-bbei-nu, Mo-she Ra-bbei-nu,*
> *Mo-she Ra-bbei-nu, Mo-she Ra-bbei-nu ...*

Let go of your little self and dive within. Experience the living knowledge of the Changeless and Ever-Present Reality.

Cease your chanting and rest within the stillness.

Slowly open up your eyes.

❧

Moses was acclaimed as the greatest of the Jewish prophets, yet he was also called the humblest human being on the face of the earth. Like Moses, let us learn how to walk in awe. Let us tap into the immense power of the Eternal Might. May we discover the passageway into the mansions of the heavens and be blessed to know God face-to-face.

Mantra for the *Shekhinah*

Our last mantra meditation evokes the presence of the *Shekhinah*. The *Shekhinah* is the name given in Judaism to the feminine aspect of Divinity. The *Shekhinah* has many different aspects to Her nature. Each component indicates another facet of Her spiritual work.

The *Shekhinah* energy is a stimulating force. Like yeast, She brings alive the spiritual life of those around Her and intensifies their inner growth.

The *Shekhinah* is a protective energy. She is likened to an eagle that carries her young upon her wings to guard them from predators (Deuteronomy 32:11). She was the protecting force in the Temple of ancient Jerusalem. Her presence shielded the land and people of Israel during biblical times.[11]

The *Shekhinah* is also the great mediator. Without the *Shekhinah,* nothing could be created. She is the Divine Mother who mediates between heaven and earth.

The mantra for the *Shekhinah* has four words: *Ve'al roshi Shekhinat El*—"And on my head is the *Shekhinah*"—the feminine Divine Presence. The words are taken from a prayer that we recite each night before going to sleep. It is a prayer that asks for the *Shekhinah*'s protection. It is an invocation of Her sacred energy and spirit.

During the meditation, we will combine chanting of the mantra with a series of visualizations. Together, they will lead us under the shelter of the *Shekhinah*'s wings.

Let us now begin.

Make yourself comfortable. Close your eyes and relax every part of your body. Start with your head and shoulders, and move all the way down to your toes.

Breathe in and out in a normal fashion, focusing your mind on the intake and outflow of your breath.

Visualize the doorway of the *heh* ה. Let the *heh* swing in one direction as you inhale and in the other direction as you exhale.

Shut out all of the outside noise. For this one moment, let nothing else exist but the movement of your breath. Become one with the *heh*. Become the doorway.

Picture the presence of the *Shekhinah* resting above your head. Visualize the light of the *Shekhinah* radiating out in all directions. Imagine that you are sitting peacefully in the midst of this beatific light.

Chant the mantra out loud:

> *Ve'-al ro-shi She-khi-nat El, ve'-al ro-shi She-khi-nat El,*
> *Ve'-al ro-shi She-khi-nat El, ve'-al ro-shi She-khi-nat El ..*

Repeat it quietly to yourself:

> *Ve'-al ro-shi She-khi-nat El, ve'-al ro-shi She-khi-nat El,*
> *Ve'-al ro-shi She-khi-nat El, ve'-al ro-shi She-khi-nat El ..*

Intone the mantra silently in your mind:

> *Ve'-al ro-shi She-khi-nat El, ve'-al ro-shi She-khi-nat El,*
> *Ve'-al ro-shi She-khi-nat El, ve'-al ro-shi She-khi-nat El ..*

Visualize the love of the *Shekhinah* shining down upon you, surrounding your whole body—enveloping you in Her loving embrace. Feel that love permeate into the depth of your being. Let it nourish you with security, comfort, and light.

Chant the mantra out loud:

> *Ve'-al ro-shi She-khi-nat El, ve'-al ro-shi She-khi-nat El,*
> *Ve'-al ro-shi She-khi-nat El, ve'-al ro-shi She-khi-nat El ..*

Repeat it quietly to yourself:

> *Ve'-al ro-shi She-khi-nat El, ve'-al ro-shi She-khi-nat El,*
> *Ve'-al ro-shi She-khi-nat El, ve'-al ro-shi She-khi-nat El ...*

Intone the mantra silently in your mind:

> *Ve'-al ro-shi She-khi-nat El, ve'-al ro-shi She-khi-nat El,*
> *Ve'-al ro-shi She-khi-nat El, ve'-al ro-shi She-khi-nat El ...*

Now visualize the awesome power of the *Shekhinah* flowing into your heart and mind. Feel Her strength coursing through your being. Feel it imbue you with courage and confidence. Know that you have the power to accomplish anything!

Chant the mantra out loud:

> *Ve'-al ro shi She khi nat El, ve'-al ro-shi She-khi-nat El,*
> *Ve'-al ro-shi She-khi-nat El, ve'-al ro-shi She-khi-nat El ...*

Repeat it quietly to yourself:

> *Ve'-al ro-shi She-khi-nat El, ve'-al ro-shi She-khi-nat El,*
> *Ve'-al ro-shi She-khi-nat El, ve'-al ro-shi She-khi-nat El ...*

Intone the mantra silently in your mind:

> *Ve'-al ro-shi She-khi-nat El, ve'-al ro-shi She-khi-nat El,*
> *Ve'-al ro-shi She-khi-nat El, ve'-al ro-shi She-khi-nat El ...*

Stop your chanting and rest quietly in the silence.

Slowly open up your eyes.

❦

The relationship between God and humanity is closely tied to the state of the *Shekhinah*. We are intimately linked with the feminine aspect of God. May we be worthy to raise up the *Shekhinah* to Her full power and beauty. May we help restore the Living Presence of God to all of humankind. One day the radiant glory of the Universal Mother will shine throughout our entire planet.

Mantra: A Lifelong Friend

A mantra is a potent spiritual tool. It is a meditation that can be utilized under any circumstances and in any location. Each mantra has a number of aspects to its practice. As we progress along the path, we will discover new levels to its meaning and power.

Daily mantra chanting will produce significant results. Over time, our relationship with our practice will deepen and evolve. Gradually, the mantra will become our steady companion, a precious friend that we take with us through life. The better we come to know this friend, the more we will appreciate its presence, and the more we will receive its grace. We will be drawn back to this enchanting inner companion, over and over again.

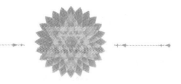

CHAPTER NINE

CONTEMPLATION

Inner Reflection upon a Transcendent Reality

*T*he Hebrew word for "wisdom," *chokhmah,* can be broken down into two words: *koach mah,* "the power of Nothingness." According to the Hasidic master Dov Baer of Mezeritch, wisdom connects us to a place that transcends understanding and physical awareness. It joins us to the place where thought begins, where it emerges out of the *Ein Sof*— the Absolute.[1]

When we delve into spiritual wisdom, we touch on the fundamental pattern of reality. We follow a pathway in the Mind of God. This pathway lifts us into the consciousness of the higher expanses, into a chamber in the Celestial Palace. Once we have entered this chamber, we pass into the interior of the palace and greet the Sovereign of sovereigns.

This journey expresses the essence of the technique of contemplation. In contemplation, we meditate upon the core truths of existence. Our reflections transport us out of our narrow perceptions up into the broad spaces where thought meets being, where thinking becomes seeing, where the human mind touches the Universal Consciousness.

The Role of Contemplation in Jewish Mysticism

Contemplation is an essential part of the life of a Jewish mystic. The Baal Shem Tov saw all aspects of religious practice as an opportunity to enter into the Divine Presence. Study of the holy scriptures, whether it is a verse from the Torah, a teaching in the Talmud, or a passage in the *Zohar,* is a tool for contemplation—a way to elevate us into the realm of the supernal worlds.

Therefore, the Baal Shem Tov gave his Hasidim specific instructions about how to go about their learning. Here are a few examples:

- The Rabbis said (*Berakhot* 8a), "God has nothing in this world except *arba amot shel halakhah*—the four cubits of Jewish law." When you sit down to learn, think in your heart that God has been contracted into this very space where you are learning and that your learning brings God's presence into the room.[2]
- Each hour that you learn, break for a few minutes and link yourself to the Almighty.[3]
- During your learning, remind yourself before whom you are learning. Keep reminding yourself of the Divine Presence at every moment and every hour, because the learning process can sometimes distance you from God.[4]
- When you are learning a passage from a particular rabbi, Hasidic master, or Kabbalist, visualize in your mind that this person is right there before you, teaching you. As he speaks, visualize that you are drawing into yourself the divine livingness in his words. And whenever you reach a point of understanding from the teaching, visualize that you are drawing the spiritual force of this understanding into yourself.[5]

All of these instructions were intended to ensure that study became a form of contemplation, and not just the dry repetition of laws or arrogant intellectual sparring.

Contemplation can lead us to pure knowledge, to the truth contained within our soul. True knowledge comes from within. Everything we learn from outside ourselves is incomplete and deficient in its very nature. As the Zen master Tokusan declared after his *satori* (enlightenment experience), "Any knowledge or learning is just like a drop of water fallen in a valley when it is compared with the depth of experience."[6]

In fact, everything that we learn from books is only a means of teaching us how to tap into the wisdom within ourselves, into the light of our own being.

Contemplation of the inner mysteries is akin to plowing a fertile field. The soil is rich in nutrients and minerals. Our task is to till the soil, plant vibrant seeds, and nurture the saplings until they grow into sturdy trees that provide a bountiful harvest.

The first chief rabbi of Israel, Rabbi Avraham Yitzchak Kook, was deeply immersed in the life of contemplation. He used the imagery of cultivation extensively in his writings. Rav Kook refers to the inspiration from contemplation as "all the holy thoughts and all exalted knowledge [which] sprout forth upon the breadth of 'the field which God has blessed' (Genesis 27:27). These arise continually, in every season and at every hour, in every moment and each fraction of a moment, new and wonderful plants, flowers and buds."[7]

Those who learn spiritual wisdom, seeking out the inner truths, are called by the Ari "laborers in the field" (*chatzadei chakla* in Aramaic). The mystics who contemplate the holy scriptures labor with their intellect and intuition to bring the truth contained in the Cosmic Mind down into this material world. Their harvest, according to Rav Kook, is transformed into ideals in the Soul of Israel, which enable the people of Israel to bind themselves to their Supernal Source.[8]

There are many levels to the divine field. The further we penetrate into its soil, the more alive our minds will become, and the more profound the truths will be that we uncover. As we dig down into the primordial levels of the field, we will touch upon eternal truths that resonate not only in the Soul of Israel but also in the Soul of humanity. When we reach the seventh and deepest level, we will reveal the supernal roots of truth in *Adam Rishon*—the Universal Soul that encompasses every sentient being.[9]

For the mystic, prayer too is a vehicle for contemplation. The Baal Shem Tov saw prayer as a contemplative ascension through the inner worlds. Prayer is an opportunity to raise up the *Shekhinah,* to lift Her into spiritual union with the Heavenly Spouse.

In fact, he saw our every mundane act as a spiritual event, a chance to contemplate the hidden truths of God's creation. Each time we link together thought and action, we are uniting the higher and lower worlds—we are joining heaven and earth.

> Our Rabbis [in the Midrash] said, "Chanokh was a cobbler and with each and every stitch he would unite the Holy One,

blessed be He, with the *Shekhinah*."[10] ... Now, thought is called *Ein Sof—Yud Heh Vav Heh,* and action is [called] *Adonai—*[the *Shekhinah*], and when he joins thought and action at the moment of acting, it is called the uniting of the Holy One and the *Shekhinah*.

   With every single movement, one should unite the Holy One and the *Shekhinah*. This means being aware of and taking care with every movement. And when he joins together thought and action, this is called union ... and if you question and doubt about this, and have doubts as to whether you are paying attention with every movement [to join] each thought and action, then the actions, accounting, knowledge, and wisdom that a person is engaged in—all [falls] into *Sheol* (the Netherworld)—the place of the *klipot* (material husks).[11]

Contemplation is not a passive experience; there is a dynamic exchange that takes place. Rav Kook envisioned two streams of thought meeting in the act of contemplation: one stream coming from above, and the other from deep within us.

These two streams combine to create all interior movement. Whenever they converge, our whole being becomes illuminated. We receive inspiration from a distant realm—from a powerful and ancient reality. We contact the celestial worlds of our Forefathers and our Foremothers—the chain of souls down through the ages.[12]

The Baal Shem Tov compares this moment of convergence to a bolt of lightning that brightens the entire sky. One bolt of spiritual insight, he declares, can illuminate us with wisdom, understanding, and knowledge.[13] It can lift us up into the Universal Consciousness and reveal the light of Truth that shines there.

Obstacles and Solutions in Contemplation

As with all the other techniques, attempting to engage in contemplation presents both challenges and opportunities. Meditation does not take place in a vacuum, and there are always a multitude of different factors that we need to take into account. This section looks at the obstacles that confront us as we dive inward in contemplation and offers some ideas on how to progress with our inner striving.

Creating a Well-Prepared Vessel

To be able to contemplate, our mind needs to be on the right vibration. As Rebbe Nachman of Breslov explains, if our imagination is on a low level, we will not be able to visualize matters of a higher nature. To contemplate the divine attributes and visualize God's grandeur, we need to have a purified creative imagination.[14]

Achieving this higher imaginative faculty demands a life of purity and holiness. We begin the voyage into the inner reality by sanctifying our lives. The first step on our journey is to take on spiritual practices and engage in spiritual disciplines. Once we have placed ourselves on the road to inner transformation, God will come flooding into our lives. The more we sanctify our lives, the more the light of our soul will shine within us, and the more the flame of our lower desires will become dim. As Sri Ramakrishna told one of his devotees, "The more you advance in one direction, the more you leave behind the opposite direction. If you move ten steps towards the east, you move ten steps away from the west."[15]

As we move forward along the path, the whole of our being becomes illuminated by the light of the soul. Over time, even the body itself becomes sanctified. Our senses sharpen and become more elevated, our desires become more refined. All of our spiritual attributes develop and become more prominent. Our yearning for purity, wisdom, and divine life grows and evolves.

Gradually, our lower nature is mastered, as one after the other, we disdain name and fame and all the matters worldly people hold dear. We become immersed in the life of the spirit, the search for holiness, and the pursuit of truth.

An Open Mind and an Expansive Consciousness

Contemplation requires an expansive consciousness and an open mind. To enter into the Universal Mind, we must reach beyond our finite awareness and enter into the awareness of the Timeless Reality. Prejudice and closed-mindedness are the signs of a material person. A narrow consciousness keeps us bound to this physical world.

In contemplation, we strive to break through the barriers between people and touch the underlying unity behind everything that exists. God is infinitely expansive and all-embracing. If we want to join with God, we need to become expansive and all-embracing ourselves.

True contemplation transcends the limitations of the lower concrete mind and lifts us into the wide spaces of the higher abstract mind. We move from studying the details of facts and figures to reflecting on the universal patterns that flow through all levels of the universe. By meditating on the broad design of Creation, we become attuned with the fundamental currents of existence. We resonate with the eternal thoughts in the Divine Consciousness.

To be a true contemplative, we need to clear away all lingering hostility toward other peoples and religions. All the great teachers transcended the hubris of their own faith. They saw the Divine in all of its manifold forms.

This is the way for us to enter into contemplation—alert, open, and free. Standing naked before God, we recognize our common humanity and our oneness of being. Stripped of our blinders, we can gaze freely upon the hidden wonders of the celestial worlds.

A Quiet Space and a Calm Mind

Unlike mantra chanting, contemplation is not a meditative technique for the busy world. We cannot engage in contemplation amid the bustle and noise of life; it demands a quiet space and a calm mind. Any agitation or distraction will block the passageway into the inner reality.

It is important to create a sacred space for our contemplation. A spot in nature is ideal. Here our mind easily expands and is effortlessly drawn inward. The beauty, energy, and serenity of the natural world lend themselves to reflection and meditation.

If we cannot be out-of-doors, then we should find a quiet spot inside where we can be alone in solitude. And if we can enter into a holy place, that is even better. In such a space, our mind can set out on its flights of creative thinking and travel through the inner planes without interruption or disturbance.

We begin our practice by placing ourselves in the presence of God. Next, we ask the Possessor of All Wisdom for inspiration and understanding. Then we turn inward and open our consciousness to impressions from the spiritual realm.

A Broad Palette

Contemplative meditation encompasses a broad palette of inner reflections. We can contemplate the meaning of a prayer, meditate on the nature of the higher worlds, imagine a scene from the scriptures, reflect on the manifestation of a divine attribute, delve into the works of creation, or ponder the enigmatic symbolism of a prophetic vision. Each of these meditations will awaken our soul consciousness and lift us into the awareness of the higher reality.

Let us now explore together the world of contemplation.

Contemplation of the *Shema*

The *Shema* is the central prayer of Judaism. It is recited every day in the morning and in the evening. The *Shema* is the first prayer we are taught when we are young and the last prayer we say before we die.

According to the tradition, Moses taught this prayer to the Children of Israel on the border of the Promised Land as an affirmation of their faith in the oneness of the Godhead—a declaration that everything is of God, in God, and from God.

The *Shema* is also a testament of our love for the Originator of All Existence and the truth that love is the path that will take us to the place of unity and oneness.

The *Shema* is an affirmation of faith, a prayer of protection, a means of healing the spirit. The *Shema* is a powerful tool for contemplation that raises our awareness and binds us to God.

In our first practice, we will work with a series of seed thoughts for you to reflect upon. The first portion of this reflection repeats the thoughts of the *Shema* mantra, as it is important to have the entire prayer in your mind. Take each seed and plant it in the field of your consciousness. Nourish it with the water of your spiritual contemplation. In this manner, the seed will grow into a beautiful plant.

Let us now begin our meditation on the *Shema*.

Close your eyes and make yourself comfortable. Relax every part of your body, beginning with your head and shoulders and moving all the way down to your toes.

Breathe in and out in a normal fashion, focusing your mind on the intake and outflow of your breath.

The Hebrew letter *heh* is pronounced like an "h." It is the sound we make when we exhale. The *heh* looks like a doorway ה. It is the doorway of our breath. As we inhale, the *heh* swings one way. As we exhale, it swings in the other direction. As we focus on our breath, we ourselves become the letter *heh*. We become a swinging door through which divine livingness flows in and out.

Inhale, and let the *heh* swing in one direction; exhale, and let it swing the opposite way.

Shut out all the noise and clamor of the world around you. For this one moment, let nothing else exist but the movement of your breath. Become one with the *heh*. Become the doorway.

Now turn your heart and mind toward the *Shema*.

The prayer begins with these words: *Shema Yisrael, Adonai Eloheynu, Adonai Echad*—"Hear, O Israel, the Lord is our God, the Lord is One."

The word *shema* means "to hear." But *shema* is not just a physical hearing; it is a deep listening from the core of your being—a vibrant hearing in the very depth of who you are. *Shema* is God calling out and telling you to hear and receive the words of this prayer in the center of your heart.

The second word of the prayer is *Yisrael*, or Israel. It tells you to whom God is speaking: to the part of you that belongs to *Yisrael*. Israel is a faith and a nation—but it is also a spiritual mission. It is a vast soul that is formed of all the people who are striving to reveal the Divine Presence on earth, to fill the world with radiant light—to help all of humanity to live and act as one. It is from this place of high aspiration that you are to listen to this prayer.

The next two words of the prayer are *Adonai Eloheynu*. *Adonai* means "Lord." However, in the Hebrew, what is written is the Ineffable Name *Yud Heh Vav Heh*. In the Kabbalah, this Name represents the aspect of Divinity that embodies compassion, the source of all compassion in the universe.

Adonai Eloheynu, then, is "The Lord of Compassion is our God." This source of all-embracing love is not in some far-off heaven, but right here with you, walking beside you through life—sharing your joys and your sorrows, your triumphs and failures. You are never alone.

The last two words of the first sentence are *Adonai Echad*—"God is One." God is both immanent and transcendent. In the Absolute, there is perfect unity—in the place of pure consciousness and being; in the place where all is peace, harmony, and bliss.

This is the first line of the *Shema*. Next comes this declaration: *Barukh shem kavod malkhuto leolam va'ed*—"Blessed be the Name of the glorious divine kingdom for ever and ever." Reflect on the meaning of these words. Think of the myriad planes of existence with all of their living beings and souls. Think of the majesty and grandeur of God's glorious kingdom.

Now contemplate the next paragraph, where you express your profound love for the Creator. This paragraph begins with the beautiful words, *Ve'ahavta et Adonai Elohekha, bekhol levavkha, uvekhol nafshekha, uvekhol meodekha*—"And you shall love *Adonai*, your God, with all of your heart, and all of your soul, and all of your might."

> *Bekhol levavkha*—"with all of your heart": To love God is to be ready to expand your heart ever wider. You expand your heart by dedicating all of your capacity to love divine service. You love with your whole heart by cherishing every human being and every living creature.

> *Uvekhol nafshekha*—"with all of your soul": Are you willing to offer up your life for God? Are you willing to put yourself completely in the hands of heaven? On another level, the *nefesh* is identified with the intellect. *Vekhol nafshekha*, then, is to turn all of your capacity to think and understand toward a higher purpose. It means to direct your mind toward knowing your Maker—toward understanding the world around you and knowing yourself.

> *Uvekhol meodekha*—"with all of your might": Give all of your strength and everything you possess to the Sovereign of sovereigns. Work to better this world and aid humanity. Strive to establish truth, peace, and justice. Take all of your heart, mind, and soul and set them as an offering before the Rock of the Ages.

> *Vehayu hadevarim ha'eleh asher anokhi metzavekha hayom*—"and these words which I command you today": Do not think of the *Shema* as a prayer that comes from long ago. God is talking to you now, at this very moment, if you open your heart and mind to hear.

> *Al levavekha*—"(shall be) upon your heart": Keep the One Refuge as a living presence upon your heart at all times.

Veshinantam levanekha—"and you shall teach them to your children": Teach your children to live a life of meaning. Instruct them to love God and serve humanity. Encourage them to aspire for the highest values and ideals.

Vedibarta bam—"and you shall speak of them": Make God a part of your every conversation. Bring the Most High into all your interactions and affairs. Draw the Divine Spirit into everything you think, say, and do.

Beshivtekha beveytekha—"when you sit in your house": When you are at home with family and friends, integrate the All-Compassionate One into your daily interactions. Infuse divine care and generosity into the atmosphere of your home, into the way you relate to others.

Uvelekhtekha vaderekh—"and when you walk by the way": When you go out in the world, don't leave God at home. Bring the sacred presence into your workplace and your business dealings. Bring the higher awareness into your encounters with the stranger in the street.

Uveshokhbekha uvekumekha—"when you lie down and when you rise": In the morning when you awake, take a moment to connect to the place of stillness inside you. Center yourself in the calm and quiet, before you start your routine—before a multitude of different thoughts and responsibilities pour into your mind. And when you lie down to sleep at night, take another moment, and go back to the silence within. Then from that place of peace and inner tranquility, enter into the land of deep repose.

Ukeshartam leot al yadekha—"you shall bind them for a sign upon your arm": Bind all of your actions to God. Turn heavenward before everything you do, and ask for help and guidance.

Vehayu letotafot bein eynekha—"and they shall be a frontlet between your eyes": Keep the inner awareness alive in your consciousness. Feel the place of contact as you go about your day. Return to touch that space at regular intervals. Hold on to the light during the hours of movement and action.

Ukhetavtam al mezuzot beytekha—"and you shall write them on the doorposts of your house": As you enter your home and as you leave your dwelling, reflect on the deepest questions of who you are and the purpose for which you have come into this world.

Uvishearekha—"and upon your gates": Place the awareness of God on the nine gates of your body and the five gates of the senses, so that everything you see, hear, taste, smell, and touch reminds you of the unity of all sentient beings and the blessings of the One who is pure compassion and love.

Now, enter into silent meditation on these profound truths.

Let go of all images and rest quietly in the silence.

Slowly open up your eyes.

The essence of the *Shema* is a proclamation of the intrinsic unity of all creation. It is a declaration that everything arises from the same divine source. The *Shema* is a testament of our undying love for the Power at the heart of existence. Love is the path that will lead us to union with the Supreme Reality.

Mi Bara Eleh—Who Has Created These Things?

"Lift your eyes on high, and behold who has created these things."
—Isaiah 40:26

The Hasidic master Avraham Dov of Astrich teaches that one of the key principles in serving God is to ask ourselves about everything that we see, be it a creature or an object, "Who has given it life and vitality? Why has it been created?"

When we look at the world around us, we are seeing more than just random arrangements of molecules—we are beholding divine creations. Each object has a use and a meaning. Each creature has its own particular role in the divine structure of Creation.

By asking these questions, we penetrate beyond the outer form and circumstances. By reflecting in this manner, we see the world each day anew. We break the hold of our physical mind-set and lift our minds onto a higher plane.

Rebbe Avraham adds another dimension to our contemplation. Our reflection, he says, should be based on the teaching in the Ethics of the Fathers (*Pirkei Avot*) 6:11: "Everything that the Holy One, blessed be He, created in His world, He created for His glory."[16]

This is a wonderful thought. Every single object was created for the sake of God's glory. Everything was designed to reveal the presence of the Creator. Each tree, each rock, each living creature was formed to bring us into contact with its divine source.

This concept becomes even more profound when it is applied to other human beings. We are more than animal creatures. Each of us is part of the One Indivisible Universal Spirit that lies behind all that exists. No one is without a higher purpose or value. No matter how difficult a person may seem to us, each individual has qualities within him or her that reveal the eternal glory in some way.

This concept of seeing the manifestation of God's glory in others is taken one step further by Sri Ramana Maharshi. When asked why he did not go out into the world and help others, he would say that he sees no others. He sees everyone and everything as the Universal Self of all being. He regards everyone and everything as his own Self.[17]

This is another way for us to understand Rebbe Avraham's teaching. The outer appearance that we perceive with our physical eyes is all an illusion; only the inner divine glory truly exists. When we inquire, "Who is it that has given this person or object life and vitality?" and when we ask, "Why has it been created?" we are striving to uncover the divine glory that is its real nature; we are trying to touch its true reality.

Let us now use these teachings as a contemplation meditation.

Close your eyes and make yourself comfortable. Relax every part of your body, beginning with your head and shoulders and moving all the way down to your toes.

Breathe in and out in a normal fashion, focusing your mind on the intake and outflow of your breath.

Visualize the doorway of the *heh* ה. Let the *heh* swing in one direction as you inhale and in the other direction as you exhale.

Shut out all of the outside noise and clamor. For this one moment, let nothing else exist but the movement of your breath. Become one with the *heh*. Become the doorway.

Now think of a living object or creature in your surroundings that is important to you, such as a favorite animal, bird, or tree. Consider its shape, function, and character.

Ask yourself the question *"Mi bara eleh?"* Who has given it life and vitality? Why has it been created? How does it manifest God's glory? What part of the Divine Design does it reveal?

Contemplate the answer to these questions.

Move on to something that is meaningful in your larger environment, something that plays a greater part in your wider horizons: a beautiful park in your neighborhood, a secluded spot in the country, a majestic chain of mountains, a mighty sea or ocean.

Ask yourself again, *"Mi bara eleh?"* Who has given it life and vitality? Why has it been created? How does it manifest God's glory? What part of the Divine Design does it reveal?

Reach out to the cosmos, to the great heavenly bodies: the planet Saturn with its magnificent rings, the sun in all its glory, a spectacular supernova at light-years' distance, or the shimmering vastness of the mammoth Milky Way.

Ask yourself, *"Mi bara eleh?"* Who has given it life and vitality? Why has it been created? How does it manifest God's glory? What part of the Divine Design does it reveal?

Delve deeper and deeper into this thought. Try to reach to the very essence of the object or entity—touch the supernal source from which it comes.

Now think of people you know and love, and ask yourself this same question, one last time: *"Mi bara eleh?"* Who has given them life and vitality? Why have they been created? How is God's glory manifested in them? What part of the Divine Design are they revealing?

Try to see them as part of your Self, as part of your own being. See them as part of the oneness of all that is. Find yourself in them, and them in you. Know that you and they are one.

(An optional additional step for this contemplation is to think of someone with whom you have had difficulty, someone who has caused you sorrow and pain, and ask yourself the same question: *"Mi bara eleh?"* Then try to see him or her as your own Self.)

Let go of all thoughts and rest quietly in the silence.

Open up your eyes.

Our conscious recognition of the divinity in another person or object has a dynamic influence. It adds to the revelation of God's glory and expands the manifestation of the Divine Presence in the world. May we perceive the beauty, wisdom, and holiness of all those around us. May we reveal the sacred light within everyone we meet, so that it can shine forth into the universe.

Contemplating the Inner Reality: The Baal Shem Tov's Technique for Ascending through the Four Worlds

According to the teachings of the Ari, there are four higher worlds or realms: the world of *Asiyah,* or Making; the world of *Yetzirah,* or Formation; the world of *Briah,* or Creation; and the world of *Atzilut,* or Emanation.

The world of *Asiyah* (Making) is the realm of action. It is the most concrete of the higher worlds.

Yetzirah (Formation) is the realm of sound. The angelic kingdom predominates in this world.

Briah (Creation) is the world of thought, the plane of the mind. In *Briah* everything is composed of mental matter.

The world of *Atzilut* (Emanation) is the realm of pure energies. In this world, nothing exists except the interaction between the divine emanations.

The central contemplative practice of the Baal Shem Tov is structured as a mental ascension through the four worlds. His practice is modeled on the mystical ascension of the Chariot from Talmudic times and the ascent through the heavenly palaces in the *Zohar.* His technique combines both visualization and contemplation. It integrates a variety of elements—including the Divine Name *Yud Heh Vav Heh,* the ten *sefirot,* and the *Shekhinah*—with the spiritual work of forming and expanding our interior space. It is a fascinating and challenging meditation.

The contemplative practice outlined below is based on the instructions for ascending through the worlds in the Baal Shem Tov's writings.[18]

The practice develops and expands on these instructions, to take us on a journey through the inner reality.

Guiding Principles of This Contemplation

As you ascend on high into the supernal worlds, ascend slowly from level to level. Do not ascend more than one world at a time. First ascend to the world of *Asiyah*, and then to the world of *Yetzirah,* and afterward the world of *Briah*, and then the world of *Atzilut*.

As you ascend to each heaven, be careful not to fall down from your very high thoughts, so that you do not plunge down below. Continually strengthen yourself with all your might to remain on high in your thoughts. However much you ascend, have the intention that you are approaching God in a very high place. As it says in the book of the *Zohar* (2:82a), "The head of the King is not like the feet of the King."

When you can no longer hold your mind on high, descend to the level below in order to rest your mind, and bind yourself to the Infinite Power with awe and love. When you feel that you have regained your strength, begin to ascend on high once more.

As you start your ascent, feel that the power you received during your time of repose enables you to now ascend to a very high place, just as a person who wants to throw a stone in the air first brings his arm down low so that the stone will rise on high.

Feel joy and freedom as you ascend, linking yourself to ever-higher worlds. Go beyond the firmaments, the angels, the thrones, the *ofanim* and *serafim*, until you reach the *Ein Sof*. Know with total faith that the Divine Presence is with you, protecting you as you rise through the worlds. Feel that you are bound with God and that God is connected to you in all your limbs and powers. Imagine that you are looking at God and that God is looking at you.

Make yourself comfortable. Close your eyes and relax every part of your body. Start with your head and shoulders, and move all the way down to your toes.

Breathe in and out in a normal fashion, focusing your mind on the intake and outflow of your breath.

Visualize the doorway of the *heh* ה. Let the *heh* swing in one direction as you inhale and in the other direction as you exhale.

Shut out all of the outside noise and clamor. For this one moment, let nothing else exist but the movement of your breath. Become one with the *heh*. Become the doorway.

Link yourself with your own soul, and prepare to ascend on high. Imagine that you are above the dome of the world, and gather your strength to ascend even higher.

Picture opposite your forehead or on your forehead in your mind's eye, the Name יהוה and the ten supernal *sefirot* stretching up into the heavens. Imagine that the *Shekhinah* fills the whole world and that Her glory is accompanying you with great power as you ascend above.

Asiyah

Ascend in your mind to the first heaven, *Asiyah*, the world of Making. Expand this heaven out in your mind in all directions. The heaven should open in your thoughts, as if it is in front of you. It should not seem like a narrow or small space, but rather the space should expand out in all directions.

Now visualize the Name *Yud Heh Vav Heh* in your mind's eye. Imagine that the Divine Presence is with you, that Her glory fills this whole world. It is a subtle substance that is finer than fine. Look upon the *Shekhinah*, just as you look upon the physical objects of the earthly world.

Imagine that you are speaking in this world. Recite a prayer before God or chant a mantra. Visualize that your words come out of your mouth as a stream of letters composed of light.

Yetzirah

When you are fully established in the first heaven, ascend to the next heaven, *Yetzirah*, or Formation, the world of the angels. Imagine that the *Shekhinah* is accompanying you in your flight with great power.

Stretch out this higher plane in your mind. Let it open up in your thoughts, as if the world is in front of you. The space should expand in all directions.

Visualize the Name *Yud Heh Vav Heh* in your mind's eye. Feel the Divine Presence with you; Her glory fills this whole world. Imagine that you are looking upon the angels who inhabit this world. Look upon the angels, just as you look upon a living creature in the earthly world.

Imagine that you are speaking in this world. Repeat a prayer before God or chant a mantra. Visualize that your words come out of your mouth as waves of oscillating energy.

Briah

When you are fully established in the second heaven, then you can ascend to the third heaven, *Briah*, or Creation, the world of the Throne. Imagine that the *Shekhinah* is by your side as you ascend above with great power.

Expand the world out in your mind in all directions. Let it open in your thoughts, as if this heaven is before you. Let the space spread all around you, filling the contours of your mind.

Picture the Name *Yud Heh Vav Heh* in your mind's eye. Feel the Divine Presence with you; Her glory pervades this whole world. Imagine that you are looking upon the Throne of Glory and the Heavenly Hosts. It is as real to your inner sight as the material world is to your physical eyes.

On this plane, there is no speech but only pure thought. Silently repeat a prayer, or chant a mantra mentally. Visualize that your thoughts emerge from your mind as vibrant spheres of scintillating light.

Atzilut

When you are fully established in the third heaven, then you can ascend to the fourth and final heaven, *Atzilut,* or Emanation, the world of Being. Imagine that the *Shekhinah* is lifting you on high with great power.

Expand this heaven out to infinity. Let the inner space flow freely in your mind. Feel the presence of the Name *Yud Heh Vav Heh*. Experience the glory of the Divine Presence permeating this whole plane.

In this world there are no mantras, no letters, no words—only pure Being. Imagine that you are immersed in a boundless ocean of light and consciousness.

Contemplate how everything, whether in the world of the heavenly *sefirot,* the world of the angels, or the world of the Celestial Throne, is nothing in comparison with God.

Attach yourself to God with total love, for the Holy Blessed One is beyond anything and everything in this universe. Whatever good things there are in any of the worlds—all have their source in the One.

Recognize that God can do whatever God wants. The All-Powerful Consciousness that has created the universe can destroy all the worlds in one instant and form them again in another. Everything receives its life and energy from the Source of all being.

Know that there is nothing to rely on but the Shield of Abraham. There is no one and no thing that we should fear. Nothing else is worthy of our love and devotion.

Let go of all thoughts and images and rest quietly in the silence.

Slowly open up your eyes.

Ascending through the worlds expands our consciousness. It opens the vast expanses of the wider reality to us. We become aware that the divine glory fills all of existence. We are infused with the truth that all the worlds are one.

Jerusalem Meditation

Jerusalem is a busy, bustling metropolis with a beautifully designed parliament, a state-of-the-art museum, a modern city hall, and a futuristic light-rail system. But it is also an ancient and holy city where everything is bathed in a special kind of light, and a sweet fragrance of the ancient kingdom of Israel fills the air. When we experience this side of Jerusalem, a tremendous love wells up inside us for the city and its people. In such moments, we touch upon the inner essence of Jerusalem, and know in our hearts that it is truly one of the holiest places in the world.

According to the tradition, there is an earthly Jerusalem and also a heavenly Jerusalem. The earthly Jerusalem is the capital of the modern State of Israel. The heavenly Jerusalem is the centerpoint of the Soul of Israel in the higher worlds—one might call it the headquarters of the Soul's work. The heavenly Jerusalem is where the power of the Divine Presence is focused. It is this higher Jerusalem that we are experiencing when we feel the city's special light and sanctity. We are touching upon her spiritual essence and are thereby transported into another realm.

There is a working relationship between the earthly Jerusalem and the heavenly Jerusalem. They are both part of a larger plan and purpose that spans many planes and worlds. The earthly Jerusalem is the lowest manifestation of this work, energy, and ideal.

The tradition tells us that in the future, Jerusalem will expand and rise up to touch the Throne of Glory,[19] so that the earthly Jerusalem and the heavenly Jerusalem unite and become one. The higher Jerusalem and the lower Jerusalem were created to build a bridge between the worlds.

The name Jerusalem, or *Yerushalayim,* is composed of two parts: *yeru* + *shalem*. The tradition tells us that Abraham, who knew that it was the place appointed to become the Temple, called it *Yireh,* for it would be the abiding place of *yirah*—the awe of God. Shem, the son of Noah, on the other hand, had previously given the city the name *Shalem*—the place of wholeness and peace. The tradition then goes on to explain that because God did not want to offend either Abraham or Shem, the Holy Blessed One decided to unite the two names together and called the city *Yeru-shalayim*—Jerusalem, the city of awe and peace.[20]

For our final contemplation meditation, we will utilize these two aspects of Jerusalem's eternal essence to tap into the spiritual power of this ancient city and its higher counterpart in the supernal worlds. This meditation combines contemplation with a powerful concluding invocation. It offers up a prayer for the peace of the Holy City and all of humankind.

Make yourself comfortable. Close your eyes and let go of all tension in your body.

Relax every part of you. Start with your neck and shoulders, and then move down through your body all the way to your toes.

Begin to breathe in and out in a normal fashion, focusing your mind on the intake and outflow of your breath.

Visualize the doorway of the *heh* ה. Let the *heh* swing in one direction as you inhale and in the other direction as you exhale.

Shut out all of the outside noise and clamor. For this one moment, let nothing else exist but the movement of your breath. Become one with the *heh*. Become the doorway.

Yeru—Awe

Now imagine that you are on your way to ancient Jerusalem, ascending through the Judean hills. Even as you climb up the approach to the city, you can feel the energy starting to build inside you. What looks like a white mountain suddenly appears before you in the heart of the city. It is the *Beit Hamikdash*—the Holy Temple.

As soon as your eyes fall upon its features, the presence of the *Shekhinah* begins to overshadow you. Feel the power of Her majesty and might.

Visualize that you are ascending to the Temple Mount and entering through its gates. Hear the cry of the shofar, the ram's horn, as it calls out from the Temple walls. Listen to the chanting of the Levites as it rises up from inside the inner courtyard. The two great pillars that guard the entrance to the Sanctuary appear before your eyes.

Now imagine that it is Yom Kippur, the holiest day of the year. The Temple service has reached its climax. After performing many rituals of purification and sanctification, the High Priest enters into the Holy of Holies with great trepidation.

The Temple courtyard is filled with hundreds of thousands of pilgrims. Everyone is waiting expectantly for the arrival of the High Priest.

The High Priest appears. His countenance is shining like the sun. He turns to bless the people with great power. As the High Priest exclaims the Ineffable Divine Name, everyone in the Temple courtyard is thrown upon his or her face by the force of his light. It is truly a day of blessing, purification, and atonement—a day of awe before God.

Shalem—Peace

One of the names for the ancient Temple was *Sukkat Shalom*—the Abode of Peace. Imagine the profound sense of peace in the inner Sanctuary of the Temple—the stillness, the silence: a vibrant silence that was filled with divine life. Any pilgrim who entered into the Temple area experienced this sense of all-embracing peace.

Feel the peace of Jerusalem envelop you. Feel its soothing presence permeate deep inside you and fill the whole of your being with peace, calm, and tranquility. Rest in that feeling of peace and serenity until you yourself become the peace.

Invocation

Now turn your mind inward and visualize a pillar of light rising from the earth up to the heavens—from the lower to the higher Jerusalem.

Link your mind with the heavenly city. Connect with all of the souls on this celestial plane who love and cherish Jerusalem. Feel the tremendous love, light, and peace emanating from the higher realm.

Turn to these great souls and ask for their help in uniting the heavenly and the earthly Jerusalem. Draw their spiritual power down into you, and then let that power flow through you out into the world.

Let go of all images and rest in the silence.

Open up your eyes.

When the earthly Jerusalem becomes one with the heavenly Jerusalem, a fundamental change in our consciousness will take place. This change in consciousness will transform our reality until everything in the world is infused with the qualities of the heavenly Jerusalem. From a human being to the smallest creature or object—all will be imbued with light, harmony, and peace.

May we be worthy to bring the love and unity of the Kingdom of Heaven down into our material plane of existence. May we be worthy to be counted among the builders of God's Temple in all of the worlds.

PART THREE

The Life of Meditation

Up until now, we have put all of the emphasis on our daily practice. Meditation, however, is about more than just thirty or forty-five minutes of turning inward. It is a whole way of life that powerfully impacts how we interact with the world. Meditation is about going through our day in a heightened state of awareness. It is about walking at all times in the presence of God.

In this third part of the book, we explore how to bring meditation into our day-to-day existence. We learn how to utilize the fruits of our inner practice to transform our reality. We discover how to infuse our entire being with the light of the Divine.

We also discuss the final stage of the meditative path: merging with our spiritual source. What occurs when we reach the level of union with God? What are the indicators that tell us that we have established a strong and lasting connection with our soul? This section explains the spiritual dynamics of union and outlines the signs that reveal we have achieved the ultimate goal.

Chapter Ten

HOLDING THE LINK

How Do We Keep Our Mind on God?

*M*any people who practice meditation for an extended period of time have some type of inner experience. However, this experience in itself is not enough. The challenge is to learn how to hold on to what we have received—both inside and outside of the meditation room. This work demands a deeper commitment to our spiritual life.

What Does It Mean to Hold on to the Link?

Holding on to the link has two separate components: the capacity to maintain our inner contact from meditation to meditation and learning to keep our inner connection as we go about our day-to-day life. Both aspects are important components of this stage of meditation. Each has its own methods and focus.

Let us begin with the work of learning to adhere to a link during meditation.

Adhering to Our Higher Contact

A spiritual link is a point of inner contact with a soul on higher planes. In a broader sense, it can be defined as a breakthrough from the finite into the Infinite. Our challenge is to learn how to reestablish our inner connection each time we sit down to meditate. This is a matter of discovering the same "place" in our consciousness where the original contact was made. We accomplish this task by developing an awareness of the dimensions of our inner space and a clear sense of what a spiritual contact feels like.

There is no simple way to express this reality; it is something that needs to be experienced in order to be understood. What can be said is that there is a point of tension that is reached where a feeling of another presence infuses our consciousness while, at the same time, our inner reality begins to expand and come alive.

Constant effort to maintain a contact during meditation deepens our familiarity with this place in our mind. We gradually become aware of its vibration and location. We get to know the impression and awareness that it creates in us.

God will aid us in this process by providing visual or other cues to help identify the inner contact. We might be given a sound that accompanies its presence, an image that sets it apart, or a name of some great spiritual figure that we learn to associate with the contact. These names or images are God's way of telling us who has come to us. It might be the actual specific figure that we see or feel. It could also be another soul who is on an equivalent line, someone who carries a similar energy and works with the same religion or path.

Alternatively, we may have none of the concrete signs mentioned above. Instead, we may experience a particular spiritual quality whenever a contact is made: a feeling of love, a flood of light, or a profound sense of peace. God has many ways of letting us know that the Divine Presence is near.

Our task is twofold. We work to keep our mind clear so we can recognize the moment of contact. And we strive to become adept at navigating our inner space. These two skills enable us to find the location in consciousness where we have made our contact and to return to that spot again and again. With time, it will become a familiar space to us—a mind state that we can come back to whenever we wish.

Once we know how to locate this inner place, we can fix our awareness there. In this way, we learn to maintain that point of contact for an extended period of time. The longer we can hold on to our link, the more fully we will receive the blessing of those on higher planes. As our connection evolves, our contact will become a spiritual doorway through which inspiration, guidance, and experience flow to us.

The Constant Remembrance of God

Many of us have had an experience of the Higher Power. It lasts for a moment and makes us think differently for a while. However, for most of us, the experience fades away over time, and with it, the change in perspective. We quickly return to our earlier values, aspirations, and behavior, and our life remains as it was before.

After we have experienced a spiritual contact, the question that we need to ask ourselves is, how do we hold on to our inner link amid the vicissitudes of worldly existence? How do we integrate God's living presence into our everyday life?

The Sufi master Jalaluddin Rumi taught, "Never be without remembrance of Him, for His remembrance gives strength and wings to the bird of the Spirit."[1]

The practice of the constant remembrance of God, what the Sufis call *Zikr*, is our main tool in keeping the spirit of God alive inside us. It teaches us how to spread our wings and rise above the mundane affairs of material life. In this discipline, we turn inward to touch the place of spiritual contact at regular intervals throughout the day. We strive at every moment to keep aware of the inner presence. And we continue on with our practice until God-remembrance becomes our natural state of being.

The practice of the remembrance of God does not rely on elaborate rituals or complex intellectual contemplations. It makes use of simple techniques of repetition and awareness. Through regular application, these techniques slowly solidify the link with our soul.

We can use an objective signpost to regulate our practice, such as "linking in" each time the chime on our watch sounds the hour; or we can respond to a subjective prompting, such as the start of an important engagement or the aftermath of a difficult encounter. There are numerous methods of achieving this heightened awareness. Each method is suited to a particular temperament and soul quality; all of the approaches lead us to the same ultimate goal.

In the Hasidic text *Likutei Ramal*, the constant remembrance of God is compared to the mindfulness maintained by a person who is carrying a precious gem in his pocket as he goes about town taking care of his affairs. No matter what else he may be doing, one part of his mind will be on the jewel for fear of losing it. It doesn't make any difference whether he is walking along the street, or going about the market making purchases, or arguing with a client, or simply relaxing and eating lunch; throughout all these activities, he will never lose awareness of the presence of the jewel.[2]

Holding on to an inner link in this manner takes a great deal of practice. We need to become so focused in our interior space that neither the sense-perceived stimuli from the world around us nor the emotional turbulence from the feelings inside us can disturb our inner balance and poise. This is not easily accomplished. It demands hard work, patience and perseverance, and an abundance of divine grace.

As we progress along the spiritual path, our power of inner concentration gradually intensifies. As the practice of constant remembrance takes possession of our consciousness, the affairs of the world require less and less of our focused attention, and communion with the Infinite absorbs more and more of our time.

Sri Ramana Maharshi used an analogy from the world of music to explain how we go about learning to live in this manner:

> When the harmonium [an Indian musical instrument similar to the accordion] is being played there is a constant note that is called the *sruti*. Along with that, other notes also come out. If the ear is fixed on this note that is constant, then, while listening to the other notes, that original note cannot be forgotten. Actually, that first note gives strength to all the other notes.
>
> So, the principle to understand is that the first note is the *adhistana* (substratum) while the other notes represent worldly activities. During worldly activities, if (awareness of) the note of the *adhistana* is continuous, whatever is spoken is then done with the authority of this *adhistana* note....
>
> The *jnani* [realized soul] keeps his attention on the first note.... When the attention is fixed properly on the first note, the effect of the other notes will not be felt....
>
> *Jnanis* fix their sight in the substratum, the *adhistana*, even during worldly activities because nothing else is real except *adhistana*. To feel that there is clay in the pot is the proper attitude (that is, see the essence and not the form).... Even when the pot is whole you can see it as the form of clay. In the same way the world can be seen as the form of *Brahman* [God].[3]

On one level, then, the constant remembrance of God is a matter of establishing a mental routine. We need to form the habit of God awareness. It is a question of building up our steadiness and resolve. We keep at our practice until God remembrance becomes an automatic response.

Some people find this approach too dry. They are looking for a path that is more personal and accessible. The Baal Shem Tov provides us with a model that is more devotional and closer to home. A central maxim of his teaching was "you are where your thoughts are."[4] He counseled his Hasidim to always bind their thoughts to the supernal world throughout the day. This, he said, is the hidden meaning of Leviticus 21:12, "And from the Temple, he shall not go out." This phrase is a lovely way of describing the practice of God remembrance. In this practice, we build a place in our mind where we can be alone with our Beloved. We fashion a little room or temple with our creative imagination, where we and the Immeasurable One can meet.

Despite this wonderful image, the Baal Shem knew that it would be hard for his Hasidim to fulfill this injunction amid the cares and worries of their mundane lives. He therefore gave them the following metaphor as a guide for their practice:

> When he speaks at length about worldly matters, his thought should be that he is journeying from the higher world below. Like a person who leaves his house and goes outside with the intention to come right back, while he is on the way, he thinks [about] when he will return to his home. So he [the Hasid] should be thinking always of the supernal world—that there is his real home—in God.[5]

This is an effective way of making the practice of constant remembrance come alive for people. Sri Ramakrishna used a similar approach when the householder devotees asked him how to keep their mind on the One True Reality while going about their worldly duties:

> A maidservant in the house of a rich man performs all the household duties, but her thoughts are fixed on her own home in her native village. She brings up her master's children as if they were her own. She even speaks of them as "my Rama" or "my Hari." But in her own mind she knows very well that they do not belong to her at all.

> The tortoise moves about in the water. But can you guess where
> her thoughts are? There on the bank, where her eggs are lying. Do
> all your duties in the world, but keep your mind on God.[6]

Despite the strong devotional aspect of these practices, the abstract
nature of inner contacts makes it difficult for many people to relate to
them. Visualization is a powerful tool that can help us with this problem. Picturing a concrete image in our mind while striving to maintain
our God remembrance can transform an inner link into a tangible reality for us.

The Hasidic text *Or Haganuz* suggests that as we go about our daily
activities, rather than thinking of our body as simply a physical entity,
we can think of it as holy ground that carries within it the light and consciousness of the soul. Our body is the support for the whole expanse of
our soul, which stretches far into the heavens above us. It is the vehicle
for the emanation of the energies of the *Shekhinah* and all the higher
worlds.[7]

The fifteenth-century Kabbalist the Shelah haKadosh suggests that we
visualize the light of the *Shekhinah* resting above our head, radiating
out in all directions around us. We then imagine ourselves seated in the
midst of this beatific light as we go about our normal routine.[8]

There is a still more direct method that we can use. In this approach,
we imagine that the spiritual figure we have identified with our inner
link (or that God has identified for us) is standing right next to us. This
great teacher is watching everything we do, listening to every word we
speak, reading all of our thoughts. He or she is always with us; we are
never alone.

This approach provides us with a very personal focus for our practice.
It makes constant remembrance more natural for us. Our inner connection will come more easily and feel more accessible. Our spiritual discipline will be brought to life.

Psalm 121:5 declares, "*Adonai tzilkha*—God is your shade." The
practice of constant remembrance is about learning how to walk in the
shade of the Divine Presence. By continually returning to the place of
our inner contact, we will start to feel God beside us throughout the day.
We will receive ever-clearer guidance and inspiration. We will know
that we are secure in our Eternal refuge, safe under the shelter of the
Shekhinah's wings.

Other Measures for Holding the Link

Solitude: Getting Away from It All

The constant remembrance of God is a potent spiritual tool. It helps us to fan the spark of our inner contact as we go about our daily lives. Yet this habitual remembrance is sometimes not enough to maintain our inner connection. The pull of the world is too all-pervasive. The challenges of our responsibilities can easily become overwhelming. Therefore, occasional periods of concentrated inner work in solitude are recommended for the spiritual seeker—a retreat where we focus one-pointedly on our inner life.

The Baal Shem Tov believes that this is the hidden meaning of the first commandment that God gave to Abraham: *"Lekh lekha me'artzekha, umimoladetekha, umibeit avikha el ha'aretz asher areka—Get you out of your country, and from your kindred, and from your father's house, to the land that I will show you"* (Genesis 12:1). The literal translation of this verse is: "(You) go to yourself, (away) from your land, and (away) from your kindred, and (away) from your father's house, to the land that I will show you." In this command, the Baal Shem explains, God is telling Abraham and every other spiritual seeker: *Lekh lekha*—go to your Self; *me'artzekha, umimoladetekha, umibeit avikha*—leave your people, your background, and your father's house, and go into seclusion, to be alone with your self; *el ha'aretz asher areka*—then God will show you the place where you are heading. The Most High will reveal to you the inner "lands" of the spiritual realm.[9]

Sri Ramakrishna also advised his householder devotees to go, from time to time, to a solitary location and commune with the Infinite. He elucidated the reason for going into solitude by comparing it to the process of making butter:

> To get butter from milk you must let it set into curd in a secluded spot: if it is too much disturbed, milk won't turn into curd. Next, you must put aside all other duties, sit in a quiet spot, and churn the curd. Only then do you get butter.
>
> Further, by meditating on God in solitude the mind acquires knowledge, dispassion, and devotion. But the very same mind goes downward if it dwells in the world....

> The world is water and the mind milk. If you pour milk into water they become one; you cannot find the pure milk anymore. But turn the milk into curd and churn it into butter. Then, when that butter is placed in water, it will float. So, practise spiritual discipline in solitude and obtain the butter of knowledge and love. Even if you keep that butter in the water of the world the two will not mix. The butter will float.[10]

A secluded spot in nature is ideal for a retreat. Such a place provides us with a beautiful setting for our practice. It offers us an environment that is completely cut off from the busy city life. In nature, the unique spiritual power of the angelic kingdom becomes readily available to us.

We should try to go into isolation at least a couple of times a year. We can begin with a long weekend and over time extend our retreat to a week or even ten days. If our life circumstances permit, we can enter into solitude for a month at a time. During a retreat, the refinement of the thought processes that we can achieve and the depth of meditation that we can experience far surpass anything we can accomplish in our day-to-day practice.

Yet periods of solitude are only a supplement to our daily meditation. They provide us with the opportunity to receive spiritual sweets and gain the fruit of our daily routine. Regular meditation and the constant remembrance of God are the staples of the seeker's spiritual diet. This two-pronged approach will transform the contours of our inner map and satiate the hunger of our soul.

First Light: The Power of the First Thought of the Day

Rebbe Ze'ev Wolf of Zhitomir was a member of the Maggid of Mezeritch's inner circle. He extols the first thought that we have on rising in the morning as a treasure of great value:

> This first thought can be given the name "first light," because all the particulars of the service and behavior that he will do and achieve during the day are bound up and dependent on it [his first thought].... Within it are contained the specific thoughts and advice that he needs to give his soul for divine arousal and to raise up the limbs of the *Shekhinah* from the totality of levels toward which he turns his consciousness. Everything is dependent on this thought called "first light."[11]

Sri Ramana Maharshi provides us with further insight into why this first instant after awakening is so vital:

> Just on rising up from sleep, and before seeing the objective world, there is a state of awareness which is your pure Self.[12]
>
> It is neither sleep nor waking but intermediate between the two.
>
> There is the awareness of the waking state and the stillness of sleep. It is called *jagrat-sushupti*. Call it wakeful sleep or sleeping wakefulness or sleepless waking or wakeless sleep. It is not the same as sleep or waking separately. It is *atijagrat* (beyond wakefulness) or *atisushupti* (beyond sleep). It is the state of perfect awareness and of perfect stillness combined. It lies between sleep and waking; it is also the interval between two successive thoughts. It is the source from which thoughts spring; we see that when we wake up from sleep.... Go to the root of the thoughts and you reach the stillness of sleep. But you reach it in the full vigour of search, that is, with perfect awareness.[13]

The experience of the "first light" is more than just a moment of intuition or inspiration. It is an altogether unique state of being, where we are still linked to the pure awareness of our true Self. First light appears in the moment before the constricting filter of the ego has gotten a grip on the mind. It is a place of perfect silence and stillness—a taste of the infinite peace of the Absolute.

It is not so much the actual first thought, then, that is of essential importance; rather, it is the state of consciousness in which we awaken— the state of rightness, of profound peace and inner contentment, of resting in our true Self. If we can retain this state, then its light and energy will infuse our entire day, guiding and directing all that we do. This is why it is called first light. When we hold on to this first moment of pure perception, it illuminates the whole of our existence.

In the continuation of his teaching, Rebbe Ze'ev Wolf makes clear that we need to retain our first thought throughout our waking activities:

> And it is incumbent on him to not let go of this first thought from his inner consciousness for even a second. Rather, he should keep this thought with him throughout his activities during the day. Even if several other good thoughts come to him during the day,

nonetheless, he should not let go of this [his first thought].... This first light is a great advantage in guiding a person in fulfilling his daily concerns.[14]

Arthur Osborne, one of Ramana Maharshi's senior devotees, outlined a similar process in his description of how he turned the first moment of thought into a potent spiritual exercise:

> Bhagavan [Ramana Maharshi] had said that the state to be aimed at is a sort of waking sleep; also that it can be experienced at the moment between waking and sleeping. I prolonged the state as long as possible. During the weeks that followed, this formed my mode of meditation: particularly, of course, while waking from sleep (while falling asleep I found it more difficult) but also throughout the day—retiring into impersonal consciousness, seeing the flow of events drift past on its surface.[15]

This approach to the first moments on arising represents a fundamental change in the way that we start our day. Ordinarily, we get up, hop out of bed, and begin our activities. In fact, even before we leave the bed, our attention is diverted to a whole gambit of thoughts, responsibilities, and problems that flood into our head.

Instead, we are being asked to wake up slowly, while keeping all personal thoughts at bay, and strive to hold on to the first moment of pure peace—our first light. We prolong that moment for as long as possible. Only after we have secured our first light in our awareness do we start our normal schedule.

Once we have entered into our daily routine, we still do not let go of our first light. Throughout our waking hours, we work to stabilize our mind in this source of blessing. And we keep referring back to this first moment of harmony and clarity until it becomes a vital presence inside us.

First light shines forth on many levels. On one level, it is a method of binding our hearts and minds to God. On another level, it is a flash of inspiration from the spiritual realm to guide us throughout the next twenty-four hours. On the highest level, it is a momentary experience of pure consciousness—the abidance in the Self.

Holding on to first light is holding on to God. If we can harness this first light, it will raise our consciousness and transform our perception of reality.

Like the first rays of dawn that sweep away the darkness and brighten the morning sky, this inner light will expel the dimness of ignorance from our mind and illuminate our entire being with the knowledge of the *Ein Sof*.

Two States of Consciousness:
Moving Between Our Higher and Lower Self

For most of us, the ability to constantly maintain our God remembrance seems an impossible and unattainable feat. The truth is that we never remain for long in any one state. Our mind fluctuates all of the time.

The Hasidic masters were keenly aware of this reality. They spoke of two different states of consciousness that a seeker experiences throughout his spiritual journey: *mochin dekatnut* (the small or lower mind) and *mochin degadlut* (the big or higher mind).

The Baal Shem Tov uses a couple of examples to portray these two states. His first example relates to our experience during our spiritual exercises. *Mochin degadlut,* or the higher mind, is when we feel a great love and awe for God, and our practices are filled with joy. *Mochin dekatnut,* or the lower mind, is when we do not experience any strong inner yearning, and all of the disciplines seem difficult and only come with great effort.[16]

The Baal Shem's second example refers to our experience when we are learning. When our study of spiritual wisdom is lifeless, where we achieve only a functional comprehension of the words but no real understanding of the text, then we are in a state of *mochin dekatnut*. When we learn with great enthusiasm and reach a profound understanding of the text, where all of the concepts become spiritually alive, then we are in a state of *mochin degadlut*.[17]

Looking at these two examples of the Baal Shem, we might broadly define these two states of being as a contracted state of consciousness, where we see everything through the lens of the concrete mind of the personality (*mochin dekatnut*), and as an expanded state of consciousness, where we view the world through the infinite awareness of the soul (*mochin degadlut*).

According to the Baal Shem, the spiritual life continually vacillates between these two states of being, like the heavenly creatures, the *chayot*, in the vision of Ezekiel, that one moment advance toward the heavenly light and then retreat a moment later (Ezekiel 1:14). These two states are an inexorable part of our dualistic reality; just as wherever there is light there must also be darkness, so we cannot remain in the spiritual light forever but must also experience the state of inner darkness. As long as we are bound to a physical mind-set, we will continue to experience these two opposing states.[18]

Swami Vivekananda was one of the leading disciples of Sri Rama-krishna. He played a key role in bringing the teachings and philosophy of Vedanta to the West. Swami Vivekananda had a wonderful manner of describing these two states of mind. He expressed the experience of these two spiritual poles this way: "When I am on the Heights, I say 'I am He' [i.e., I am Brahman], and when I have a stomachache, I say 'Mother, have mercy on me.'"[19]

When we are overshadowed with the full power of God's presence, we are filled with amazing inner strength and extraordinary confidence. Then we are ready to declare, "I am He"—I am the Imperishable, Eternal Self.

When God withdraws the Divine Presence, however, we are left as the emotionally limited and spiritually imperfect animal creatures that we are. In such moments of fragility, we cry out instead, "Mother, have mercy on me."

King David also expressed a similar dynamic of opposing states of awareness in the book of Psalms. Psalm 23:4 triumphantly exclaims, "Though I walk in the valley of the shadow of death, I shall fear no evil, for You are with me." Psalm 30:8, on the other hand, meekly confesses, "Lord … when You concealed Your countenance, I was afraid."

The balance between these two states is intimately bound to our ability to hold on to our inner link. It is an ever-changing and evolving process.

At the beginning of our spiritual journey, we try to sustain our link for a scant few moments, so that we can remain in a higher state of mind and gain a glimpse of the Truth. At this stage, our experience of *mochin degadlut* is rare. We spend most of our time in a state of *mochin dekatnut*.

Over time, however, we are able to preserve our connection for longer periods of time. Our ability to enter into *mochin degadlut* slowly increases. The state of *mochin dekatnut* dominates our life less and less.

If we are steady in our practice and persevere in the work of self-transformation, then we will eventually reach a stage where we can maintain our link fairly steadily. Now the majority of our day is spent in *mochin degadlut*, and we feel the Holy One with us most of the time.

There still are moments, however, when God feels far away, moments when we are denied the joy of the Divine Presence. Yet, slowly we begin to realize that even in these moments of absence, a guiding force is there. There is a kind of "knowing" on a deeper level, a steady flow of energy and an almost imperceptible line of awareness that extends from the supernal power to us. As we assimilate this truth, we arrive at a different place within ourselves where we just "are"—where we rest in our sustaining Source no matter what the circumstance.

Now, whenever the higher reality becomes distant, we no longer cry out like a frightened creature; rather, like a helpless child, we reach up toward the arms of our unseen Protector and call, "Mother, please embrace me."

Obstacles and Solutions in Trying to Hold on to Our Link

Trying to maintain our link pits us against both internal and external obstacles. It is a different kind of difficulty that we face. The issues we confront present us with more of a constant struggle than immediate individual problems. The solutions require a shift in our consciousness and a change in our approach to life.

This section looks at several crucial areas in this spiritual battle and offers some ideas on how to negotiate our way to victory on the field of life.

The World: How Do We Counter the Negative Influences of Our Daily Reality?

The greatest obstacle that we face in holding on to our spiritual contact is the disruptive effect of worldly existence on our thought life. Wherever we turn, we are bombarded with a barrage of sensory input. The whole of our awareness is constantly being drawn outward and away from the inner reality. We are continually urged to focus on the appearance of our body, the number of our possessions, and the record of our material achievements. Everything about our Western society is arranged to keep us immersed in a physical state of mind.

The various techniques described in this section are essentially different methods for overcoming the downward pull of material living. They each confront this issue in a different way.

At the same time, the paradox is that our problem is also our solution. The greatest ally we have in countering the effect of the world on us is the same inner link that we are trying to maintain. Sri Ramakrishna used to say that if we whirl round and round, we will get dizzy and fall unless we hold on to a pillar as we turn, in which case we will keep our balance despite the rapid spinning movement.[20]

A solid inner link creates a powerful counterbalance of positive spiritual vibration to offset the negative influence of the energies around us. It enables us to work from a different place within ourselves, to watch events as a witness and observer. This, in turn, detaches us from the emotional whirlwind of the moment, so that we can stop and reflect before we act, react, and interact.

The Bhagavad Gita (6:19) compares the mental condition of an individual who can rest in God to a light in a windless place. Our inner link allows one part of ourselves to be in another world or dimension that is untouched by the environment around us. It lifts us into a region beyond time and space that is unaffected by the winds that blow through our material reality.

If we build a firm link with our soul, then the problem of worldly distractions will simply disappear on its own. As Sri Ramana Maharshi would reply whenever one of his devotees expressed a desire to leave family life and become a wandering mendicant:

> Renunciation is always in the mind, not in going to forests or solitary places or giving up one's duties. The main thing is to see that the mind does not turn outward but inward. It does not really rest with a man whether he goes to this place or that or whether he gives up his duties or not. All that happens according to destiny…. The only freedom you have is to turn your mind inward and renounce activities there.[21]

Once we have learned to keep the mind turned inward, nothing can disturb us. Our being becomes anchored in the sacred space inside us, like a central pillar or rock on which all else rests. Externally, we may still go through the tumult and chaos of life, but we will remain clear and calm within.

The Effects of Spiritual Stimulation

When the energy of God flows into us, it greatly stimulates everything that is inside us. On the one hand, all of our positive qualities are given an enormous boost: the love in our heart pours out in great abundance, the understanding of our mind expands and deepens, our inner light shines with a powerful radiance and beauty. At the same time, all of our imperfections are also stimulated: our inner conflicts are stirred up, our animal desires are awakened, and all of our hidden fears and doubts inundate our mental space.

If we look at the lives of the saints and holy ones of the different religions, we will see that their spiritual experiences were rarely kind or gentle. God entered their lives like a tempest, uprooting everything around them, inside and out. When the Infinite and Eternal enters into the finite and temporal, difficulty, disruption, and imbalance are the inevitable result.

One day, one of Sri Ramana Maharshi's young attendants asked him why his body shook so much, even though he was at the time only in early middle age. The Maharshi explained, "What is there so strange in it? If a big elephant is tied down in a small hut, what else will happen to that hut except troubles of all sorts? This is the same."[22]

The power of the Presence is sometimes more than a person can handle. There are many stories about prophets and holy ones who wandered like madmen and madwomen when in the throes of divine intoxication. And there are even more tales about spiritual seekers who lost their sanity after trying to break through into the spiritual realm.

In the Talmud (*Chagigah* 14b), there is a story about four rabbis who entered the heavenly *Pardes* (the supernal orchard in the higher worlds). In the wake of this experience, one died, one went mad, and one became an atheist. God is a consuming fire, and we need to be humble and pure before we attempt to enter into the divine realm.

The Need for Balance

Though we have spoken at length about the constant remembrance of God, as well as other practices that keep our mind on high, we need to be alert and thoughtful when striving to hold on to an inner contact. Balance is an essential part of the spiritual life.

A story from the Buddhist sutras beautifully illustrates this truth. A young man named Sona Kolivisa, who was the son of a rich merchant, joined the Buddha's order of monks. Due to his great desire to attain enlightenment, Sona had been walking on thorns in an excess of zeal. The path where he walked was covered with blood. Then, exhausted by his austerities, Sona began to think to himself. "Maybe it would be better if I were to return to my home and use my wealth in doing good deeds." Soon he was in a whirlwind of confusion.

Knowing his thoughts, the Buddha went to him and asked,

"When you were at home, Sona, could you play the lute?"

"Yes, Master," Sona replied.

"When the strings of the lute were over-taut, did your lute give proper sounds?"

"No, Master," he answered.

"When the strings of your lute were neither over-taut nor over-slack, the lute gave the proper sounds. Was it not so?"

"It was so, Master," he acknowledged.

"Even so, Sona," explained the Buddha, "... have an evenness of zeal, master your powers in harmony. Be this your aim."[23]

To fine-tune the instrument that is a human being is a very delicate process. On one hand, we will break if our spiritual life is too intense; on the other hand, we will accomplish very little if we are unfocused and diffuse.

We need to take care of our instrument. We purify and refine our body, mind, and soul. We try to strike a balance between the physical and the spiritual, between the body and the soul, between activity and relaxation, between asceticism and overindulgence. By walking along this middle path, we can do effective work.

The Baal Shem Tov also believed in the middle path. Once again, he utilized the image of the heavenly creatures who "rush forward and then retreat" in Ezekiel's vision as his metaphor to teach us this spiritual truth. Just as all things long to go back to their source, he explains, one part of us is always rushing toward God. However, if we are too fully immersed in the spiritual realm, we can become destabilized by the power of the divine light. Therefore, we need to take a break from our spiritual practices from time to time and occupy ourselves with mundane matters. In this way, our body and mind will get a rest from the intensity of our inner life, a period of quiet when we can reflect and recharge. The spiritual path is founded on this dual motion: we first strive toward the heavens, then we retreat back into the physical world to integrate our advances, and then we ascend back up into the higher worlds again.[24]

If we can hold on to our spiritual link, then we will go through the day with a sense of peace and well-being, no matter what difficulties life may bring our way. We will find joy in even the most insignificant activity. We will feel a profound love for everyone and everything. The world around us will shine with vibrancy, beauty, and light.

CHAPTER ELEVEN
MERGING WITH OUR SPIRITUAL SOURCE
The Final Fulfillment of the Quest

*W*e now come to the final stage in the meditation process: merging with our spiritual source. This stage is the culmination of the spiritual path. It is the precious fruit, harvested after intense labor, often spanning many lifetimes. Even during the life when this process comes to its fulfillment, the union usually occurs after years of dedicated effort. Yet sometimes it happens in a moment in the midst of a worldly existence. It is all a matter of God's grace and divine purpose.

Full union happens only to a rare few. At the same time, each and every one of us can aspire to this supreme goal. It is the spiritual birthright of all human beings. Everyone will eventually attain union in some future incarnation.

Two Types of Union

We need to distinguish between two levels of union. The highest form is union with our spiritual source. And while such a union happens only to a chosen few, there is another level of union that is more within our grasp. This is a union in one of the centers of our spiritual body.

Union in a Center

As explained earlier in the book, we each have a subtle body of spiritual centers that underlies our physical form—what the Kabbalah calls the

Etz haChayim, the Tree of Life. This body of *chakras* or *sefirot* contains seven major centers aligned along the spinal column. Each center has its own particular energy. Each center evokes a specific state of awareness.

A *sefirah* is formed in embryo as a nucleus of spiritual force with a left-hand, a right-hand, and a central component. This sefirotic structure parallels the network of three energy pathways that run through our body of spiritual centers. There is a right-hand passage called the path of *chesed,* or mercy. There is a left-hand passage called the path of *din,* or judgment. And there is a middle passage called the path of *rachamim, or compassion; this pathway is also referred to as the path* of the *Shekhinah*.

A constant stream of energies flows in and out of the centers. Some of this energy pours into the left-hand component of the centers and is stored there, and some is directed to the right-hand aspect of the centers and collects there. Each *sefirah* has a different balance of energies. Certain *sefirot* have a strong left-hand side, while others are predominantly right-handed. It all depends on the nature of the energy that we imbibe and the state of our spiritual development. Our every encounter and experience affects the quality and refinement of the energy in our centers. Everything we think, say, and do has an effect on us.

At any given point in time, our awareness is focused in one particular *sefirah*. Its quality and character influence our perception of reality. As we evolve along the path, our consciousness ascends from one center to another of the *Etz haChayim*. The shift into a new *sefirah* can take a whole lifetime or longer to achieve. Some *sefirot* are more prevalent among the masses of humanity, while others are less commonly developed. And only the exceptional person will have his or her awareness fixed in the two highest centers of *chokhmah/binah* (wisdom and understanding) and *keter* (the crown).

Our spiritual goal is to raise our consciousness up to the next *sefirah*. For this to happen, the energy in both the left-hand and the right-hand components of that *sefirah* need to be purified and properly balanced, as do the energy pathways themselves. Once this has occurred, the energies in the right-hand and the left-hand subtle passages ascend to meet in the designated *sefirah*, while a powerful influx of *Shekhinah* energy comes flooding through the middle passage to boost the whole of the center with its creative force. This tremendous spiritual outpouring fuses the left-hand and right-hand components into a single unified whole. Our consciousness then surges up into this new center as we are lifted into an entirely different state of being. After the union with the higher center has been completed, the energy of the *Shekhinah* descends back to the lowest center once again.

This higher center now becomes the foundation of our experience. Its attributes and "color" infuse all aspects of our life. As a result of this union, we are reborn into a new spiritual reality. We take another step forward along the journey to Self-realization.

What Occurs When We Reach Union in a Center?

While there is no fixed pattern for spiritual development, union in a center generally follows a proscribed process and takes a certain amount of time.

We become aware of the process beginning long before it comes to full fruition. First, there is an intensification of our practice. Our meditations become deeper and our inner connection more powerful.

Next, a strong line of energy starts to build between our mind and the point of higher contact. A vast vortex of spiritual force draws us magnetically toward it. The presence of the overshadowing soul becomes increasingly tangible and alive.

Then, as the process nears its completion, our mind comes under intense internal pressure. Our head starts to feel as if it is caught in a vise. Our body may begin to tremble and shake from the impact of the energy. The point of inner contact becomes our sole reality, and everything else fades from sight.

Finally the climactic moment arrives. A tremendous burst of energy comes pouring through us, expanding our awareness outward and upward in a rush of joy and light. All the tension disappears from our mind and body as we emerge into a zone of unimaginable freedom and bliss. Though our individual self remains, we are aware that we have entered into another greater consciousness. We are enveloped by its presence and dwell in the radiance of its light.

We may remain in this state for hours, or it can come and go in a few seconds. The effects of our experience, however, are powerful and lasting. The initial joy and wonder can stay with us for days, weeks, or even months.

How Do We Know When Such a Union in a Center Has Occurred?

In the period of time after such an experience, we will become aware of a change in our perception. We will begin to see the people and the world around us in a different, clearer light. We will experience a novel way of thinking and a fresh manner of knowing; a broader understanding will engulf our mind.

Our words will have a stronger impact and a greater authority. New and original thoughts will unexpectedly drop into our mind. An image or a few words of poetry will spontaneously arise from deep inside us. A new direction for our life will suddenly open up.

Matters that formerly disturbed us will no longer bother us. A profound peace and contentment will descend upon the mind. Others will begin to notice that an inner radiance emanates from us. A profound love for others will awaken in our heart.

These and many other wonderful experiences are the signs that we have attained union in a higher center. The blessings that God bestows during initiation are many and varied. The only certainty is that we are unworthy of them. They are all gifts of divine love.

This is a description of what happens during union in one of the seven centers. We will now explore the spiritual processes that occur when we attain union with our Soul Father, the One who embodies the highest aspect of our soul. Our Soul Mother is an essential part of this experience. She bestows the precious energy that makes it possible for us to ascend to our supernal source.

Full Union

Union with the source of our soul is the highest achievement of the religious life. It is the distinguishing characteristic of the great prophets and teachers of humankind. This union is portrayed in a symbolic manner in the mystical literature. The Kabbalah depicts the mystical union of the bride and groom and the celestial meeting of the Queen and King. The Hindu scriptures describe the joining of the Deity with his female *Shakti,* or power. Christians speak about the mystical union of Christ with his bride. All of these images are in reality describing a scientific process that takes place in the body of spiritual centers, whereby a human being is united with God.[1]

As we evolve along the spiritual path, our consciousness rises from center to center, uniting the left and right components in each of the *sefirot*. When this process reaches the highest center, the *Shekhinah* energy ascends through the middle passage to the *sefirah* of *keter*, the crown center, and a corresponding infusion of divine energy pours down into the top of the head from the highest aspect of the soul.

When these two streams of energy, from above and from below, merge together, all of the centers fuse into one great *sefirah* in the head, and the body becomes filled with light. The power of this fusion bridges the gap between the physical and spiritual planes, and we become conscious in the Kingdom of Heaven.[2]

As a result of this spiritual union, we are transformed from an ordinary human being into a God-realized soul. Our will is now totally bound to the divine will. Our separate identity is submerged in the Infinite Consciousness that underlies all of existence. Enough personality is retained to enable us to function in the world, but this is only a facade. In truth, the individual personality no longer exists. All that remains is a pure divine instrument.

As Swami (Papa) Ramdas explains:

> The state of the *Jivanmukta* [realized soul] is compared to that of a drop which becomes one with the ocean. That, of course, is the state which all *Jivanmuktas* attain. Still there remains a divinised individuality. It is the divine power and will that causes the *Jivanmukta*'s body to talk, walk, and move about. His illumined personality persists even after the body is cast off.[3]

The Nature of the Experience of Full Union

Given the rare nature of this kind of experience, the details of what occurs are not easy to determine. Most of the individuals who have attained this state have left no record of what happened. There are, however, a few examples that have been transmitted down the centuries. Most notable are the records from the great Indian teachers of the last few generations.

Sri Ramana Maharshi

Sri Ramana Maharshi's greatness is widely acknowledged across India and around the globe. His realization of and permanent abidance in the Source of All Being is considered to be a spiritual attainment of the highest degree.

You can feel yourself one with the One that exists: the whole body becomes a mere power, a force-current: your life becomes a needle drawn to a huge mass of magnet and as you go deeper and deeper, you become a mere centre and then not even that, for you become a mere consciousness, there are no thoughts or cares any longer— they were shattered at the threshold; it is an inundation; you, a mere straw, you are swallowed alive, but it is very delightful, for you become the very thing that swallows you; this is the union of *jiva* [the individual soul] with Brahman, the loss of the ego in the real Self, the destruction of falsehood, the attainment of Truth.[4]

The Prophet Jeremiah

We get a glimpse of this absorption into God, or Brahman, in the words spoken by the All-Powerful to the prophet Jeremiah at the beginning of his prophetic ministry:

> "You shall go to all whom I shall send you, and whatever I command, you shall speak. Do not be afraid of them: for I am with you to deliver you," says the Lord.
>
> Then the Lord put out His hand and touched my mouth. And the Lord said to me, "Behold, I have put My words in your mouth. See, I have this day set you over the nations and over the kingdoms, to root out, and to pull down, and to destroy, and to throw down, to build, and to plant....
>
> "Therefore, gird your loins, and arise, and speak to them all that I command you: do not be dismayed at them, lest I dismay you before them. For, behold, I have made you this day a fortified city, and an iron pillar, and walls of brass against the whole land, against the kings of Judah, against its princes, against its priests, and against the people of the land. And they shall fight against you; but they shall not prevail against you; for I am with you," says the Lord, "to deliver you." (Jeremiah 1:7–10, 17–19)

Realized souls are God's instruments. Wholly merged into the Timeless and Boundless Awareness, they have no will of their own. Their mouths are God's mouth, and their words are God's words.

Sri Ramakrishna

Sri Ramakrishna was a unique figure in the annals of religious history. The living form of the Universal Mother became fully alive and real for him. His strong attachment to the Mother, however, blocked his path forward to full realization. This passage describes the moment when he overcame this inner obstacle, and entered into the Reality that transcends all names and forms.

> In spite of all my attempts I could not altogether cross the realm of name and form and bring my mind to the unconditioned state. I had no difficulty in taking the mind from all the objects of the world. But the radiant and too familiar figure of the Blissful Mother, the Embodiment of the essence of Pure Consciousness, appeared before me as a living reality. Her bewitching smile prevented me from passing into the Great Beyond. Again and again I tried, but She stood in my way every time. In despair I said to Nangta [his Advaitic teacher]: "It is hopeless. I cannot raise my mind to the unconditioned state and come face to face with Atman [the non-dual Self]." He grew excited and sharply said: "What? You can't do it? But you have to." He cast his eyes around. Finding a piece of glass he took it up and stuck it between my eyebrows. "Concentrate the mind on this point!" he thundered. Then with stern determination I again sat to meditate. As soon as the gracious form of the Divine Mother appeared before me, I used my discrimination as a sword and with it clove Her in two. The last barrier fell. My spirit at once soared beyond the relative plane and I lost myself in samadhi [superconscious state].[5]

Mataji Krishnabai

Mataji Krishnabai was the primary disciple and successor to Swami Papa Ramdas. He often said that she had attained the same level of enlightenment as he. She was known for her selfless service to the needy—whether they were in human or animal form. Papa Ramdas was the central focus of her devotion. She identified "Papa" with the Universal Consciousness that underlies all that exists. In her autobiography, Krishnabai provides us with one of the most detailed accounts of a realization experience:

> As usual, when I sat for meditation that night, suddenly I felt at the tip of the toes a sensation as if ants were creeping up. As this gradually spread upward, the already affected lower parts

became dead, as it were, and the parts above became lighter. When this sensation reached the heart, I had a frightening shock.

O all-pervading Papa! Now I mentally debated with you within me in this way: "You said that you pervaded me internally and externally, but my state now is really fearful. However, I shall not give up until I fully realise your immutable and immortal Being."

The fear then disappeared and a sort of joy welled up in my heart, and I saw a light. Then I practised saying as you had taught me: "I am neither fear nor joy nor light. I am beyond these." Both these feelings of fear and joy and also the light then disappeared. When the power rose above the neck, all my thoughts ceased and with it my contention with you.

O all-merciful Papa! Thus the power ascended from the neck to *Bhrukuti (Ajna)* [the third eye]. From there, by your infinite grace, it rose up with more speed and brilliance than that of lightning. About the experience I had at that time nothing could be said except that I had indescribable bliss. How did this happen? What is all this? Even for these thoughts the mind was not there as it had dissolved in your eternal Being. How long I remained in this state on that night I did not know. When I came out of it, that is, to the awareness of the external world, I felt: "I am the universe and also beyond it."

So long as I had the body-idea, I used to feel that I was the body from head to foot and that it was mine. In the same way, now I got the experience that I was the entire universe, it was mine and I was beyond it.[6]

Krishnabai added some further clarification about her experience in the final stage of raising the energy in a conversation recorded by one of her devotees:

Mataji said that all she could tell of the final ascent of the *Kundalini* was that it shot from *Bhrukuti (Ajna Chakra)* to the *Sahasrara*, the apex [the crown], like a flash of lightning. The state that she then attained was simply indescribable. It was beyond all expression. So lost she was in that state, for God knows how many hours, she was loath to come down. In fact, she prayed to Papa that she remain in that state itself forever.[7]

The Prophet Elijah

The various components of Krishnabai's meditation remind us of the prophet Elijah's experiences on Mount Horeb (1 Kings 19:1–12). During his flight into the desert, Elijah is sustained for forty days and nights on energy alone, just like Moses is. He then enters into a cave on the mountain and dives deep into meditation. The extraordinary events that take place there can be understood in terms of the different stages of inner awakening that precede spiritual union.

Isaiah 29:6 proclaims, "There shall be a visitation from the Lord of Hosts with thunder, and with earthquake and great noise, with whirlwind and tempest, and the flame of a devouring fire." These four forces represent the four stages that Elijah passes through on the mountain.

In the beginning, Elijah encounters a great wind that shatters the rocks on the mountainside, but, the Hebrew Bible tells us, "God is not in the wind" (1 Kings 19:11). In this stage of his meditation, Elijah becomes aware of the unseen energies flowing through his body. He feels multiple currents radiating all around him. Elijah experiences a whirlwind of force and the presence of great power, but he has not met the Supreme Being.

Then Elijah encounters an earthquake. In this phase of meditation, the passage of energy through the centers creates a powerful reaction in his physical body. An extraordinary tension builds up inside him as the Almighty approaches and tries to forge a mental contact. Elijah's whole body shakes and trembles from the effects of the energy. God is fast approaching, but the Higher Power has still not entered through the door.

Then the earthquake is gone, and there is a fire that rages inside Elijah. He now feels the presence of the One who has come. Light pours forth into his mind and fills the whole of his being. It is both blissful and blinding at the same time. Elijah feels the divine attributes that precede the divine glory. God is very close, but the Holy Blessed One has not yet arrived.

The fire then passes, and a still, small voice sounds forth. Elijah has now reached the moment of true communion. In this place of complete stillness, no barrier is left between him and his supernal source. Full contact is made at the core of his being. He touches That which is without Beginning or End. In this state of ceaseless meditation, Elijah's mind is joined to the Universal Mind of God.

Immediate Aftermath of Union

In the immediate aftermath of the union experience, a profound transformation takes place in the behavior and consciousness of the realized soul. Though these changes can vary, they follow along certain lines. Again, we will primarily use the testimonies of several modern-day Indian spiritual teachers as our reference.

Sri Ramana Maharshi

Sri Ramana Maharshi's enlightenment occurred swiftly and suddenly as he sat alone in his uncle's house. In a few short moments, a great change took place inside him, and the young school boy was transformed into a full-blown sage.

> At the time there was a flash of excitement, it may be roughly described as heat, but it was not clear that there was a higher temperature in the body, nor was there perspiration. It appeared to be like an *avesam* or some [divine] spirit possessing me. That changed my mental attitude and habits. I had formerly a preference for some foods and an aversion to others. This tendency dropped off and all foods were swallowed with equal indifference, good or rotten, tasty or tasteless. Studies and duties became matters of utter indifference to me and I went through my studies turning over pages mechanically just to make others who were looking on think that I was reading.
>
> In fact my attention was never directed towards the books, and, consequently, I never understood their contents. Similarly, I went through other social duties possessed all the time by this *avesam*, i.e., my mind was absent from them, being fascinated and charmed by my own Self. I would put up with every burden imposed on me at home, tolerating every slight with humility and forebearance. Periodically, interest in and introspection on the Self would swallow up all former feelings and interests.[8]
>
> The soul had given up its hold on the body when it renounced the "I-am-the-body" idea and it was seeking some fresh anchorage; hence the frequent visits to the temple and the outpouring of the soul in tears. This was God's play with the soul. I would stand before Iswara, the Controller of the

universe and of the destinies of all, the Omniscient and Omni-
present, and sometimes pray for the descent of His Grace upon
me so that my devotion might increase and become perpetual
like that of the sixty-three Saints. More often I would not pray
at all but silently allow the deep within to flow on and into the
deep beyond.[9]

Sri Ramakrishna

Sri Ramakrishna's realization brought about a drastic change in his behavior and his experience of reality. He struggled to retain awareness of the
outer world as unsought spiritual powers spontaneously manifested in him.
Concern for the caste restrictions of orthodox Hinduism vanished from his
mind, so that he lost all fear or inhibition in his dealings with others.

> When I first had my exalted state of mind, my body would radiate
> light. My chest was always flushed.[10] I became inert. I could not
> feel the form of my own head.[11] I cannot utter a word unless I
> come down at least two steps from the plane of samadhi.[12]
>
> Oh, what a state of mind I passed through! When I first had
> that experience, I could not perceive the coming and going of day
> or night.[13] I could not observe any caste restrictions. The wife of
> a low-caste man used to send me cooked greens, and I ate them.
> I touched my head and lips with the leaf-plates from which the
> beggars ate their food in the guest-house of the Kali temple.[14]
>
> In that state I sometimes ate the leavings from a jackal's meal,
> food that had been exposed the whole night, part of which might
> have been eaten by snakes or other creatures.... Sometimes I rode
> on a dog and fed him with luchi [fried bread], also eating part of
> the bread myself. I realized that the whole world was filled with
> God alone.[15]
>
> One day, in that state of divine intoxication, I went to the bathing-
> ghat on the Ganges at Baranagore. There I saw Jaya Mukherji [a
> devotee] repeating the name of God; but his mind was on something
> else. I went up and slapped him twice on the cheeks.[16]

The Baal Shem Tov

Though this particular episode occurred later in his life, we find in the
following account from the Baal Shem Tov the disposition and behavior
that is characteristic of the aftermath of union:

It was a *Rosh Chodesh,* the day of the celebration of the new moon. The morning prayers began in the same way as any other prayer service. The Baal Shem Tov entered the synagogue and went to his place among the worshipers and the reader recited the first blessings. Suddenly, the Baal Shem began to tremble, but this too was nothing new. The spiritual current that ran through the Rebbe during *davening* [prayer] would often cause a slight quiver in his body. Today, however, the Baal Shem was shaking fiercely from head to toe. When it came time for the Baal Shem to leave his place and go to the front of the synagogue and lead the prayers, he remained motionless at his place, immobilized by the intensity of his inner state. When one of his Hasidim approached the Baal Shem to try and help him, he saw that the Rebbe's face was glowing like the sun, his eyes two giant orbs staring off into empty space.

Another Hasid stepped forward to aid the master. Together the two Hasidim guided the Baal Shem to the reader's desk. For a long time he just stood there motionless. Then, in a quavering voice, the Baal Shem started to recite the prayers, as his body shook and trembled. He continued chanting out loud until he finished *Hallel,* the special prayers of praise, and the reader's *Kaddish.* Now the Baal Shem withdrew inward once again. While his mind soared in the heavens, his body continued to shake and shudder. Finally his body grew still, his face returned to its normal appearance, and the Baal Shem opened his eyes. The Hasidim then continued on with the service, reading from the Torah scroll and completing the rest of the morning prayers without incident. It was a *Rosh Chodesh* like no other before or after.[17]

Mataji Krishnabai

Before achieving union with God, Mataji Krishnabai had been the perfect example of a life of activity and service. In the immediate aftermath of her realization experience, however, Mataji lost all interest in the outer world and its activities. Even the service of her beloved Papa no longer drew her attention. The inner reality had completely taken possession of her mind.

O Papa, you are without beginning and without end. Since I was absorbed the whole night in your true Being [in the realization experience described earlier], in the morning I had not any initiative to get up or to do any work and so I could not do your service as usual. When you pressed me to take food I took a little of it. As I had no desire to see anything, with a view to remain absorbed in you, I used to lay myself down with eyes closed. As I lost all external consciousness I did not know how time passed....

I was in this state for several days and when I was coming to the awareness of the external world, I was doing your service and absolutely necessary work for taking care of my body or any service of others. I was doing so in a spirit of indifference. At this time, in spite of my being immersed in your Being all the time, I could not find joy in doing any work or service. I did not like to get back to the awareness of the external world from the state of obliviousness of it and the consciousness of immobility and eternity. Therefore, I was feeling that I should remain always forgetful of the body because I got so much joy in that state.[18]

The Psalms

When we are bathed in the glory of the divine light, everything else simply drops away. Nothing else really matters to us. Our only remaining desire is to stay in the state of oneness and peace forever. This spiritual mood is beautifully portrayed for us by the words of King David in Psalm 27.

One thing I have asked of the Lord, this I seek, that I may dwell in the House of the Lord all the days of my life, to behold the beauty of the Lord, and to visit His Sanctuary. (Psalm 27:4)

Signs of Union

Sri Ramakrishna used to say that just as the eastern horizon becomes red at the approach of dawn, there are certain signs that appear when individuals approach God-realization.[19] Such a spiritual union produces dramatic effects on their state of consciousness and behavior. It radically transforms their way of living in the world.

To provide both inspiration and perspective, some of the inner and outer signs that tell us that we have achieved the supreme goal will be outlined in this section.

During earlier stages of the meditative life, we may exhibit some of these character traits. At that time, however, these qualities will be uneven or last for only a short period and then disappear. In the final stage of union, these divine attributes become our permanent possession. They become our very own.

Outer Signs of Union

There are both inner and outer signs that reveal that the culmination of the spiritual journey has been attained. First, the personal characteristics of the awakened ones will be enumerated. Then, the more esoteric dimensions of those who live in the state of permanent divine knowledge will be explored.

Integrity: All the Parts of a Realized Soul Are Integrated Together

Integrity is the first sign of a realized soul. Integrity is more than a sense of uprightness; it is when the essence of who we are permeates all aspects of our being. When we possess integrity, we do not have to make a display of truthfulness or uprightness, because it emanates into everything we do. We are our true Self, and this is clear to everyone who meets us. We may act as a wise counselor or as an innocent child, but whatever we do, it appears completely natural.

Knowers of God are different from people who are merely powerful personalities. Powerful personalities may be a force in the world yet still have many personal imperfections—parts of them that are at odds with the strength and even greatness that they exhibit in their chosen field.

This is not so with knowers of God; their greatness permeates every aspect of their being, from the smallest details to the broadest expressions of life. The reason for this is that illumined teachers are not just highly developed persons; they are spiritually transfigured personalities, wholly taken over by the power of the soul. Spirit has become the dominant force, overriding any vestiges of personality traits.

This is why there is a sense of wholeness and naturalness to enlightened teachers. The power of the soul draws all the disparate parts of them together into one single, integrated whole. It is this sense of completeness, of *shleymut,* that distinguishes realized souls from other people. Their inner balance and harmony are conveyed to everyone who comes into the radius of their influence.

Enlightened beings have a unique capacity for perfection in both the spiritual and the physical realm. This quality is based on a balanced and still mind. It produces an extraordinary faculty for clear perception, sharpens the powers of the mind and the intuition, and heightens the awareness of every thought, word, and deed. This perfection is visibly manifest in the description of a prophet by the medieval Jewish thinker and teacher Moses Maimonides, commonly known as the Rambam:

> Such a person will undoubtedly perceive nothing but things very extraordinary and divine, and see nothing but God and His angels. His knowledge will only include that which is real knowledge, and his thought will only be directed to such general principles as would tend to improve the social relations between man and man.[20]

Natural Sanctity: There Is a Beauty and Holiness to Everything Realized Souls Do

The light of God flows out from the realized ones into every situation and every person, no matter what they are doing. Therefore, what they are doing no longer is important, because whatever they do is meditation and everywhere they go is illuminated by the Divine Presence.

The Hasidic text *Divrei Moshe* asserts that whenever tzaddikim are engaged in mundane affairs, they imbue them with holiness at every moment. When they are talking to a shopkeeper and negotiating over the price of an article, they are infusing holiness into that person. If they are speaking to someone about the weather, they are saturating that individual with spiritual light. Whomever they encounter, whatever objects they handle or use—all will become permeated with sanctity.[21]

We see this truth poignantly expressed in the following testimony from one of the disciples of Rebbe Dov Baer, the Maggid of Mezeritch:

> Rabbi Leib, son of Sarah, the hidden tzaddik who wandered over the earth, following the course of rivers, in order to redeem the souls of the living and the dead, said this: "I did not go to the maggid in order to hear Torah from him, but to see how he unlaces his felt shoes and laces them up again."[22]

Great spiritual figures have a natural air of sanctity that envelops them at all times. They are able to teach profound truths through the ordinary experiences of daily life. They exhibit an extraordinary capacity to bring the power and consciousness of the Kingdom of Heaven into every situation and circumstance.

Humility: Realized Souls Walk Humbly in the World

Those who have realized their identity with the Supreme Being walk in the world with a deep sense of humility. Moses, who spoke "face-to-face" with God, the Torah tells us, was "very humble, more so than any man on the face of the earth" (Numbers 12:3). When the patriarch Abraham stood in the presence of God, he proclaimed, "I have taken upon myself to speak to the Lord, I who am but dust and ashes" (Genesis 18:27).

Saint Francis of Assisi also possessed a humility that was born out of direct experience. One night, one of Saint Francis's disciples discovered him lying flat on his face in prayer. "O my dearest Lord and God," Francis cried out, "what are You, and what indeed am I, your little, useless worm of a servant?"

When the disciple asked Francis the meaning of these words, he was told:

> In that prayer which you heard, two lights were manifested to me: one light in which I knew the Creator, and one in which I knew myself. When I said, "What are You, my Lord and God, and what am I?" then I was in the light of contemplation, in which I saw the infinite depth of the Divine Godhead and my own wretched abyss of misery.[23]

In the beginning, the humility of Rebbe Dov Baer of Mezeritch was not as readily visible to others as was the meekness of Saint Francis of Assisi. It became openly revealed to all of the Hasidim, however, after the Baal Shem Tov's passing:

> Before the Baal Shem Tov passed away, the Hasidim asked him who would take his place as their Rebbe. The Baal Shem answered: "Whoever can teach you how to break pride; he is the one who is destined to be the next Rebbe."
>
> After the Baal Shem's death, the Hasidim went to each of the Baal Shem's inner circle and asked them how to overcome pride. When they put the question to Reb Dov Baer, he closed his eyes and withdrew inward. Heaving a deep sigh, he opened his eyes and replied: "Psalm 93:1 declares, 'The Lord reigns; He is clothed

in pride.' Pride belongs to God; therefore no mere human can fully overcome it. Pride is something that we need to struggle with our whole life long." When they heard these words, the Hasidim understood that Dov Baer was the Baal Shem's chosen successor.[24]

Equanimity: Realized Souls Are Unaffected by Praise or Blame

Psalm 16:8 proclaims, *"Shiviti Adonai lenegdi tamid*—I have set the Lord always before me."* The Baal Shem explains that the word *shiviti* refers to the state of *hishtavut*—equanimity. Individuals who live in God's presence at all times will possess firm equanimity. They will not be unsettled whether they are praised or blamed, whether they are given food fit for royalty or just plain bread and water. They will not become excited when people think that they are great scholars or when people think that they are ignoramuses. They will be at peace both when they succeed and when they fail. This is the state of realized souls.[25]

We see this type of unshakable equanimity in the behavior of Sri Ramakrishna. One day, Trailokya, one of the owners of the temple where Sri Ramakrishna lived, decided to banish Ramakrishna's attendant from the temple grounds because of a misdeed. In his rage at the attendant's indiscretion, Trailokya also made a remark that implied that it would be a good thing if Ramakrishna left, too.

> Accordingly one of the temple officials came to Ramakrishna and ordered him to leave at once. Without the least sign of resentment or dismay, Ramakrishna picked up his towel, slung it over his shoulder, and walked unprotestingly out of the room which had been his home for the past twenty-six years. He had almost reached the gate of the compound when Trailokya came running after him, crying, "Sir, where are you going?" "But didn't you want me to go away?" Ramakrishna asked him innocently. "No—they misunderstood—I never meant that," Trailokya assured him, "I beg you to stay!" At this, Ramakrishna smiled; [he] turned without saying a word, went back to his room, sat down, and continued a conversation he had been having with some devotees, as if nothing unusual had taken place.[26]

Rebbe Zusya of Anipoli was also known for his equanimity. He accepted whatever circumstances he was placed in, however he was treated, without the slightest show of anger or resentment.

Once, Reb Zusya and Reb Elimelekh spent the night in an inn where a wedding was being celebrated. The guests were of a rough character and had drunk rather a bit too much. In a mischievous mood, they looked around the room for a way to have some fun. Spotting Reb Zusya and Reb Elimelekh sitting perched in a corner of the inn, they came over and grabbed Reb Zusya by the collar and started throwing him around. After they had given Zusya a good beating, they flung him back in the corner beside his brother, and went back to their dancing.

Feeling for his brother's suffering, Reb Elimelekh turned to Zusya and said: "You are the one sitting closer to them, so they took hold of you. Let us change places so that, next time, they will take me instead. Lie down in my place and try to get some rest."

A short while later, the ruffians returned to continue their "game." One of them was about to seize Reb Elimelekh, when his friend cried out: "That is no way to treat our special visitors! You are giving all of the honor to the same guest!" With that, they let go of Reb Elimelekh, and grabbing onto Reb Zusya, they declared: "You too shall receive your share in our joy!"

Reb Zusya laughed. Lifting his hands in resignation, he turned to his brother Elimelekh and exclaimed: "If a person is destined to receive blows, they will find him wherever he lays himself down."[27]

Courage: Realized Souls Have the Courage to Face Anything

Those who dwell in the House of God work with certainty, not mere words or ideas. This endows them with tremendous courage. They will confront any situation without fear; they will face any obstacle; they will willingly walk through fire to fulfill the task that God has appointed to them.

The prophet Elijah escaped into the wilderness when King Ahab sought to kill him. But three years later, when he was filled with the Holy Spirit, Elijah summoned the king and the prophets of Baal to a spiritual battle before the entire nation on Mount Carmel. There, Elijah faced off against 450 prophets of Baal in front of a gathering of thousands and called down a fire from heaven to affirm that *Adonai*, the Holy One of Israel, is the one true God.

Saint Teresa of Avila fearlessly confronted the great nobles of Spain. As she wrote regarding her exchanges with the ladies of the court:

> The Lord showed me such great favours while I was there and that in turn gave me so much liberty of spirit and made me so despise what I saw, that in my dealings with these great ladies whom I might have considered it an honour to serve, I kept as much liberty as if I had been their equal.[28]

Similarly, in sending a message she received from God to King Philip II, the powerful ruler of Spain, she did not mince words: "Remember, Sire, that Saul, too, was anointed, and yet he was rejected!"[29]

The Rambam includes courage as one of the qualities of a prophet:

> The prophets must have had these two forces, courage and intuition, highly developed, and these were still more strengthened when they were under the influence of the Active Intellect [Divine Mind]. Their courage was so great that, e.g., Moses, with only a staff in his hand, dared to address a great king in his desire to deliver a nation from his service. He was not frightened or terrified, because he had been told, "I will be with you" (Exodus 3:12).[30]

After killing an Egyptian who was beating a Hebrew slave, Moses fled to Midian in fear for his life. But after the revelation of the burning bush, he returned to Egypt to single-handedly face the Pharaoh and the whole might of Egypt. His encounter with God had infused him with fearlessness.

Inner Signs of Union

Until now, we have looked at the outer indications that an individual has reached realization. These external signs portray the transformations that occur in the character of those who are in union with God. Momentous changes also take place in their interior reality. These inner signs announce to the world that these souls have merged with their spiritual source.

Seeing through the Mind of God

Perhaps the greatest of the inner changes that emerge after union is the ability to see through the Universal Mind of God. Enlightened souls can be taken up into the Mind of God at any time. In this rarified atmosphere, they come into contact with the realm of pure ideas. Here, ideas are not learned, but rather the fundamental reality that an idea embodies is directly experienced. This "living truth" immediately penetrates into their very being. Only later does it become transformed into thoughts and words.

In this state of union with the Mind of God, the whole world and all of the heavens are in the grasp of these transcendental actors. They can receive visions from the higher planes. They can penetrate the veil of physical reality and come face-to-face with those in the Kingdom of Heaven. They can be transported to any location around the globe and see that place as if they were physically present. Every event is now experienced through the medium of the Divine Mind.

We are given a fleeting image of the workings of this divine vision in the book of Ezekiel:

> And it came to pass in the sixth year, in the sixth month, in the fifth day of the month, as I sat in my house, and the elders of Judah sat before me, that the hand of the Lord God fell upon me. Then I beheld, and lo a figure as the appearance of fire: from the appearance of his loins and downward, fire; and from his loins and upward, as the appearance of brightness, as the color of electrum [an alloy of silver and gold]. And he put forth the form of a hand, and I was taken by a lock of my head; and a spirit lifted me up between the earth and the heavens, and brought me in the vision of God to Jerusalem, to the door of the gate of the inner court that looks toward the north. (Ezekiel 8:1–3)

Givers of Peace

When Sri Ramana Maharshi was asked how to recognize a genuine holy man, he responded, "By the peace of mind found in his presence."[31] The ability to give others peace has been a characteristic of the illumined soul since the beginning of time. The music of the young David brought solace to the troubled mind of King Saul. The Buddha infused a feeling of tranquility in all those who surrounded him. And Sri Ramana himself was known for the great serenity and inner stillness that people felt in his presence.

When individuals carry this energy, its power is felt as soon as they enter the room. There is a tangible change that occurs. The chaos and noise in our mind immediately disappears, and all internal tension vanishes. In its place, there is calm, quiet, and relief.

The mystic and philosopher Paul Brunton beautifully describes this experience in his account of his first visit to the Maharshi:

> I become aware of a silent, resistless change that is taking place within my mind. One by one, the questions which I prepared in the train with such meticulous accuracy drop away. For it does not now seem to matter whether they are asked or not, and it does not matter whether I solve the problems which have hitherto troubled me. I know only that a steady river of quietness seems to be flowing near me, that a great peace is penetrating the inner reaches of my being; and that my thought-tortured brain is beginning to arrive at some rest.[32]

A disciple of Rebbe Dov Baer of Mezeritch recounted how the Hasidim would undergo a similar transformation whenever one of them visited their teacher:

> Whenever we rode to our teacher—the moment we were within the limits of the town—all our desires were fulfilled. And if anyone happened to have a wish left, this was satisfied as soon as he entered the house of the maggid [Rebbe Dov Baer]. But if there was one among us whose soul was still churned up with wanting—he was at peace when he looked into the face of the maggid.[33]

Bliss: Spiritual Joy

> "You have anointed my head with oil, my cup runs over."
>
> —Psalm 23:5

Those who dwell in the state of union are overflowing with incredible joy. Rebbe Levi Yitzchak of Berditchev speaks of the thrill of God's presence as greater than any physical pleasure. It is a happiness that grows and deepens over time.[34] Sri Ramakrishna spoke of spiritual joy as an all-encompassing, all-embracing bliss that permeates every pore of our being.[35]

When Sri Ramakrishna was in a state of divine ecstasy, he would stagger about like a drunkard, reeling from the intoxication, unable to even hold up his body cloth. When the Baal Shem was flooded with divine light, not only would he be uplifted, so would all of his Hasidim. In fact, the whole of his community would be filled with unbounded elation.

We find another example of the powerful contagious quality of spiritual joy in the story of King Saul and the disciples of Samuel in the Hebrew Bible. After his heroic battle with Goliath, David became increasingly beloved in the eyes of the people. Jealous of this fame and adoration, King Saul conspired to murder David. When word was sent to the king of David's whereabouts, Saul sent his soldiers to capture him.

> And it was told Saul, saying "Behold, David is at Naioth in Ramah." And Saul sent messengers to take David; and when they saw the company of the prophets prophesying, and Samuel standing over them, the Spirit of God came upon the messengers of Saul, and they also prophesied. And when it was told to Saul, he sent other messengers, and they also prophesied. And Saul sent messengers again the third time, and they also prophesied. Then he also went to Ramah, and came to the great cistern that is in Secu; and he asked and said, "Where are Samuel and David?" And one said, "Behold, they are at Naioth in Ramah."
>
> And he went there to Naioth in Ramah; and the Spirit of God came upon him also, and he went on, and prophesied, until he came to Naioth in Ramah. And he also stripped off his clothes, and he also prophesied before Samuel, and lay down naked all that day and all that night. Wherefore they say, "Is Saul also among the prophets?" (1 Samuel 19:19–24)

Radiating the Power of Spirit

Enlightened sages dwell in the full knowledge that they are one with the living God. This Self-knowledge permeates everything that they say and do. It uplifts and empowers all those who meet them. Simply by being in the vicinity of a realized soul, we are suffused with confidence, trust, and faith.

The Spirit of God is a tangible presence in people who are in union. It radiates forth from them. It is a quality that can be felt, experienced, and received. Once again, it is a story from the life of the prophet Elijah that testifies to this truth.

Before Elijah parted from his disciple Elisha, he turned to Elisha and said:

> "Ask what I shall do for you, before I am taken away from you."
>
> Elisha thought a moment and then replied, "I pray you, let a double portion of your spirit be upon me."

And he said, "You have asked a hard thing; nevertheless, if you see me when I am taken from you, it shall be so unto you; but if not, it shall not be so."

And it came to pass, as they still went on, and talked, that, behold, there appeared a chariot of fire, and horses of fire, which parted them both asunder; and Elijah went up by a whirlwind into heaven. And Elisha saw it, and he cried, "My father, my father, the chariots of Israel and their horsemen!" And he saw him no more; and he took hold of his own clothes, and tore them in two pieces.

He also took up the mantle of Elijah that fell from him, and went back, and stood by the bank of the Jordan. And he took the mantle of Elijah that fell from him, and struck the waters, and said, "Where is the Lord, the God of Elijah?" And after he too had struck the waters, they were divided in two; and Elisha went over.

And when the sons of the prophets that were at Jericho some way off saw him, they said, "The spirit of Elijah rests on Elisha." And they came to meet him, and bowed down to the ground before him. (2 Kings 2:9–15)

This inner radiance has a powerful effect on whoever comes into contact with these spiritual transmitters. For some, it engenders love and admiration; for others, it evokes fear and awe, as is seen in this passage from the book of Exodus:

And it came to pass, when Moses came down from Mount Sinai with the two Tablets of the Covenant in Moses's hand, when he came down from the mountain, that Moses knew not that the skin of his face shone while he talked with Him. And when Aaron and all the Children of Israel saw Moses, behold, the skin of his face shone; and they were afraid to come near him. And Moses called to them; and Aaron and all the rulers of the congregation returned to him, and Moses talked with them. And afterwards all the Children of Israel came near, and he gave them in commandment all that the Lord had spoken with him on Mount Sinai. And when Moses had finished speaking with them, he put a veil on his face. But when Moses went in before the Lord to speak with Him, he took the veil off, until he came out. And he came out, and spoke to the Children of Israel that which he was commanded. And the

Children of Israel saw the face of Moses that the skin of Moses's face shone; and Moses put the veil upon his face again, until he went in to speak with Him. (Exodus 34:29–35)

This outer luminosity is the expression of an inner condition. It is a reflection of the purity of mind, body, and spirit of these selfless distributers of divine wealth. Rabbi Dov Baer, the Maggid of Mezeritch, once begged Heaven to show him a man whose every limb and every fiber was holy. Then they showed him the form of the Baal Shem Tov, and it was all of fire. There was no shred of substance in it. It was nothing but flame.[36]

Mastery of the Body

Another quality of realized souls is their ability to completely transcend body awareness. As Latu Maharaj, one of the disciples of Sri Ramakrishna, once explained to his devotees, "When that knowledge dawns, body consciousness disappears, the mind stops and even the intellect vanishes; only an uninterrupted Consciousness flows."[37]

We find two striking examples of this capacity of transcendence in the lives of the Indian saint Sri Ramana Maharshi and the Hasidic master Zusya of Anipoli.

Sri Ramana Maharshi was renowned for his total identification with the Self and his disassociation from the body. The depth of this identification became clear in the final years of his life, when he suffered from a terrible debilitating cancer.

In one moving account, a devotee describes the experience of being in the Maharshi's presence during one of the operations on the cancerous growth on his arm. The blissful peace that everyone felt and the Maharshi's attitude of complete indifference to his body astounded everyone present in the hospital, including the doctors who were responsible for performing the operation.[38]

Reb Zusya too was known for his ability to rise above the conditions in which he found himself. One day, Reb Zusya received the inner command to go to a village not far from Anipoli and guide a tax collector on the path of *teshuvah* (repentance). So he went to the village and found the man selling vodka to peasants. Zusya attempted to intervene, to turn the man's thoughts to God and prayer, but the collector just ignored him. In spite of his rejection, Reb Zusya continued to exhort the man to repent, and even laid a hand on his arm to get his attention. In response, the collector took hold of Zusya and forcibly shoved him out the door into the courtyard. It was the middle of the Polish winter and Zusya was soon shivering from head to toe. Catching sight of an old wagon wheel resting on the ground, he pulled it against his body. In an instant, the dilapidated wheel was transformed into a Wheel of Fire from the Heavenly Chariot. Encompassed in its warmth, Zusya fell into a state of spiritual bliss. In the morning, the tax collector discovered Reb Zusya still lying in the courtyard, a brilliant inner radiance emanating from him. The sight of the rebbe in this exalted state had a profound effect on the collector. He realized that he had forgotten the true purpose of life, and vowed to repent and change his ways.[39]

The secret of this story is not the miraculous transformation of the old carriage wheel into a wheel of fire from the Heavenly Chariot. Rather, it is Reb Zusya's use of the spiritual potency of a divine thoughtform, together with the creative power of the higher mind, to transport himself beyond the confines of body awareness and become impervious to the freezing cold.

For these great souls, the mind-body complex was not intrinsically negative or impure. It was merely another limiting factor that needed to be transcended, like time or the weather. Those who have been liberated from the bonds of birth and death live ever free in the boundless consciousness of the Absolute. They are one with God, and nothing can disrupt that eternal bond.

Mastery of Time and Space

The Hasidic master Nachum of Chernobyl teaches that tzaddikim live on a level above time. Therefore, not only can they access the teachings of their own generation, but they can also draw on the wisdom of future generations.[40]

These unique human beings dwell in a unity of consciousness that spans the higher planes. They are able to glimpse into the Universal Mind at will. They are joined to the overshadowing Divine Presence at every moment. They experience time in the Eternal Now.

The awakened ones are not only beyond time, they are also beyond space. The Baal Shem Tov teaches, "You are where your thoughts are."[41] The individual in union can be anywhere.

This is how the Baal Shem employed *kefitzat haderekh* (teleportation) to get to a destination. This is also how he was able to be in more than one place at a time (bilocation). It is not a question of learning a secret name of God or a magic formula; rather it is a matter of knowing how to link the mind into a place above time and space.

These souls who have broken the bonds of physical consciousness act, at once, in the moment and in the Eternal and Infinite. They can be simultaneously in this world, with those on higher planes, and also beyond both. Through their agency, the dwellers on this physical plane are able to touch upon the higher reality, and the souls in the Kingdom of Heaven can contact those in incarnation upon earth. They are masters of time and space.

Universal Vision: Seeing the Divinity in Everyone

Above all else, those who are established in the consciousness of oneness have universal vision. They see the divinity in every human being. Enlightened individuals can discern how each person fits into the greater whole, how each is an essential piece of the puzzle that we call life. They understand that both the saint and the sinner, the virtuous person and the scoundrel, the wise man and the fool, are part of the play of this material existence. They know that all of these actors are part of the wondrous manifestation of God's Eternal Spirit in this finite physical world.

In one of his books the Trappist monk Father Thomas Merton describes his sudden experience of this profound spiritual truth while walking down a busy street in Louisville, Kentucky:

> I was suddenly overwhelmed with the realization that I loved all those people, that they were mine and I theirs, that we could not be alien to one another even though we were total strangers....
>
> Then it was as if I suddenly saw the secret beauty of their hearts, the depths of their hearts where neither sin nor desire nor self-knowledge can reach, the core of their reality, the person that each one is in God's eyes. If only they could all see themselves as they really *are*. If only we could see each other that way all the time....
>
> At the center of our being is a point of nothingness which is untouched by sin and by illusion, a point of pure truth, a point or spark which belongs entirely to God.... It is like a pure diamond,

blazing with the invisible light of heaven. It is in everybody, and if we could see it we would see these billions of points of light coming together in the face and blaze of a sun that would make all the darkness and cruelty of life vanish completely … the gate of heaven is everywhere.[42]

We find the same great love for all people expressed by the Baal Shem Tov. He articulates his love in simpler, more concrete terms. "The lowest of the low you can think of," he once told one of his Hasidim, "is dearer to me than your only son is to you."[43]

Swami (Papa) Ramdas, in contrast, provides us with a dramatic picture of this universal vision. His words reveal the full breadth of the all-encompassing love of these radiant beacons of Divine light:

A stage was soon reached when this dwelling in the spirit became a permanent and unvarying experience with no more falling off from it, and then a still more exalted state came on; his [Ramdas always speaks of himself in the third person] hitherto inner vision projected outwards. First a glimpse of this new vision dazzled him off and on. This was the working of divine love. He would feel as though his very soul had expanded like the blossoming of a flower and, by a flash as it were, enveloped the whole universe embracing all in a subtle halo of love and light. This experience granted him a bliss infinitely greater than he had in the previous state. Now it was that Ramdas began to cry out, "Ram [God] is all, it is He as everybody and everything."[44]

The ancient Jewish sources echo this cry of a modern Indian saint. The words of the prophet Isaiah portray a world where such universal vision prevails:

The wolf shall dwell with the lamb, and the leopard lie down with the kid; and the calf and the young lion and the fatling together; and a little child shall lead them. And the cow and the bear shall graze; their young ones shall lie down together: and the lion shall eat straw like the ox. And a babe shall play on the hole of the cobra, and an infant shall put his hand on the viper's nest. They shall not hurt nor destroy in all my holy mountain; for the earth shall be full of the knowledge of God, as the waters cover the sea. (Isaiah 11:6–9)

PART FOUR

Broader Meditation Issues

*I*n the first three parts of the book, we explored the stages of the path of meditation: preparation, intention, forging a connection, holding the link, and merging with our spiritual source. These five stages form the central core of the contemplative life.

The fourth and last part of the book investigates a number of broader issues related to the practice of meditation. The purpose of this section is to give us a deeper understanding of the spiritual processes that occur when we dive into the inner realm. It places meditation in the wider context of the Kabbalistic view of reality and the mystical conception of God. It explains how our individual practice fits within the evolutionary framework of the universe. The following topics are explored in part 4:

1. **Two Paths to the Supreme:** Some of us are searching for a path to a personal God. Others do not believe in a personal Deity and are looking for another way to connect to the Higher Power. This chapter looks at the personal and impersonal

paths of meditation and the similarities and differences between them.

2. **The Dynamics of Inner Experience:** What happens when we enter into our inner reality? What takes place in our consciousness when we meditate? This chapter explores the dynamics of the meditation process utilizing the teachings of the sixteenth-century Kabbalist the Ari as our guide.

3. **The Psychic:** This chapter investigates what happens when our meditation goes wrong. It explains how to identify when we have entered into the lower realms and how to deal with the resulting consequences for our spiritual life.

4. **Individual versus Group Practice:** We can meditate either on our own or in a larger group. There are distinct differences between the two experiences. This chapter outlines the advantages and disadvantages of each form of practice.

5. **Individual and Collective Evolution:** In our evolution as human beings and as souls, there is spiritual work we do as part of our individual journey, and there is also a greater mission in which we participate as part of a larger collective. Our meditative life is an integral component of this process of inner development. This final chapter looks at the interplay between these two aspects of our reality in this world.

Chapter Twelve

Two Paths to the Supreme

Personal and Impersonal Meditation

S ri Ramakrishna would often tell a parable about a man who saw a chameleon:

> Once a man went into a wood and saw a beautiful creature on a tree. Later he told a friend about it and said, "Brother, on a certain tree in the wood I saw a red-coloured creature." The friend answered: "I have seen it too. Why do you call it red? It is green." A third man said: "Oh, no, no! Why do you call it green? It is yellow." Then other persons began to describe the animal variously as violet, blue, or black. Soon they were quarrelling about the colour.
>
> At last they went to the tree and found a man sitting under it. In answer to their questions he said: "I live under this tree and know the creature very well. What each of you has said about it is true. Sometimes it is red, sometimes green, sometimes yellow, sometimes blue, and so forth and so on. Again, sometimes I see that it has no colour whatsoever."[1]

This parable explains the nature of the experience of God. There are two paths toward the Supreme: the personal path and the impersonal path. The personal approach is like the various colors of the chameleon. The impersonal route is when the chameleon has no color at all.

On the personal path, we strive toward the Sovereign of the Universe using personal imagery and devotion. We speak of the individual soul, the group Soul, and God. On the impersonal path, there is no soul; there is no other. We commune with the Infinite and become one with the Absolute.

On the personal path, we draw near to the Omnipotent and Omniscient by building an intimate relationship. We talk with God as naturally as we would with a family member or a dear friend. We see our relationship as that of a child and parent, or as a servant and master, or as two lovers. We feel the Divine Presence beside us, walking with us through life. We share our hopes and dreams with God, as well as our fears and disappointments. Through our devotion, we forge a spiritual link with our holy Beloved. The One Who Is Pure Love then turns toward us to bestow blessings and inspiration.

On the impersonal path, we are not looking for a personal Deity to call our own; we yearn to unite with the Infinite. We want to touch and then abide in a Reality that is beyond all thought or image. We seek the Timeless Consciousness that fills and transcends the whole of the universe but that cannot be named or described.

On this austere path, we do not go toward any personal aspect of the Godhead, but reach, instead, toward God in the abstract. We concentrate on the *Ein Sof*—That which is without Beginning or End—and strive to ascend into the realm of unity and oneness as far as we are able. Rather than forming a relationship with our Creator, we desire to become one with the Boundless Ocean of Being.

In meditation, we use these two paths to attune ourselves to the Higher Power and to align ourselves with our true essence. To meditate in the personal mode, we visualize a sacred symbol, repeat a Divine Name, or chant a mantra associated with a particular aspect of Divinity. The symbol or word acts as a mental signal that ascends to the spiritual source with which it is identified. By use of this signal, we bind ourselves to our supernal source and join with it. This is a path of the mind as well as the emotions. Contemplative prayer is the archetypical example of this approach.

The impersonal mode, in contrast, is predominantly a method of the mind. It is not love or any other divine attribute that we seek, but the joining of our individual mind with the Universal Mind. There is no "I-Thou" relationship; rather, our goal is the immersion of our separate identity in the Illimitable Spirit. Through a still, one-pointed mind, we merge with the One that has no second. Meditating on the indwelling Self is a classic practice of this path.

Both of these approaches are used in the major world religions. Different religions emphasize different paths. Normative Hinduism and Catholic Christianity follow a highly personal approach. Forms and images are a natural part of their worship. Judaism and Islam also believe in a personal God with attributes but without form. In these two religions, no images whatsoever are allowed. In the mystical teachings of Judaism, however, the varied aspects of the Indivisible Godhead are further explored.

Classical Buddhism, on the other hand, follows a purely impersonal approach. Buddhists do not believe in a personal God, nor do they accept the existence of a separate individual soul. This is similar to the approach of the Hindu philosophy of Vedanta. For non-dual Vedantists, Brahman, or Pure Being, is the only Reality; everything else is the product of *maya,* or illusion. That which is reality must be eternal and non-changing.

Yet even this distinction between the personal and impersonal paths is not absolute. For example, the impersonal practice of Self-enquiry calls for an investigation into our personal identity, which gives way in the end to the underlying universal Identity. As Sri Ramana Maharshi has said, "He [God] is always the first person, the I, ever standing before you."[2]

These two approaches are not conflicting truths; rather, they represent two aspects of one reality. In the personal mode, we ascend toward the Infinite through a progression of divine aspects. On the impersonal route, we look past all changing temporal manifestations and identities and strive to merge with the substratum of Pure Consciousness that underlies all that is. There are two separate paths, but both paths ultimately lead to the same Eternal Source, where all distinction between personal and impersonal becomes obliterated.

CHAPTER THIRTEEN

THE DYNAMICS OF INNER EXPERIENCE

What Happens When We Meditate?

*T*he sixteenth-century Kabbalist Rabbi Yitzchak Luria, more commonly known as the Ari (the Lion), was a dynamic and inspiring spiritual teacher. He was at the center of the mystical movement in Safed and its driving force. For the past five hundred years his teachings have powerfully influenced Jewish communities around the world. His works are more widely known and studied than any other Jewish esoteric wisdom, except perhaps the book of the *Zohar*.

According to the traditional biography of the Ari, he spent seven years meditating in a hut by the Nile River in Egypt before migrating to the Holy Land and beginning his vocation as a spiritual teacher.[1] This intensive spiritual practice was crucial for his inner development. In fact, the Ari's whole Kabbalistic system is based on his experiences during meditation.

The teachings of the Ari are extraordinarily insightful when they are applied to the world of meditation. They illuminate the inner dynamics that take place in our consciousness when a higher contact is made within the Kingdom of Heaven and beyond.

Shevirat Hakelim (the Breaking of the Vessels) and Veiling

According to the Ari, in the beginning of Creation, the Almighty poured the light of the Infinite into the finite vessel of the nascent universe. This divine light, however, was too great for the fragile form to hold. As a result, the vessel broke and the infant universe was destroyed.[2]

After this initial shattering, God decided to place a multitude of veils between the infinite light and our finite physical reality. These veils allowed both the universe and ourselves to exist as separate entities.[3]

The practice of meditation aims to reverse this process. It is an attempt to draw back the veils and ascend through the myriad planes of consciousness into the oneness of the *Ein Sof*.

For us to be able to integrate each step along this spiritual journey, the process of "unveiling" has to be slow and gradual. It can be compared to the situation of someone who has been blind her whole life and is suddenly given an operation to restore her sight. We would not place such an individual immediately into a room filled with bright sunlight, but would slowly and gradually let her habituate to the light. Also, we would not bombard her with images, but rather we would expose her to a few images at a time, until she was able to comfortably assimilate these powerful impacts on her brain and mind.

A similar situation exists regarding the experience of inner contacts within the higher realms of being. Originally, we might say that the Holy Blessed One provided us with "blinders" to shade the light. During meditation, those blinders are removed one by one.

Embodying States of Consciousness

The Ari's *yichudim* (metaphysical unions) provide a structure for the inner experiences that occur during meditation. His Kabbalistic system of the five levels of the soul and the *tikun*, or spiritual repair, of the soul and the universe explain the dynamics of the evolution of consciousness, be it the awareness of an individual human being or the Mind of God.

In truth, there is no up or down, no in or out—just different states of being. Meditation, then, is in essence a process of infinite expansion, where we enter into more and more expansive states of consciousness. Once we have integrated a given way of perceiving into our own mind, we can hold that space for others. Each of us dwells in a separate state of awareness, which embodies the reality of a specific "location" in the Universal Mind.

A good analogy for this process is Jacob's ladder. In Jacob's dream or vision, there are angels ascending and descending the rungs of the ladder and the Controller of All looking down from above. The ladder is the universe stretching from the finite out to the Infinite. Each rung is another state of consciousness along this continuum of existence. On each rung or state of awareness, there is an angel or being that carries and maintains that particular divine thoughtform in its mind.

According to the Ari, there are five levels to the soul: *nefesh*—our personality; *ruach*—our individual soul; *neshamah*—the group soul of which we are a part; *chayah*—the group soul of our group soul; and *yechidah*—our spiritual root in the Universal Soul, *Adam Kadmon*.

Each of these aspects of our soul embraces a particular state of awareness. Our spiritual evolution is designated by our movement from one level of the soul to another until we reach oneness in the *Ein Sof*.

Yichudim (Metaphysical Unions)

The Ari's system of *yichudim* describes the process whereby we establish a link in consciousness and then make that link our own. This process is divided into six stages. First there are three stages of spiritual intimacy or union.[4] This is followed by three stages of consolidation and growth.[5]

Three Stages of Intimacy or Union

The first stage in the process of *zivug*, or union, is called *neshikin*—kisses. This is the first contact, the beginning of our soul experience where we are touched by the energy, light, and love of God. There is an exchange of breath, so to speak.

In *neshikin,* a link is forged or awakened between the personality and the soul. The *ruach* (spirit or breath) from our soul enters into our consciousness, and a bond is formed in mental matter. Everything else depends on this bond and develops from it. If this connection is broken, then we must start all over again.

The second stage is *chibbuk*—the embrace. In *chibbuk*, we experience the embrace of God's overshadowing presence. We are immersed in the divine attributes, enveloped in love, light, and compassion. This phase takes the contact that began in *neshikin* one step further toward union.

The third stage is *zivug yesod beyesod*—full union. This is the true union where there is a merging of the two souls—an intimate and direct knowing. In *zivug yesod beyesod*, we become one with the source that we have contacted. It is now our task to maintain this new state of consciousness, so that the soul that held this spiritual space before us can go on to higher levels of being and work.

Three Stages of Consolidation and Growth

The first of the three stages of consolidation is called *ibbur*—pregnancy or period of gestation. This phase is often spent in isolation or solitude. The Ari sets the length of *ibbur* at forty days, reminiscent of the forty days of solitude that Moses spent on Sinai. This isolation is necessary because we are not yet fully established in our higher vision. We need a period of protection and nurturing for the new awareness to solidify.

The second step is *yenikah*—breast-feeding. Now we are spiritually born and go out into the world. However, we still need to be closely attached to our Soul Mother. We need to be breast-fed by Her—directly nourished from our supernal root. A steady line of consciousness joins us to our soul, through which we are fed knowledge and energy. We cannot wander far from our inner contact. We continue to require a certain degree of shielding and care.

The final unfolding is *gidul hamochin*—the development of the mind. At this point, we have grown fully into our higher state of consciousness. We no longer need to stay in close proximity to our inner source. We can find spiritual food on our own and "wander" wherever we wish. We live in the rarified air of our new spiritual home and have ourselves become a source of energy and spiritual influence for those dwelling on the rungs of the ladder below our own.

The Wider Picture

This model of the evolution of consciousness is extended by the Ari to the whole of creation and the entire spiritual realm. In the higher worlds, the process of *yichud,* or union, is taking place between the different *Partzufim,* or Divine Countenances: *Arikh Anpin*—the Greater Countenance; *Ze'eir Anpin*—the Lesser Countenance; *Abba* and *Imma*—the Supernal Father and Mother; and the *Shekhinah*—the Feminine Divine Presence, as well as other lesser *Partzufim.* They all are part of the interlinking chain of being, the grand progression of the manifest universe toward union with God in the Absolute.

Everything is ascending upward, striving to merge with that which is higher than itself. This is a process that is happening on both the personal and the cosmic levels, but the essential dynamics remain the same.

From a spiritual point of view, all this movement is an effort to reverse the catastrophic shattering that took place at the beginning of Creation. It is an attempt to construct a stronger vessel that can hold the light of the Infinite. When this process reaches its completion, our universe will have fulfilled the divine purpose for which it was created, and a new stage of reality will begin to unfold.

CHAPTER FOURTEEN
THE PSYCHIC

The Danger of Delving into the Inner Realm

*T*he spiritual life is a great adventure. Meditation takes us to extraordinary places and opens up vast new worlds. At the same time, this inner exploration carries with it many dangers. Delving deeply into our internal world when we are not yet ready to do so can unbalance us physically, emotionally, and mentally. Excessive meditation can sometimes cause a tremendous surge of psychic energy to flow into our centers, with unexpected and hard-to-control effects.

This section attempts to address some of the problems that can arise in such a situation. It provides understanding and advice about how to proceed under these circumstances.

The Potential and Problem of the Psychic Energy

As mentioned in chapter 4, there are three energy pathways that run through our spiritual body. The Kabbalah speaks of them as three pillars or columns. The left-hand pathway is called the column of *din,* or judgment. The right-hand is the column of *chesed,* or mercy. And the power of the *Shekhinah,* the feminine Divine Presence, ascends along the middle column.

The left-hand energy is also referred to as the psychic. Psychic energy provides the medium for supernatural experience. It gives form to vision and inspiration. It opens the door to other planes of existence and enables us to contact those planes.

The psychic therefore plays an important role in the inner life of all spiritual seekers. As we start out on our journey, it is the psychic energy that provides us with much needed encouragement in the way of spiritual experiences. Then, at a later stage, the psychic becomes our gateway into the Kingdom of Heaven and the conscious experience of the divine realms.

In its role as a spiritual doorway, however, the psychic also introduces certain dangers. Since the psychic energy merely provides an open passage into other worlds, we can end up anywhere, including planes beneath our own.

Contact with lower planes occurs more often than most people realize. When people interact with the lower psychic, they become hypnotized by the energy. Immersed in a world of illusion and half-reality, they are lost in a state of semi-trance.

This is not the only hazard. In their eagerness to get close to God, some seekers are drawn into a relationship with disembodied beings from these planes. These spirits play on their egos, convincing these individuals that they are great spiritual beings. They are misled into believing that they have contacted the higher worlds of the Kingdom of Heaven. As a result, their inner development becomes misdirected and their spiritual growth is derailed.[1]

In the worst cases, such individuals can be persuaded by their so-called inner guides to commit terrible crimes and engage in immoral acts. The Hebrew Bible speaks about the corrupt cults of ancient Canaan where adherents threw their children into the fire for the god Molekh and took part in wild orgies in the name of the goddess Ashtoret. All of these base forms of idol worship were a product of such lower psychic alliances.

The Protective Influence of the Divine Kingdom

Because of these perils, the psychic energy should not be developed on its own. The right-hand energy needs to be developed in tandem with the left-hand force. The energy of *chesed,* or mercy, brings in the overshadowing protection of the divine kingdom. The presence of the Divine makes certain that the proper door is opened and that the correct plane is contacted. It ensures that we are guided to our spiritual home.

Providing such protection is one of the major roles of the traditional religions. When Jews pray to God as *Yud Heh Vav Heh*, or Christians pray to Jesus, or Buddhists meditate on the Buddha, they are connected to their spiritual source by a pathway that is formed of all the souls who are on their particular line. Jews connect with all of the prophets, rabbis, and great souls who have come to help and guide the Jewish people. Christians link in with all of the Christian saints. Buddhists join with all the incarnations of the Buddha and bodhisattvas.

In this way, our prayers have a specific address to which they go. They are not just a message in a bottle haphazardly blown across the waves of an ocean, arriving, if we are lucky, on a distant and random shore. Our prayers are like a letter taken from our hand by the postman and passed on directly to the post office. We are guaranteed that it will go to the right place and the right person, because it has a name, an address, and a zip code.

Great Ones who have founded or revitalized a religion act as a "safe pair of hands" to oversee our petitions. They make sure that our prayers arrive at the right destination. This is also the role of spiritual teachers. They watch over us during our inner journey. The firm spiritual link that they have established provides a clear pathway into the supernal realm. Like a switchboard operator, these meditation guides connect us to the divine telephone service. They know when we need careful overseeing and when we are capable of pursuing inner contacts on our own. Many of the enlightened sages have written down clear instructions to help us distinguish between higher spiritual contacts and lower psychic phenomena.

Conditions for Receiving Reliable Guidance

There are certain conditions that need to be present for us to be confident that the inner guidance we are receiving is reliable. Following are a number of the key requirements for the safe reception of inspiration from on high.

Life of Purity and Holiness

The best defense against spiritual problems, the Baal Shem tells us, is a dedicated life of purity and holiness.[2] As indicated above, the psychic energy opens a door onto other planes of existence. The plane we contact will reflect our own spiritual vibration. The more refined our vibration, the higher the plane we will reach. The more we imbue our life with godliness, the less the lower psychic can gain a hold upon us.

Development of the Heart: The Right-Hand Energy

Another line of protection comes from developing the heart aspect. If our heart is open, the Source of All Goodness can overshadow and protect us. When we show love to others and perform acts of kindness for them, it draws the Holy Spirit toward us. The right-hand path of divine virtues seals the door to the lower psychic realms.

Attunement with God

To be worthy of higher contacts, the Baal Shem Tov explains, it is necessary to attune our minds with the higher reality. We start by establishing a strong inner link with our soul, and then we keep that inner connection flowing at all times: "Only if he is linked to God in his thoughts at all times, only then will God make it possible for him to always know [what to do] ... but a person who is haphazard in his relationship with God, God will also be haphazard with him."[3] Once we naturally turn to the All-Merciful for every need and at every moment, we can begin to trust the inner guidance that we receive.

Surrender

If we want the Eternal One to send us inner inspiration and guidance, the Baal Shem stipulates, we have to let go of all our thoughts and schemes and surrender them to the Source of All Knowledge.[4]

As long as we think that we ourselves know what to do, God will allow us to sort out our own lives by using our intelligence. The Ever-Present Witness will let us strive and struggle to find the path forward—growing and evolving through the decisions that we make.

However, if we "cast our burdens on the Lord," as it says in Psalm 55:23, then the Compassionate One will take up responsibility for our lives. The Fashioner of Destiny will guide us during times of trial and tribulation and point the way forward when we lose our way.

It is not easy to achieve this kind of total submission. As Latu Maharaj, a direct disciple of Sri Ramakrishna, once replied to a devotee who asked him about self-surrender, "Surrendering oneself to God means that one should move at his command. Do not do anything without his command. Even if it means a great loss for you, do not stray from that. Only when you have attained this state can you say that you have truly surrendered yourself to God."[5] Whenever Latu Maharaj faced a decision, he looked to the Provider of All for guidance. If necessary, he would wait a whole year for instruction to come. Until he felt certain of the right direction, he simply refused to act.[6]

Such profound renunciation is difficult to attain. Even if we have not yet achieved this state, we can have full surrender as our goal. With this objective in mind, we can strive to live with awe and humility. Cultivating these traits will ready us for the moment when we can receive divine inspiration.

Practical Guidelines for Judging Our Spiritual Experience

Learning how to judge our inner experience is a most complicated question, even for seekers who are very evolved. If we want to have faith in our inner experience, then we need to have clear guidelines set out for us.

Inspiration Appears When We Are Unattached and in a High Spiritual State

The first guideline that the Baal Shem lays down is that true inspiration only comes when we are in a high spiritual state: "When he is bound to God, and a thought falls into his head about something, then it is true—just as it has fallen into his thoughts. And this is a touch of *ruach kodesh*—divine inspiration."[7]

Real inspiration does not normally appear when we are thinking about a particular subject. Rather, it falls unexpectedly into our head while our thoughts are turned in a completely different direction. Saint Teresa's writings underline this point. In genuine inspiration, "the soul has not been thinking of what it hears—I mean that the voice comes unexpectedly ... often it refers to things which one never thought would or could happen." By contrast, in false locutions, "someone seems to be composing bit by bit what the soul wishes to hear."[8]

Here, wishful thinking plays a significant role. One of the temptations that everyone faces in the spiritual life is the deluding effect of wishful thinking. We all want to experience the Divine Presence. Everyone is searching for guidance and inspiration. The problem is that our own desires can obstruct our ability to discern what is real and what is imaginary—what is from God and what is not. Vigilant examination of that which we hear or see will greatly aid us in this task.

Assessing our mental state at the time of our experience is therefore crucial in determining its veracity. The Baal Shem specifies that true inspiration occurs when we are so concentrated in prayer that no distracting thoughts arise. Only such a state of profound inner focus will produce reliable guidance.

> And when he is speaking [with God in prayer or meditation] without any distracting or disturbing thoughts, in a state of being firmly joined with the higher worlds, and a thought comes to him like a bit of prophecy—certainly it is true. And this thought comes from the divine utterances that are declared in the heavens.[9]

Inspiration Comes with Clarity and Authority

We also need to look at the exact nature of our experience. Did the inspiration come in dribs and drabs or in a single flash? Were the words or visions clear and distinct, or were they vague and distorted? Again, Saint Teresa is illuminating: "The genuine locution is so clear that, even if it consists of a long exhortation, the hearer notices the omission of a single syllable, as well as the phraseology which is used." In fanciful locutions, in contrast, "the voice will be less clear and the words less distinct; they will be like something heard in a half-dream."[10]

The spiritual vitality of the experience is also important. Do the words come with authority and power, or are they lifeless whispers that leave no lasting effect? As Saint Teresa explains, "The first and truest [sign] is the sense of power and authority which they bear with them, both in themselves and in the actions which follow them."[11]

Inspiration Has a Profound and Lasting Effect

This passage points to yet another factor in analyzing our experience: the effect that the words or visions have on us. A real experience will wipe away our fears and doubts and fill us with peace and serenity. As Saint Teresa expresses it, a single word of this kind to a troubled soul "takes all its fear from it, and it is most marvellously comforted, and believes that no one will ever be able to make it feel otherwise.... A great tranquillity dwells in the soul, which becomes peacefully and devoutly recollected, and ready to sing praises to God."[12]

True inspiration infuses us with renewed strength to serve and strive toward the Most High. As Rebbe Levi Yitzchak of Berditchev teaches:

> When a person wants to know if God receives joy from his service, the test is if a person sees that his heart is on fire and burning to

serve God, and he has fervor and strong motivation in his divine service; then it proves with certainty that God is pleased with his worship.[13]

True inspiration makes a lasting impression upon our mind. As Saint Teresa remarked, "These words do not vanish from the memory for a very long time: some, indeed, never vanish at all."[14] A real spiritual experience remains with us for the rest of our lives. It continues to guide and inspire us for all of our days. In an instant, whole new worlds of understanding become accessible. A greater truth is imparted than any words can possibly convey: "One single word may contain a world of meaning such as the understanding alone could never put rapidly into human language.... Not only can words be heard, but, in a way which I shall never be able to explain, much more can be understood than the words themselves convey."[15]

The *Zohar* tells us that Jacob's vision of a ladder ascending to heaven became the focus of his spiritual life. He would teach the mystical truths revealed therein to everyone who came to him.[16] Certainly, the words that the Jewish people heard at Mount Sinai have remained forever in our collective memory. They have been reverberating in our national consciousness ever since.

Even with all of these guidelines, real dangers still remain with respect to spiritual experience. Extreme caution is required before we follow our inner guidance. Any words of inspiration should be balanced by a heavy dose of reason and common sense. Above all else, a profound sense of humility and a strong commitment to transforming our lower nature are vital prerequisites if we wish to walk along this path.

Signs of a Psychic Problem

We have laid out a series of guidelines for knowing whether or not we have received genuine inspiration. However, how do we know when we or someone else has gone astray?

People with a psychic problem exhibit a variety of different signs in their behavior and attitude. For example, there is an absence of mental clarity, coupled with strong willfulness. They are emotionally high-strung and fragile. The slightest spiritual input causes them to fall into a trance.

They may stop eating and sleeping, saying that to do so would interfere with their inner state.

They also possess a huge ego about their spiritual attainments. They declare that they are great spiritual beings and make grandiose proclamations such as, "I am an enlightened soul; I am the Messiah/*Shekhinah*; I have come to change the world."

They display all sorts of scruples in their behavior. For instance, they demand that all actions be done in a specific manner, insisting that certain acts need to be done only with the right hand and others only with the left one. They are adamant that a specific color of clothing has to be worn on a particular day and at a precise time. Whatever they do, they look for signs and symbols to guide them, often making totally irrational decisions based on this input. All these different forms of volatile and erratic behavior and thinking are signs of a psychic crisis.

Advice for the Individual with the Problem

The books of the Christian mystic Saint Teresa of Avila contain an abundance of information about life in a contemplative community. Her methods of dealing with disturbed nuns provide much practical advice for working with seekers who have become unhinged by the psychic.[17]

No Spiritual Practices

The first matter that Saint Teresa makes clear is that the nun in question must be prevented from spending too much time in meditation and prayer.

People with a psychic problem need to give up all inwardly focused spiritual practices: no prayer, no esoteric study or contemplation. They have to stop listening to and asking for higher input. In fact, they should totally ignore all inner messages or perceived energy intake. This means, for example, that they should not use their instincts to intuit the answer to who is calling when the doorbell or cell phone rings or what the visitor's arrival might foretell. The best approach is to cease looking for signs altogether and to pay no attention to any spiritual symbolism that does arise in the mind.

Down-to-Earth Activities

The next thing that Saint Teresa suggests is to give the nun lots of practical work to occupy her.

In general, individuals who are struggling with the psychic should engage in activities that ground them in the body. Some examples of such pursuits are gardening, cooking, and physical exercise. Apart from these endeavors, it is important for them to eat and sleep well.

The crucial issue is that whatever they are doing, their mind must not be inwardly directed; rather, it should be occupied with either outer activity or intellectual study. At all times, their mind should be in the "here and now." This outward focus is a vital discipline. It will keep them from falling into a hypnotic trancelike state.

The emphasis on mindfulness has an additional positive effect. It builds a mind that has great willpower and emotional fortitude, which will enable them to remain steady and detached. Such a finely tuned and concentrated mind is a potent tool in the spiritual and physical life of any seeker.

Self-Awareness

It is hard for us to imagine the insidious manner in which the psychic is used to manipulate the ego and the depth of the self-delusion that takes place. When the psychic overshadows, the hold is strong and runs deep. To counter this tendency, the troubled individuals need to keep a watch over their ego. They need to look at how the psychic has inflated their ego in the past to ensnare them, how it has used their pride and arrogance to lead them astray. This "ego analysis" will guard them from possible future troubles and keep them ever humble and self-aware.

Advice for the Spiritual Guide

Do Not Argue with Them

The willfulness of a person under psychic influence is a very serious problem. In dealing with such individuals, Saint Teresa warns us not to argue with them about their visions and heavenly voices. It will only make matters worse. The soundest counsel, she says, is to pay absolutely no attention to their psychic experiences; only in this manner will they quiet down.

Recognize the Seriousness of the Danger

Saint Teresa recounts how in some instances, the grip of the psychic was so fierce that she had to apply very harsh treatment to these disturbed souls. It caused her great pain to do so, she admits, but the danger to them and the other nuns around them was too great to chance any other course.

The psychic can totally undermine anyone's spiritual development. The afflicted souls can become lost in the lower realms for months or even years. They can poison the thoughts and practice of the other seekers around them. They can destroy the harmonious relationship between all of the members in a spiritual group. An uncontrolled lower psychic influence is a grave threat to a contemplative community.

A Long-Term Process

Dealing with individuals who have fallen into the clutches of the psychic is a long and challenging process. It requires both a firm and a lovingly patient hand. Saint Teresa informs us that in most cases she was able to gradually restore her wayward sisters to health and inner well-being. Her writings provide us with an excellent example of the power of an evolved spiritual teacher to watch over and guide those in her care.

Despite the many pitfalls that exist in the meditative life, real spiritual experiences are a great blessing when they come. Divine revelations inspire and uphold us. They are moments of the miraculous that nourish and sustain our soul. These precious encounters lift us into another level of consciousness, a state of heightened awareness where we know with profound certainty that God is the guiding force directing our lives.

The ability to drive a car gives us great freedom and mobility but also the capacity to cause great harm to others and ourselves. Meditation is our spiritual vehicle. If we steer our divine vehicle with caution and drive along secure routes, then we will arrive at our supernal destination safe and sound.

Individual versus Group Practice

Are We Better Off Meditating Alone or with Others?

*M*ost people think of meditation as a purely solitary activity. However, there is important work that takes place when we meditate in a group. What we can achieve as individuals is not the same as what we can accomplish as a collective. A group broadens our field of spiritual activity; it augments the bank of energies that are accessible to us. Both forms of meditation have advantages and disadvantages. Each of these modes of practice has its place in our spiritual life.

The Importance of Spiritual Companionship

"I find it hard to describe the joy that we experienced in those days.... Day after day, as though overpowered by a strange, spiritual fervour, we kept on doing our meditation and experiencing intense joy ... day and night we had no talk between us other than about spiritual life—about renunciation, devotion and how to acquire the knowledge of God.... Sometimes we were not even aware of how the days were passing."

—Reminiscences of a monk in the Ramakrishna Order[1]

Psalm 133:1 declares, "How good and pleasant it is for brothers [and sisters] to dwell together in unity." There is a great joy in being with others who love God. It is like being in the next world, where we are with those who love us unconditionally and know us as we truly are.

When spiritual brothers and sisters meet, they treat each other with the utmost respect and sensitivity. They work together in harmony and mutual support. They feel great happiness just to be in each other's presence.

Spiritual companionship is hard to understand for someone who has not experienced it. It is an all-encompassing and totally transforming camaraderie. Saint Teresa of Avila uses the following analogy to try to explain the nature of spiritual friendship: "It is a wonderful thing when a sick person finds another wounded with the same sickness; how great the consolation to find you are not alone. The two become a powerful help to each other in suffering and meriting. What excellent backing they give to one another."[2]

A spiritual seeker is lovesick for God. Like a person who is hopelessly in love, the spiritual seeker thinks only of his Beloved and cannot focus his mind on anything else. It is a state of "intoxication" to which most people cannot relate.

The Baal Shem Tov tells a parable about a group of people listening to the playing of a superb musician. Inspired by the beauty of his music, they jump for joy and weep or laugh out loud. Then, a deaf man accidently happens on the scene and sees them dancing in wild abandon. Unable to hear the music, he comes to the conclusion that they all are stark raving mad.[3]

With this parable, the Baal Shem is underlining the importance of keeping the company of those who "hear the music." In such company, we can lower our guard and drop all pretense and facade. We can be ourselves and speak as we truly believe without fear of misunderstanding. With our spiritual friends, we can explore ideas and share experiences that we could not or would not dare to talk about outside our circle. Especially at the beginning of our journey, it is vital for us to spend time in the company of fellow seekers.

There is another reason for spending time in holy company. Everyone leaves spiritual vibrations wherever they have been. More evolved souls impart positive vibrations, while less developed souls leave a negative residue. This is a fundamental law of spiritual science.

Without knowing or necessarily desiring it, we absorb the energy and thoughtforms of those around us. Therefore, it is essential that we choose carefully the company that we keep. If we spend our time with people who do not share our views about life, gradually their influence will change the way in which we see the world. Eventually, we will find that we are taking a path that we never intended and living a life that is not our own.

Sri Ramakrishna used a visit to the museum to illustrate this point to his devotees: "I visited the museum once. I was shown fossils. A whole animal has become stone! Just see what an effect has been produced by company! Likewise, by constantly living in the company of a holy man one verily becomes holy."[4]

Spiritual companions are the antidote to this problem. Holy company will not only make sure that we are placed in the emanation of positive spiritual vibrations; it will also counteract the negative effects of the materialistic society in which we live. Holy company is an indispensable part of the spiritual life. It is a priceless treasure for all those who are striving on the path.

Rebbe Nachman of Breslov urged his Hasidim to share their spiritual experiences and Torah insights with each other. He commanded them to gather together on a regular basis to speak about their love for God and love for their teacher.[5]

Rebbe Elimelekh of Lizhensk advised his Hasidim to share not only their insights and spiritual experiences but also their faults and imperfections: the strange thoughts that come into their hearts during prayer and learning, the images and desires that arise as they are lying in their beds, the temptations that they have faced while going about the business of their daily life. "Hold back nothing from each other," he told them. "Do not let fear or shame keep you from sharing your struggles."[6]

Swami Brahmananda spoke similarily to his disciples:

> It benefits an aspirant if he talks about spiritual life with a person of a similar nature. Fellow pilgrims can help each other. A person can escape danger on his journey if he gets acquainted with a traveler who already has followed that path and knows its problems. If you have a good guide, he will show you important things on the way and you will not have to face any troubles. Moreover, you will be able to accomplish your objective in a short time and reach your destination quickly.[7]

Swami Chidananda also extolled the benefits of uplifting company:

> That fraternity [of spiritual companions] is your greatest protection and is your greatest guarantee of always being in the light and attaining the goal.... In such company, faith becomes confirmed, questions become answered, and weakness is replaced by strength....
>
> Gurudev [Swami Sivananda] used to say that one hour in the company of holy people, seekers and lovers of God, is equal to a hundred baths in the holy river Ganges or pilgrimages to all the holy places of the world.[8]

The Spiritual Power of Group Work

There is yet another level of meaning behind the gathering of spiritual seekers beyond all those mentioned above. This aspect of its purpose is made clear to us in a story about the Baal Shem Tov.

The Baal Shem was known for his deep states of prayer that could last for hours. On one occasion, the Baal Shem went on for so long with his prayers that the Hasidim got up and left. Later in the day, they returned to the house of prayer. When all of the Hasidim were present, the Baal Shem admonished them for leaving while he was still praying. Then he recounted the following parable.

There once was a rare and magnificent bird that perched on the top of an incredibly high tree in a certain kingdom. The tree was so high that nobody could climb to the top. When word of this extraordinary creature was brought to the king, he gathered hundreds of his subjects at the foot of the tree and then commanded them to stand one on top of the other to form a human ladder. In this manner, they reached to the top of the tree, captured the bird, and brought it to the royal court.

When the Baal Shem finished telling the parable, he turned to his Hasidim and declared, "When we join together in prayer, we become a single chain of spiritual longing that reaches up into the highest heaven. When you abandoned me during my prayers, however, the cosmic ladder that we were building collapsed and the precious gift that we might have brought to the King of kings was lost."[9]

Holy company is about more than mutual support and encouragement. When spiritual friends join together, they create a spiritual structure that is greater than the sum of their parts. They build a heavenly edifice that reaches far into the higher worlds. They become part of the vast network of souls throughout all the planes, who emanate God's infinite light.

This is the reason behind the halakhic insistence on the gathering of a minyan, a quorum of ten people, for prayer services. Ten individuals establish a spiritual whole that empowers the inner work. They harness the full potency of the ten celestial *sefirot*.

Holy company strengthens our yearning and puts us in touch with our supernal source. A gathering of spiritual companions nurtures the seekers on earth and brings joy to the souls in heaven.

The Benefits of Solitary Meditation

While there are many benefits to meditating together with others, there are also some drawbacks. Personality interactions within a group can interfere with the inner work. Clashes between group members can lead to disharmony and spiritual dissonance. These dynamics can disrupt our lives both in and out of the meditation room.

Individuals can disturb us with their movement during a sitting or with the noise that they make before and after meditation. Socializing can unravel our mental preparations. A callous remark can unsettle our heart.

If we are on our own, there is no one to draw us into superficial conversation or to impinge their thoughts and emotions on us. There is no one to dampen our energy flow or throw our centers out of balance. We can reach far into the spiritual realm with our one-pointed individual practice.

A number of practical problems arise when we meditate with others. It takes an enormous effort to organize a group of busy people. Juggling everyone's needs and schedules can be a real headache. Meditating on our own, we do not need to rely on anyone. We can practice whenever we want. We can benefit from the serenity and peace of meditating in solitude. We can let go of all externals and completely forget the world.

The reality is that for most of us, regular group meditation is not possible. We do not live in communities where group meditation is part of the daily routine. We can meet with our spiritual friends once or twice a week if we are lucky. In our individualistic society, meditation is primarily a solitary pursuit.

This self-dependence has its advantages. It builds perseverance, endurance, and inner discipline. However, for those of us who find it difficult to take personal initiative and who thrive on the company of others, meditating alone can be a real challenge. We miss the tangible energy boost that comes from collective practice. It is much harder for us to get down on the meditation mat.

Our modern world offers unique solutions for combating these issues. Group meditation over the Internet is surprisingly alive and effective, especially if there is someone who guides the sitting. The vibrations of the sound waves carry the energy across cyberspace. The leader's voice joins everyone together and acts as a unifying spiritual force.

We can also arrange to meditate together with a fellow practitioner at a mutually convenient time. Though each of us is in our own abode, our energy waves will mingle in the higher realm. In addition, the very thought of our joint effort will help to motivate and stimulate us as we engage in our shared spiritual endeavor.

Both individual and group meditation have a role to play in our practice. A healthy balance between the two makes for a rich spiritual life. Belonging to a meditation group will provide us with support and encouragement. Meditating on our own will allow us to penetrate deep into our inner reality.

Eventually, the two aspects of our practice meld into each other. When people have been part of a meditation group for many years, an inner bond forms between them. There is an attunement and resonance that develops among the members. They always feel connected, whether they are together or apart. They become individual limbs that all belong to the same resplendent spiritual body, working together in the plan of God.

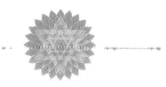

CHAPTER SIXTEEN

INDIVIDUAL AND COLLECTIVE EVOLUTION

Is Meditation a Selfish Indulgence or a Noble Endeavor?

"This I tell you: decay is inherent in all conditioned things.
Work out your own salvation, with diligence."

—The Buddha[1]

"In the same way that there was an exile and then redemption in Egypt for the whole of the people of Israel, so there is [an exile and redemption] for each individual person. This is the interpretation of Psalm 69:19, 'Draw near to my soul and redeem it.' Therefore, before we pray for universal redemption, we must first pray for the redemption of our own soul."

—Baal Shem Tov[2]

Personal and Universal Salvation

What motivates the search for personal salvation? Is it merely a selfish desire, or is it an essential part of the process of humanity's redemption? Is it a sign of arrogance, or is it an expression of humility and a realistic understanding of the human condition?

Rebbe Yehudah Aryeh Leib Alter of Ger was a dynamic nineteenth-century Hasidic leader. He taught that the real exile is the exile of the soul in the body. The depth of our present exile, he says, is reflected in the fact that we are totally focused on the body and on all things physical, while the soul and its needs have been cast to the side. Before the redemption of the world can be achieved, he concludes, we must first free ourselves from our bondage to the *yetzer hara*—to our lower self.[3]

When someone asked Sri Ramana Maharshi a question that implied a desire to reform the world, the Maharshi sharply replied:

> You imagine you are going to mend the world with your questions. Who are you to meddle with the world? Look after yourself first. Do you know yourself? Do you know what you really want? How can you know what the world needs when you are blind to your own true needs? First set yourself right.[4]

Sri Ramakrishna also similarly rebuked a devotee who wanted to "do good to the world":

> You people speak of doing good to the world. Is the world such a small thing? And who are you, pray, to do good to the world? First realize God, see Him by means of spiritual discipline. If He imparts power, then you can do good to others; otherwise not.[5]

Yet it is not only because they understood humanity's faults and weaknesses that all these great teachers put their emphasis on the work of personal redemption. They also saw the incredible potential for good in a person who has broken free from the hold of the lower self and has realized God. In one of his letters, Swami Vivekananda wrote:

> Neither numbers, nor powers, nor wealth, nor learning, nor eloquence, nor anything else will prevail, but purity, living the life, in one word, *anubhuti*, realization. Let there be a dozen such lion-souls in each country, lions who have broken their own bonds, who have touched the Infinite, whose whole souls are gone to Brahman, who care neither for wealth, nor power, nor fame, and these will be *enough* to shake the world.[6]

Rebbe Mordekhai of Nesvizh, a disciple of Rebbe Shlomo of Karlin, had a unique capacity to use everything he did to elevate his soul. He declared that a person with perfect faith can raise the dead, turn silver to gold, and change the patterns of nature.[7]

The Hasidic master Menachem Mendel of Kotzk, who lived in the late eighteenth to early nineteenth century, was known for the intensity of his search for authenticity and the profundity and sharpness of his spiritual remarks. Once, one of his Hasidim asked Rebbe Menachem Mendel how he knew the answers to questions about commerce and other mundane matters when he lived apart from the world and had nothing to do with business. The Kotzker swiftly retorted, "Only a person who is outside the world can look inside it. How will a person who is standing inside look and see?"[8] When we are above the turmoil of this world, we can see things as they really are. After we have swept aside the veil of glamor that covers this material world, we can begin to act with clarity and effectiveness.

Some people may think that realized souls benefit only themselves and do nothing for others. But that is only because they do not understand the wider influence of such a life.

A visitor once remarked to Sri Ramana Maharshi, "Some say that to make an effort for one's [own] liberation is selfish, and that instead of that, one should do good to others by selfless service." The Maharshi replied,

> Those people believe that *jnanis* [realized souls] are selfish and that they themselves are selfless, but this is not a true belief. The *jnani* lives in the experience of Brahman and the effect of this experience spreads all over the world. A radio transmission is done from one point but its effect can be felt all over the world. Those who would like to benefit from it can do so. Similarly, the Self-realisation of the *jnani* spreads everywhere and whosoever wants can tune into it. This is not a lesser service.[9]

According to Rebbe Gedalyahu of Linitz, one of the members of the Baal Shem Tov's circle, the Baal Shem not only taught that there is both personal salvation and collective salvation, but he also saw a direct link between the two: when everyone has been redeemed personally, then the collective redemption will follow automatically.[10]

The Baal Shem Tov understood that all the goodwill in the world would ultimately come to nothing unless it is accompanied by the hard work of inner perfection. Only when we have freed ourselves from the hold of the lower self can we become effective divine instruments to transform the world. Without individual self-transformation, humanity will never be redeemed.

Alignment of the Individual and the Collective

There are two aspects to the spiritual life: service and contemplation. Some religions stress one aspect, and some emphasize the other, but both aspects are equally important to our spiritual development.

Swami Vivekananda enshrined this idea in the motto of the Ramakrishna Order: "For one's own salvation, and for the welfare of the world." In Judaism, we speak about *tikun neshamah,* "fixing our soul," and *tikun olam,* "fixing the world."

We have come into this world to evolve and grow as individuals and as souls. Conjunct to this purpose, we also are born with a specific spiritual task to fulfill in the plan of God. Some of us have a major part to play on the stage of life's drama, and others have a smaller role behind the scenes, but all of us are part of the plan, and all of us contribute toward the goal of moving humanity forward in its evolution.

The major elements of each of our *gilgulim,* or incarnations, are mapped out for us before we come down into this world. Whatever is required for us to develop and grow in this incarnation will be incorporated into the script for our life. Opportunities will open up and encounters will be arranged to supply us with exactly what we need for our spiritual evolution. All the many and varied experiences of our life will be tailored to propel us forward onto the next step in our soul journey.

The specific needs of our own personal evolution will be coordinated with the workings of God's Eternal Plan. A life task will be designated for us that both furthers our individual growth and fulfills a function in the larger collective mission. Our labors will be watched over and guided by the great souls on the higher planes who are responsible for the unfolding of the divine purpose. Their work takes place in a unity of mind that is suffused with the light of the Universal Consciousness.

Discovering the personal growth we need to achieve and the spiritual task that is ours to realize is the challenge before each of us. The tzaddikim, or enlightened beings, are the masters of this process. They align the individual with the collective evolution. They draw the people who are connected to their own souls toward them like a magnet. All the great teachers of humankind have brought with them a group of individuals to help with their work. These realized souls take up incarnation together with their "eternal companions" for the salvation of the world.

Sri Ramakrishna had a vision of a higher realm from which he called down his intimate disciples to come and incarnate with him.[11] He also told two of his disciples that in an earlier incarnation, they had both been devotees of Jesus in ancient Israel.[12]

According to the Kabbalistic tradition, Rabbi Yitzchak Luria and his followers were the incarnation of Rabbi Shimon bar Yochai and his circle in the *Zohar*.[13] The Baal Shem Tov once told his Hasidim that his soul had refused to come down to this world until God promised him sixty advanced souls to incarnate with him, to watch over the Baal Shem and aid him in his work.[14]

These group incarnations show us the kind of potent vortex of spiritual power that is created when the work of *tikun neshamah* and *tikun olam* mesh together. They exemplify the work that can be achieved when there is both inner and outer alignment between human beings.

Each of us seeks meaning to our lives. Each of us desires to know and understand the purpose of our existence. We have come into this world to work out our own salvation, but we are also part of a larger spiritual reality. Our personal spiritual evolution is part of a broader mission. Our individual effort contributes to the fulfillment of a greater cosmic goal.

In Exodus 25:8, God commands the Children of Israel, "Build Me a sanctuary (*mikdash*), and I will dwell in your midst." The Baal Shem Tov teaches that this *mikdash* is a place that we build inside ourselves.[15] This sacred space is dedicated by sanctifying our lives and infusing our actions with divine virtues. It is vitalized through the practice of meditation and prayer.

This process of purification and vitalization transforms us into potent divine instruments. It enables the supernal energies to pour into us from the higher planes and then flow out from us into the world. In this manner, we become active participants in God's body of manifestation—living *mikdashim*, or temples, walking in the world.

Appendix A

Hebrew Transliteration Pronunciation Guide for Chanting

Vowels

a and ah = (ah) as in "father"
ay or ai = long i (i) as in "kayak" or "sky"
e = short e (eh) as in "bed"
ey or ei = long a (ay) as in "obey" or "eight"
i = long i (ee) as in "yogi" or "tree"
o = long o (oh) as in "go"
u = long u (oo) as in "tune"

Consonants

All consonants sound as they do in English except for:
ch or kh = throaty h sound as in Scottish "loch" or German "Bach"
tz = ts as in "mats"
Note:
g = always hard g as in "God"
h after a vowel at the end of a word = silent, as in "mitzvah"
sh = pronounced as in English, as in "shalom"

Appendix B

Further Reading on the Meditative Life

*T*his is by no means an exhaustive list. There are many wonderful books on meditation in every tradition, and it is impossible for me to enumerate them all. The titles I have included are useful books that each present a different dimension of practice and living. *Meditation from the Heart of Judaism: Today's Teachers Share Their Practices, Techniques, and Faith*, edited by Avram Davis, introduces many contemporary Jewish meditation teachers. *Jewish Mysticism and the Spiritual Life: Classical Texts, Contemporary Reflections*, edited by Lawrence Fine, Eitan Fishbane and Or N. Rose, supplies a wealth of wisdom on the meditative life from some of the most creative and thoughtful teachers in Judaism. *Inner Space* and *Meditation and the Bible* by Aryeh Kaplan provide an enlightening understanding of our "inner space" and a fascinating perspective on the role of meditation and spiritual practices in the lives of the ancient prophets. *Visions of a Compassionate World* is an unusual Hasidic text from prewar Poland that teaches a unique path to the expansion of our consciousness and inner awareness. *The Pillar of Prayer* contains the Baal Shem Tov's teachings on contemplative prayer and study. Saint Teresa's *Interior Castle* furnishes valuable information about the life of the spirit. The various Eastern books listed below offer a wide range of practices and insights to illuminate and enrich the Jewish teachings and place them in the broader context of humanity's eons-long search for the living presence of God.

Baal Shem Tov. *The Pillar of Prayer: Guidance in Contemplative Prayer, Sacred Study, and the Spiritual Life, from the Baal Shem Tov and His Circle.* Edited by Aubrey Glazer; translated by Menachem Kallus. Louisville, KY: Fons Vitae, 2011.

Bhajananda. "Meditation and Concentration." Parts 1–5. *Prabuddha Bharata,* July–November 1980.

———. "Types of Meditation." Parts 1–2. *Prabuddha Bharata,* May–June 1981.

Chetanananda, trans. *A Guide to Spiritual Life: Spiritual Teachings of Swami Brahmananda.* St. Louis: Vedanta Society of St. Louis, 1988.

Davis, Avram, ed. *Meditation from the Heart of Judaism: Today's Teachers Share Their Practices, Techniques, and Faith.* Woodstock, VT: Jewish Lights Publishing, 1999.

Ekstein, Menachem. *Visions of a Compassionate World: Guided Imagery for Spiritual Growth and Social Transformation.* Translated by Yehoshua Starrett. Jerusalem: Urim Publications, 2001.

Lawrence Fine, Eitan Fishbane and Or N. Rose, eds. *Jewish Mysticism and the Spiritual Life: Classical Texts, Contemporary Reflections.* Woodstock, VT: Jewish Lights Publishing, 2011.

Godman, David. *Be as You Are: The Teachings of Sri Ramana Maharshi.* London: Arkana/Penguin, 1985.

Kaplan, Aryeh, *Inner Space: Introduction to Kabbalah, Meditation and Prophecy.* Edited by Avraham Sutton. Brooklyn, NY: Moznaim Publishing, 1991.

———. *Meditation and the Bible.* York Beach, ME: Samuel Weiser, 1988.

"M." *The Gospel of Sri Ramakrishna.* Translated by Swami Nikhilananda. New York: Ramakrishna-Vivekananda Center, 2007.

Ramana Maharshi. *Who Am I?* Translated by Dr. T. M. P. Mahadevan. Tiruvannamalai, India: Sri Ramanasramam, 1986.

Satchidananda. *The Gospel of Swami Ramdas.* 2 vols. Kanhangad, India: Anandashram, 2006.

Sivananda. *Concentration and Meditation.* Shivanandanagar, India: The Divine Life Trust Society, 2011.

Suzuki, Shunryu. *Zen Mind, Beginner's Mind.* Edited by Trudy Dixon. New York: Weatherhill, 1995.

Teresa of Avila. *The Interior Castle.* Translated by E. Allison Peers. New York: Image Books, 1989.

Appendix C

Index of
Meditation Practices

Contemplation

Notes

Introduction: The Path of Meditation

1. Nachman of Breslov, *Likutei Etzot, Tefillah* 75 (New York: Breslov Hasidim Publications, 1976), and *Likutei Maharan* 21, section on *daat* at the end of the teaching.

2. Shlomo Efrayim of Luntchitz, *Olelot Efrayim*, article 166, cited in Ya'acov Yosef of Polonnoye, *Toldot Ya'acov Yosef*, Torah portions *Shemot* 6 and *Shofetim* 11.

3. *Chakra* is the Sanskrit word for "wheel." The term is used in Tantric and Yogic texts to describe the subtle energy centers located along the spine. The chakras are first mentioned in the Vedas—the Rig Veda, for example. The Sri Jabala Darshana Upanishad, the Yoga-Shikka Upanishad, and the Shandilya Upanishad are other early Yogic texts that discuss the chakras.

4. *Sefer Yetzirah* 1:2. It is unclear where the term *sefirah* comes from. One possibility is that the word *sefirah* comes from the Hebrew word for "sapphire"—*sapir*. The *sefirot*, or spiritual centers, are like brilliant jewels that radiate energy and light. Interestingly, the Torah tells us in Exodus 24:9–10 that Moses, Aaron, and the seventy elders of Israel ascended Mount Sinai, where they beheld the God of Israel, and "under His feet there was a kind of paved work of sapphire stone (*livnat hasapir*)." The *sefirot* are God's footstool ("under His feet"), the medium by which the Infinite Divine Oneness is made manifest in the finite universe of innumerable forms. Another speculation is that the word *sefirah* is related to the word *mispar*, "number." The *sefirot* are the basic building blocks or numbers of the universe.

5. Baal Shem Tov, *Tzava'at haRivash*, p. 21, quoted in Nachman Tsherin, *Derekh Chasidim, Dibur* 20 (New York: Breslov Hasidim Publications, 1977), p. 54.

Chapter 1: Preparation

1. Elimelekh of Lizhensk, *Noam Elimelekh*, Torah portion *Beha'alotkha*, on Numbers 11:10, "Moses heard the people weeping with their families."

2. This practice was taught to me by my teacher, Rabbi Shlomo Carlebach.

3. Alan Brown, John Rankin, Angela Wood, *Religions: A Study Course for GCSE*, ed. Alan Brown, 3rd ed. (Harlow, Essex: Longman Group, 1992), p. 132. This process follows a precise ritual called *wuzu* or *wudhu*. The worshipers wash their hands up to the wrist three times, rinse their mouth three times, wash their nostrils and blow their nose three times, wipe their face three times, wash the right hand and arm up to the elbow three times, left hand and arm up to the elbow three times, wet the hands and run them over the head and neck once, wash their ears once, the right foot as far as the ankle three times, and finally the left foot as far as the ankle three times.

4. Elimelekh of Lizhensk, *Noam Elimelekh*, Torah portion *Beha'alotkha*, on Numbers 11:10, "Moses heard the people weeping with their families."

5. Asher Tzvi of Ostraha, *Ma'ayan haChokhmah*, Torah portion *Beshallach*, quoted in Nachman Tsherin, *Derekh Chasidim, Tefillah* 127.

6. *Minhagei haArizal, Petura d'Abba*, p. 3b, quoted in Yitzchak Buxbaum, *Jewish Spiritual Practices* (Northvale, NJ: Jason Aronson, 1990), p. 115.

7. *Nachman of Breslov, Kitzur Likutei Maharan*, Teaching #2, section 3, *Likutei Maharan* #17, section 5, *Likutei Maharan Tanina* #4, sections 1, 2, and 3.

8. Avraham of Trisk, *Magen Avraham*, Torah portion *Bo*, quoted in Yitzchak Matityahu Luria, *Avkot Rokhalim*, 2nd ed., *Tefillah* 23 (Jerusalem: Foundation of Yitzchak Matityahu Luria, 1978), p. 17.

9. Elimelekh of Lizhensk, *Likutei Shoshana*, on Talmud, *Berakhot* 30b, "The pious men of old would wait."

10. Nachman of Breslov, *Otzer haYirah, Tefillah, Mahadura Batra* 2 (New York: Breslov Hasidim Publications, 1969).

11. Natan of Nemirov, *Otzer haYirah, Tefillah; Shacharit, Minchah, Maariv* 2.

12. Levi Yitzchak of Berditchev, *Kedushat Levi, Vayechi*, on Genesis 49:8, "Judah, you shall your brothers praise."

13. *Shulchan Arukh, Orech Chayim: Hilkhot Beit haKnesset, siman* 151:1.

14. *Zohar* 2:59b, quoted in Thomas C. Hubka, *The Resplendent Synagogue: Architecture and Worship in an Eighteenth-Century Polish Community* (Lebanon, NH: Brandeis University Press, 2003), p. 140.

15. Ibid.

16. *Shulchan Arukh, Orech Chayim: Hilkhot Beit haKnesset, siman* 150:5.

17. Baal Shem Tov, *Tzava'at haRivash*, p. 4b, quoted in *Baal Shem Tov al haTorah, Amud haTefillah* 36, comp. Shimon Menachem Mendel Shub of Gavortshov (Jerusalem, 1974).

18. Ritajananda, *Swami Turiyananda* (Madras [Chennai], India: Sri Ramakrishna Math, 1973), p. 14.

Chapter 2: Intention

1. The central portion of the *Shema* prayer reads as follows: "Hear [*Shema*], O Israel, the Lord is our God, the Lord is One. And you shall love the Lord your God with all of your heart, and with all of your soul, and with all of your might. And these words which I command you today shall be upon your heart. You shall teach them to your children, and you shall speak of them when you sit in your house and when you walk by the way, when you lie down and when you rise. You shall bind them as a sign upon your arm, and they shall be for a reminder between your eyes. And you shall write them on the doorposts of your house and upon your gates" (Deuteronomy 6:4–9).

2. Nachman of Breslov, *Likutei Etzot*, *Temimut* 2.

3. Ya'acov Yosef of Polonnoye, *Toldot Ya'acov Yosef*, Torah portion *Chayei Sarah*.

4. Dov Baer of Mezeritch, *Or Torah*, Torah portion *Ki Tissa*.

5. Nachman of Breslov, *Likutei Etzot*, *Tefillah* 54.

6. Ibid., *Tefillah* 61.

7. Ibid., *Tefillah* 93.

8. Chidananda, *Seek the Beyond*, 1st ed., chapter titled, "The Importance of Joy," (Shivanandanagar, India: The Divine Life Trust Society, 2005), Ch. 9, p. 39.

9. Chetanananda, trans., *A Guide to Spiritual Life: Spiritual Teachings of Swami Brahmananda* (St. Louis: Vedanta Society of St. Louis, 1988), p. 91.

10. Chidananda, *An Instrument of Thy Peace: Swami Chidananda in the West*, 1st ed. (Shivanandanagar, India: The Divine Life Trust Society, 2007), pp. 53, 57.

11. Nachman of Breslov, *Likutei Etzot*, *Tefillah* 52.

12. Ya'acov Yosef of Polonnoye, *Ben Porat Yosef*, introduction, quoted in Shub, *Baal Shem Tov al haTorah*, Torah portion *Pekudei* 1.

13. Baal Shem Tov, *Keter Shem Tov* 2:20a–b, quoted in Shub, *Baal Shem Tov al haTorah*, Torah portion *Bereshit* 82.

14. Elimelekh of Lizhensk, *Tzeitel Katan*, quoted in Shlomo Eliezer Margoliut, *Erkhai Kodesh: Yichudim* (Jerusalem, 1969), p. 47.

15. *Shulchan Arukh*, *Orech Chayim: Hilkhot Kriyat Shema*, siman 61:1, 61:4–6.

16. Natan of Nemirov, *Likutei Halachot*, *Hilchot Genayvah*, halakhah 5:7.

17. Baal Shem Tov, *Tzava'at haRivash*, p. 14b; quoted in Shub, *Baal Shem Tov al haTorah*, *Amud haTefillah* 26.

18. Lobsang P. Lhalungpa, trans., *The Life of Milarepa* (Boston: Shambhala, 1984), pp. 17–43.

Chapter 3: Forging a Connection

1. Baal Shem Tov, *Tzava'at haRivash* 135, Chabad version (Brooklyn, NY: Otzer haChasidim, 1997).

2. Baal Shem Tov, *Keter Shem Tov* 2:2c; quoted in Shub, *Baal Shem Tov al haTorah*, Torah portion *Shemini* 6.

3. Ramana Maharshi, "Peace Is the Sole Criterion," in *Spiritual Stories as Told by Sri Ramana Maharshi*, 2nd ed., ed. Joan Greenblatt (Tiruvannamalai, India: Sri Ramanasramam, 1986), p. 16.

4. Ya'acov Yosef of Polonnoye, *Toldot Ya'acov Yosef*, Torah portion *Chayei Sarah*, on Genesis 24:1, "'And Abraham was old, advanced in years, and God had blessed Abraham with everything': Meaning to say, that he merited to bind himself to the Supernal Days."

5. *Avot de Rabbi Natan* 6.

6. Marcelle Auclair, *Saint Teresa of Avila*, trans. Kathleen Pond (Petersham, MA: St. Bede's Publications, 1988), p. 72.

7. Chidananda, The Divine Life Society, "Thought for the Day," February 10, 2011, Sivanandaonline.org. (Although Chidananda did not seem to realize he was quoting Saint Teresa.)

8. Sister Gargi (Marie Louise Burke), *A Disciple's Journal: In the Company of Swami Ashokananda* (New York: Kalpa Tree Press, 2003), p. 102.

9. Mirka Knaster, *Living This Life Fully: Stories and Teachings of Munindra* (Boston: Shambhala Publications, 2010), p. 127.

10. Nachman of Breslov, *Otzer haYirah*, *Tefillah*, *Mahadura Batra* 7.

11. Yitzchak Ya'acov Rabinowicz of Biala, *Divrei Binah*, Torah portion *Beha'alotekha*.

12. "M," *The Gospel of Sri Ramakrishna*, 7th ed., trans. Swami Nikhilananda (New York: Ramakrishna-Vedanta Center, 1984), p. 113.

13. Ibid., p. 112.

14. Sister Gargi, *A Disciple's Journal*, p. 60.

15. Efrayim of Sadilkov, *Degel Machaneh Efrayim*, haftorah of Torah portion *Ki Tetzei*, quoted in the name of the Baal Shem Tov.

16. Nachman of Breslov, *Otzer Hayirah*, *Tefillah*, *Mahadura Batra* 2:13.

17. Swami Brahmananda in the name of Ramakrishna, quoted in Prabhavananda, *The Eternal Companion: Brahmananda, His Life and Teachings*, 3rd ed. (Hollywood: Vedanta Press, 1970), p. 213.

18. Natan of Nemirov, *Otzer haYirah*, *Meniyot* 1.

19. Ibid., *Meniyot* 5, 13.

20. Sister Gargi, *A Disciple's Journal*, p. 248.

21. Mordekhai of Chernobyl, *Likutei Torah*, in the *likutim*.

22. Nachum of Chernobyl, *Meor Eynayim*, Torah portion *Vayetzei*, on Genesis 28:11, "and he lighted upon the place."

23. Prabhavananda, *The Eternal Companion*, p. 183.

24. Sri Munagala S. Venkataramiah, *Talks with Sri Ramana Maharshi*, 8th ed. (Tiruvannamalai, India: Sri Ramanasramam, 1989), talk 319.

25. Avraham of Avritch, *Bat Ayin*, Torah portion *Vayiggash*, quoted in Yitzchak Matityahu Luria, *Avakot Rokhalim*, 2nd ed., *Emunah veChesed* 39 (Jerusalem, 1978).

Chapter 4: Stilling the Mind I

1. *Bereshit Rabbah* 14:11.

2. Dov Baer of Mezeritch, *Likutei Amarim*, p. 37, quoted in Nachman Tsherin, *Derekh Chasidim*, *Yirah* 55.

3. Baal Shem Tov, *Tzava'at haRivash* 8b and *Keter Shem Tov* 2:17c, quoted in Shub, *Baal Shem Tov al haTorah*, *Amud haTefillah* 15, 16.

4. Nachman of Breslov, *Likutei Etzot*, *Tefillah* 58; *Likutei Maharan* 65/7.

5. "M," *The Gospel of Sri Ramakrishna*, trans. Nikhilananda, pp. 253–54.

6. Nachman of Breslov, *Likutei Maharan* 205; *Likutei Maharan Tanina* 24.

7. Taken from the description of the life of the first Modzitzer Rebbe, Rabbi Yisrael Taub, http://modzitz.org.

Chapter 5: Stilling the Mind II

1. Baal Shem Tov, *Tzava'at haRivash* 7a, quoted in Shub, *Baal Shem Tov al haTorah*, *Amud haTefillah* 101.

2. Menachem Mendel of Vitebsk, *Pri haAretz*, Torah portions *Tetzavveh*, *Ki Tissa*, *Korach*.

3. Suri Nagamma, *Letters from Sri Ramanasramam*, 4th ed., trans. D. S. Sastri, vol. 2, letter 4 (Tiruvannamalai, India: Sri Ramanasramam, 1995), pp. 241–42.

4. Ramana Maharshi, *Who Am I?*, 14th ed., trans. T. M. P. Mahadevan (Tiruvannamalai, India: Sri Ramanasramam, 1986), pp. 4–5, 7–8.

5. Nachman of Breslov, *Likutei Maharan Tanina* 50.

6. Natan of Nemirov, *Otzer haYirah*, *Machshavot* 3:15.

7. Nachman of Breslov, *Otzer haYirah*, *Machshavot*, *Mahadura Batra* 5.

8. A. Devaraja Mudaliar, *Day by Day with Bhagavan* (Tiruvannamalai, India: Sri Ramanasramam, 1968, 2002), pp. 162–63.

9. Venkataramiah, *Talks with Sri Ramana Maharshi*, talk 354.

10. Arthur Osborne, *Ramana Maharshi and the Path of Self-Knowledge*, 2nd ed. (Tiruvannamalai, India: Sri Ramanasramam, 2002), pp. 7–8.

11. Natan of Nemirov, *Likutei Halakhot, Orech Chayim, Shabbat*, halakhah 7:75, quoted in Natan Tzvi Koenig, *Torat Natan*, Torah portion *Lekh Lekha*, 6th teaching (Bnei Brak, Israel: Torat Natan Foundation, 1998), p. 86.

Chapter 7: Concentration

1. Sivananda, "Concentration," in *Bliss Divine*, 3rd ed. (Shivanandanagar, India: The Divine Life Trust Society, 1974), p. 78.

2. *Keter Shem Tov* 2:4, quoted in Shub, *Baal Shem Tov al HaTorah*, Torah portion *Ekev* 48.

3. Dov Baer of Mezeritch, *Lekutim Yekarim*, p. 3c, quoted in Shub, *Baal Shem Tov al HaTorah*, Torah portion *Ekev* 46.

4. Dov Baer of Mezeritch, *Lekutim Yekarim*, p. 15b, quoted in Shub, *Baal Shem Tov al haTorah*, Torah portion *Ekev* 48.

5. Baal Shem Tov, *Tzava'at haRivash*, p. 7a, quoted in Shub, *Baal Shem Tov al haTorah*, Torah portion *Ekev* 49.

6. Elimelekh of Lizhensk, *Noam Elimelekh*, Torah portion *Balak*, on Numbers 25:7, "And when Phinehas, the son of Eleazar, the son of Aaron the priest, saw it."

7. Sivananda, "Meditation," in *Bliss Divine*, pp. 381–83.

8. Baal Shem Tov, *Tzava'at haRivash* 8b and *Keter Shem Tov* 2:17c, quoted in Shub, *Baal Shem Tov al haTorah, Amud haTefillah* 15, 16.

9. Nachman of Breslov, *Likutei Etzot, Tefillah* 58; *Likutei Maharan* 65/7.

10. "M," *The Gospel of Sri Ramakrishna*, trans. Swami Nikhilananda, p. 744.

11. *Reminiscences of Raja Maharaj*, from the Publication Archives of Sri Ramakrishna Math, Madras, pp. 136–48, quoted in *Swami Brahmananda As We Saw Him*, ed. Atmashraddhananda (Chennai, India: Adhyaksha, 2010), p. 282.

12. Nachman of Breslov, *Likutei Maharan Tanina* 50.

13. Bhajanananda, "Concentration and Meditation," pt. 1, *Prabuddha Bharata Journal*, July 1980, pp. 8–9.

14. Baal Shem Tov, *Keter Shem Tov* 2:17c, quoted in Shub, *Baal Shem Tov al haTorah, Amud haTefillah* 16.

15. Baal Shem Tov, *Tzava'at haRivash* 4b, quoted in Shub, *Baal Shem Tov al haTorah, Amud haTefillah* 25.

16. Baal Shem Tov, *Keter Shem Tov* 2:2d, quoted in Shub, *Baal Shem Tov al haTorah, Amud haTefillah* 88.

17. Elimelekh of Lizhensk, *Noam Elimelekh*, Torah portion *Shelach-Lekha*, on Numbers 15:38, "Speak to the children of Israel and bid them that they make them throughout their generations fringes."

18. "M," *The Gospel of Sri Ramakrishna*, trans. Nikhilananda, p. 256.

19. The Name *Yud Heh Vav Heh* is of a slightly different construction than the precise name written in the Hebrew Bible at the burning bush *Eheyeh* (*Aleph Heh Yud Heh*). We do not know how to pronounce this name, so we call it *Havayah*. *Havayah* is the root verb of both formulations, *Eheyeh* and *Yud Heh Vav Heh*. Its simple meaning is "Being" or "Existence."

Chapter 8: Mantra Recitation

1. Sivananda Radha, *Mantras: Words of Power* (Porthill, ID: Timeless Books, 1980), pp. 4–5.

2. *Shulchan Arukh, Orech Chayim, Hilkhot Kriyat Shema, siman* 61:6.

3. Baal Shem Tov, *Keter Shem Tov* 2:17c, quoted in Shub, *Baal Shem Tov al haTorah, Amud haTefillah* 16.

4. Ramdas, *Swami Ramdas on Himself*, 3rd ed. (Kanhangad, India: Anandashram Publications, 2003), see pp. 26, 68, 74, and 139–40; and Swami Ramdas, *Hints to Aspirants*, 5th ed. (Kanhangad, India: Anandashram Publications, 1998), p. 149.

5. Sivananda Radha, *Mantras: Words of Power*, pp. 106–7.

6. Translation adapted from the *Koren Hebrew Bible* (Jerusalem: Koren Publishers, 1977).

7. Chayim Vital, *Etz Chayim, Heykhal haNekudim, Shaar Shevirat haKelim, shaar* 9.

8. In Hebrew, the letter "b" is interchanged with the letter "v" in Abraham's name.

9. Gikatilla, *Shaarei Orah, shaar* 3, name of *Netzach* and *Netzachim*.

10. Ya'acov Yosef of Polonnoye, *Tzafnat Paneach*, Torah portion *Beshallach*.

11. Gikatilla, *Shaarei Orah, shaar* 1, on *Shekhinah*.

Chapter 9: Contemplation

1. Dov Baer of Mezeritch, *Likutei Amarim*, p. 11, quoted in Nachman Tsherin, *Derekh Chasidim, Daat veChokhmah* 3.

2. Baal Shem Tov, *Tzava'at haRivash* 14b, quoted in *Baal Shem Tov al haTorah*, Torah portion *Va'etchannan* 21.

3. Baal Shem Tov, *Tzava'at haRivash* 4a, quoted in *Baal Shem Tov al haTorah*, Torah portion, *Va'etchannan* 24.

4. Baal Shem Tov, *Tzava'at haRivash* 6b, quoted in *Baal Shem Tov al haTorah*, Torah portion *Va'etchannan* 28.

5. Dov Baer of Mezeritch, *Lekutim Yekarim* 4d, quoted in *Baal Shem Tov al haTorah*, Torah portion *Va'etchannan* 30.

6. Zenkei Shibayama, *A Flower Does Not Talk: Zen Essays*, trans. Sumiko Kudo (Rutland, VT: Charles E. Tuttle, 1970), p. 39.

7. Avraham Yitzchak Kook, *Orot haKodesh*, vol. 1, *Hahofa'ah haNishmatit* 16 (Jerusalem: Mossad Harav Kook, 1968), p. 180.

8. Ibid.

9. Ibid.

10. *Midrash Yalkut Reuvani*, in the name of the *Asarah Ma'amarot*.

11. Ya'acov Yosef of Polonnoye, *Toldot Ya'acov Yosef*, Torah portion *Vayera*, quoted in Shub, *Baal Shem Tov al haTorah*, Torah portion *Bereshit* 179; and Yitzchak of Kamarna, *Otzer haChayim*, Torah portion *Kedoshim*, quoted in n. 154.

12. Avraham Yitzchak Kook, *Orot haKodesh*, vol. 1, *Hahofa'ah haNishmatit* 23–24, pp. 187–88.

13. Ya'acov Yosef of Ostroh, *Reb Yeybei al haTorah*, Psalms, *kepitel* 18, quoted in Nachman Tsherin, *Lashon Chasidim, Daat veChokhmah* 28.

14. Nachman of Breslov, *Otzer haYirah, Tefillah, Mahadura Batra* 9.

15. Kankurgachi Yogodyana, *Ram Chandra Mahatmya*, pp. 17–18, quoted in Chetanananda, *They Lived with God: Life Stories of Some Devotees of Sri Ramakrishna* (St. Louis: Vedanta Society of St. Louis, 1989), p. 81.

16. Avraham Dov of Astrich, *Bat Ayin*, on Sukkot, quoted in Yitzchak Matityahu Luria, *Avkot Rokhalim, Avodah* 149.

17. Reminiscences of T. K. Sunderesa Iyer, quoted in *Arunachala's Ramana: Boundless Ocean of Grace*, vol. 3, comp. Iyer (Tiruvannamalai, India: Sri Ramanasramam 2007), p. 436; David Godman, *The Power of the Presence*, 1st ed., vol. 1 (Tiruvannamalai, India: David Godman, 2000), p. 235.

18. Many of the Baal Shem Tov's instructions for contemplative prayer have been gathered together in a section called *Amud haTefillah*, "The Pillar of Prayer," in the book *Baal Shem Tov al haTorah*. There are also many other teachings on prayer scattered throughout the book. Two places where such teachings can be found are the Torah portions of *Shemini* and *Ekev*.

19. *Midrash Shir haShirim Rabbah* 7.

20. *Midrash Bereshit Rabbah* 56:10.

Chapter 10: Holding the Link

1. Adapted from William C. Chittick, *The Sufi Path of Love: The Spiritual Teachings of Rumi* (Albany: State University of New York Press, 1983), p. 158.

2. *Likutei Ramal*, attributed to Moshe Lev of Sassov, Torah portion *Vayakhel*, quoted in Nachman Tsherin, *Derekh Chasidim*, *Yirah* 467.

3. Godman, *The Power of the Presence*, vol. 1, pp. 250–51.

4. Ya'acov Yosef of Polonnoye, *Toldot Ya'acov Yosef*, Torah portion *Chayei Sarah*.

5. Baal Shem Tov, *Tzava'at haRivash* 9b, quoted in *Baal Shem Tov al haTorah*, Torah portion *Shemini* 1.

6. "M," *The Gospel of Sri Ramakrishna*, trans. Swami Nikhilananda, p. 81.

7. Avraham Tzvi Hirsh haKohen of Apt, *Or Haganuz*, Torah portion *Shemot*, on Exodus 2.25, "And God saw the children of Israel, and God took cognizance of them."

8. The Shelah: Isaiah ben Avraham Ha-Levi Horowitz, *Shenei Luchot haBrit*, mentioned in *Oneg Shabbat*, chap. 2, quoted in Nachman Tsherin, *Derekh Chasidim*, *Yirah* 515.

9. Ya'acov Yosef of Polonnoye, *Ben Porat Yosef*, Torah portion *Vayechi*.

10. "M," *The Gospel of Sri Ramakrishna*, trans. Nikhilananda, p. 82.

11. Ze'ev Wolf of Zhitomir, *Or haMeir*, *Bemidbar*, *Megilat Ruth*.

12. Venkataramiah, *Talks with Sri Ramana Maharshi*, talk 311.

13. Ibid., talk 608.

14. Ze'ev Wolf of Zhitomir, *Or haMeir*, *Bemidbar*, *Megilat Ruth*.

15. Arthur Osborne, *My Life and Quest*, 1st ed. (Tiruvannamalai, India: Sri Ramanasramam, 2001), p. 155.

16. Ya'acov Yosef of Polonnoye, *Ketonet Pasim*, p. 11b, quoted in Shub, *Baal Shem Tov al HaTorah*, Torah portion *Bereshit* 68.

17. Baal Shem Tov, *Tzava'at haRivash* 15b, quoted in Shub, *Baal Shem Tov al HaTorah*, Torah portion *Bereshit* 69.

18. Ya'acov Yosef of Polonnoye, *Toldot Ya'acov Yosef*, Torah portions *Yitro* and *Chukkat*, quoted in Shub, *Baal Shem Tov al haTorah*, Torah portion *Bereshit* 7 and 70.

19. His Eastern and Western Admirers, *Reminiscences of Swami Vivekananda*, p. 384, quoted in Chetanananda, *God Lived with Them: Life Stories of Sixteen Monastic Disciples of Sri Ramakrishna* (St. Louis: Vedanta Society of St. Louis, 1997), p. 60.

20. Ramakrishna, *Sayings of Sri Ramakrishna*, 7th ed. (Mylapore, India: Sri Ramakrishna Math, 2001), saying #283.

21. Mudaliar, *Day by Day with Bhagavan*, p. 245.

22. Joan and Matthew Greenblatt, comp. and designer, *Bhagavan Sri Ramana: A Pictorial Biography*, 2nd ed. (Tiruvannamalai, India: Sri Ramanasramam, 1985), p. 73.

23. Adapted from *The Dhammapada*, trans. Juan Mascaro (London: Penguin Books, 1988), p. 25.

24. Ya'acov Yosef of Polonnoye, *Tzafnat Paneach*, Torah portion *Bo*, quoted in Nachman Tsherin, *Lashon Chasidim, Yirah* 243.

Chapter 11: Merging with Our Spiritual Source

1. For an example in the Kabbalah, see the Sabbath prayer *Lekha Dodi*, which describes this union in several of its verses. For an example in the Hindu teachings, see "M," *The Gospel of Sri Ramakrishna*, p. 500. For an example in the Christian tradition, see Marcelle Auclair, *Saint Teresa of Avila*, pp. 239–41.

2. "M," *The Gospel of Sri Ramakrishna,* trans. Nikhilananda, pp. 499–500.

3. Satchidananda, *The Gospel of Swami Ramdas*, 3rd ed., vol. 1 (Kanhangad, India: Anandashram, 2006), p. 189.

4. Daivratha, "Realization and Bodily Experience," in *Talks with Sri Maharshi*, quoted in *Arunachala's Ramana: Boundless Ocean of Grace*, vol. 1, p. 382.

5. "M," *The Gospel of Sri Ramakrishna*, trans. Nikhilananda, p. 29.

6. Krishnabai, *Guru's Grace (Autobiography of Mother Krishnabai)*, 3rd ed., trans. Ramdas (Kanhangad, India: Anandashram, 1964), pp. 76–77.

7. Shuddhananda, *With the Divine Mother*, 2nd ed., vol. 1 (Kanhangad, India: Anandashram, 2001), pp. 18–19.

8. From *The Mountain Path* (journal of Sri Ramanasramam), April 1981, p. 67.

9. Osborne, *Sri Ramana Maharshi and the Path of Self-Knowledge*, p. 14.

10. "M," *The Gospel of Sri Ramakrishna*, trans. Nikhilananda, p. 831.

11. Ibid., p. 767.

12. Ibid., p. 733.

13. Ibid., p. 231.

14. Ibid., p. 548.

15. Ibid., p. 544.

16. Ibid., p. 119.

17. Adapted from Martin Buber, *Tales of the Hasidim,* vol. 1, trans. Olga Marx (New York: Schocken Books, 1991), p. 49.

18. Krishnabai, *Guru's Grace*, pp. 77–78.

19. "M," *The Gospel of Sri Ramakrishna*, trans. Nikhilananda, p. 674.

20. Moses Maimonides, *The Guide for the Perplexed*, 2nd ed., trans. M. Fried-lander (London: Hebrew Literature Society, 1904), p. 351.

21. Moshe of Dolinah, *Divrei Moshe*, Torah portion *Chayei Sarah*, quoted in Shub, *Baal Shem Tov al ha Torah*, Torah portion *Bereshit* 107 and n. 87.

22. Buber, *Tales of the Hasidim*, vol. 1, p. 107.

23. Adapted from *Little Flowers of Saint Francis*, quoted in Johannes Jorgensen, *Saint Francis of Assisi*, trans. T. O'Conor Sloane (New York: Image Books, 1955), pp. 244–45.

24. Adapted from Buber, *Tales of the Hasidim*, vol. 1, p. 100.

25. Baal Shem Tov, *Tzava'at haRivash*, pp. 1–2.

26. Christopher Isherwood, *Ramakrishna and His Disciples*, 2nd ed. (Hollywood, CA: Vedanta Press, 1980), p. 183.

27. Adapted from Buber, *Tales of the Hasidim*, vol. 1, pp. 239–40.

28. Auclair, *Saint Teresa of Avila*, p. 185.

29. Ibid.

30. Maimonides, *Guide for the Perplexed*, trans. Friedlander, chap. 38.

31. Venkataramiah, *Talks with Sri Ramana Maharshi,* talk 282.

32. Paul Brunton, *The Maharshi and His Message*, 12th ed. (Tiruvannamalai, India: Sri Ramanasramam, 2000), pp. 9–10.

33. Buber, *Tales of the Hasidim*, vol. 1, p. 102.

34. Levi Yitzchak of Berditchev, *Kedushat Levi*, Torah portion *Tetzavveh*, on Exodus 29:9, "And thou shalt consecrate Aaron and his sons."

35. "M," *The Gospel of Sri Ramakrishna*, trans. Nikhilananda, p. 346.

36. Buber, *Tales of the Hasidim*, vol. 1, p. 49.

37. Chetanananda, *How a Shepherd Boy Became a Saint* (St. Louis: Vedanta Society of St. Louis, 1980), pp. 122–23.

38. Godman, *The Power of the Presence*, vol. 2, pp. 245–46. A similar portrayal of the Maharshi's attitude and reaction to pain is also found in the accounts of many other devotees. See, for example, Osborne, *Ramana Maharshi and the Path of Self-Knowledge*, chapter titled "Mahasamadhi."

39. Adapted from Buber, *Tales of the Hasidim*, vol. 1, p. 248.

40. Nachum of Chernobyl, *Meor Eynayim*, tractate *Shabbat*, first teaching: "Amar Reish Lakish."

41. Ya'acov Yosef of Polonnoye, *Toldot Ya'acov Yosef*, Torah portion *Chayei Sarah*.

42. Thomas Merton, *Conjectures of a Guilty Bystander* (New York: Doubleday Books, 1966), pp. 156–58.

43. Buber, *Tales of the Hasidim*, vol. 1, p. 72.

44. Ramdas, *In the Vision of God*, 10th ed., chap. 1: iv "The True Vision," (Kasaragod, India: Anandashram, 2011), pp. 13–14.

Chapter 12: Two Paths to the Supreme

1. "M," *The Gospel of Sri Ramakrishna*, trans. Nikhilananda, p. 859.

2. David Godman, *Be as You Are: The Teachings of Sri Ramana Maharshi* (London: Arkana/Penguin, 1985), p. 201.

Chapter 13: The Dynamics of Inner Experience

1. Gershon Scholem, *Kabbalah*, pt. 3, "Personalities" (Jerusalem: Keter Publishing House, 1974), p. 421.

2. Chayim Vital, *Etz haChayim, Hekhal Nikudim, shaar 2, shaar 9, Shaar Shevirat haKelim*, chap. 2.

3. Chayim Vital, *Etz haChayim, Hekhal Nikudim, shaar 3, shaar 10, Shaar haTikun*, chaps. 3–4; see also Nachman of Breslov, *Likutei Maharan, Torah 65*, and Rebbe Natan of Nemirov, *Likutei Halakhot, Tefillat Aravit, halakhah* 4:13.

4. Chayim Vital, *Etz haChayim, Hekhal 5, Hekhal Ze'eir Anpin, shaar 14, shaar 20, Shaar Partzufim, drush 2*.

5. Moshe Chayim Luzatto, *Clalim Rishonim, clal 23*, and *Petach Shearim, Ze'eir Anpin 11*, brought in the commentary of Michael Bornstein to *Mishnat Chasidim*, the commentary to *Hekhal 7*, chap. 1, mishnah 1, n. 56, "*ibbur, yenika* and *gadlut*."

Chapter 14: The Psychic

1. Chayim Vital, *Shaar haGilgulim*, introduction 22; also Gershon Scholem, "Kabbalot of R. Jacob v R. Isaac haKohen B'ne R. Jacob haKohen," in *Mada'ae HaYahadut*, vol. 2, pp. 254–55, quoted in Bernard Jacob Bamberger, *Fallen Angels* (Philadelphia: Jewish Publication Society, 1952), pp. 174–75.

2. Menachem Mendel of Vitebsk, *Pri haAretz*, quoted in Shub, *Baal Shem Tov al haTorah*, Torah portion *Ekev* 34. Here the Baal Shem Tov compares the process of joining together two pieces of silver to joining with God. To achieve *devekut*, there must be nothing between God and us—no imperfections or impurities—or we will not be able to "stick" to God.

3. Baal Shem Tov, *Tzava'at haRivash*, p. 4a, quoted in Shub, *Baal Shem Tov al haTorah*, Torah portion *Ekev* 51.

4. Dov Baer of Mezeritch, *Lekutim Yekarim*, p. 2a, quoted in Shub, *Baal Shem Tov al haTorah*, Torah portion *Ekev* 53.

5. Chetanananda, *How a Shepherd Boy Became a Saint*, p. 105.

6. Chandrashekhar Chattopadhyay, *Swami Adbhutananda as We Saw Him*, trans. Satswarupananda (Chennai, India: Adhyaksha, 2011), p. 288.

7. Baal Shem Tov, *Tzava'at haRivash*, p. 4a, quoted in Shub, *Baal Shem Tov al haTorah,* Torah portion *Ekev* 51.

8. Teresa of Avila, *Interior Castle*, trans. E. Allison Peers (New York: Image Books, 1989), p. 145.

9. Baal Shem Tov, *Tzava'at haRivash*, p. 4a, and Dov Baer of Mezeritch, *Lekutim Yekarim*, pp. 3c and 15b, quoted in Shub, *Baal Shem Tov al haTorah*, Torah portion *Ekev* 52.

10. Teresa of Avila, *Interior Castle*, p. 145.

11 Ibid , p 141

12. Ibid.

13. Levi Yitzchak of Berditchev, *Kedushat Levi*, Torah portion *Mishpatim*, on Exodus 24:17, "And the appearance of the glory of the Lord was like a devouring fire."

14. Teresa of Avila, *Interior Castle*, p. 142.

15. Ibid., p. 146.

16. The Midrash speaks at length about the revelations given to Jacob through the vision of the ladder. He is said to have seen the future history of the world shown to him. See Louis Ginzberg, *The Legends of the Jews*, vol. 1, trans. Henrietta Szold (Philadelphia: Jewish Publication Society, 1937, 1968), pp. 350–52. See also *Zohar* 1:149b–150b, which discusses Jacob's ladder and the prophecies and wisdom he saw and learned from it; *Tikunei Zohar* 43, which speaks of the ladder as a symbolic teaching given to Jacob about the ascent through the four worlds; and the writings of the Shelah, Rabbi Isaiah Horowitz, on Jacob's ladder, in his monumental work *Shenei Luchot haBrit.*

17. See Pere Silverio of St. Teresa, shorter edition of *The Works of Saint Teresa*, Saint Teresa of Avila, *The Foundations*, chap. vii, quoted in Marcelle Auclair, *Saint Teresa of Avila*, pp. 218–20. Saint Teresa uses the term "melancholia" to describe this condition. Marcelle Auclair refers to it as "neurasthenia." I am looking at it from a completely spiritual perspective as behavior which results from a problem with the psychic.

Chapter 15: Individual versus Group Practice

1. Akshaya-chaitanya, *Reminiscences of Swami Brahmananda*, trans. Bhaskarananda (Mylapore, India: Sri Ramakrishna Math, 2006), pp. 8–9.

2. Tessa Bielecki, *Ecstasy and Common Sense: Life of Saint Teresa* (Boston: Shambhala, 1996), p. 17.

3. Efrayim of Sadilkov, *Degel Machanei Efrayim*, in the name of the Baal Shem, Torah portion *Yitro*, on Exodus 20:14, "and all the people saw the voices."

4. "M," *The Gospel of Sri Ramakrishna*, trans. Swami Nikhilananda, pp. 400–401.

5. Nachman of Breslov, *Likutei Etzot, Hitchazkut* 3.

6. Elimelekh of Lizhensk, *Tzeitel Katan*, quoted in Shlomo Eliezer Margoliut, *Erkhai Kodesh*, Rav veChaver, pp. 126–27.

7. Chetanananda, trans., *A Guide to Spiritual Life: The Spiritual Teachings of Swami Brahmananda*, p. 94.

8. Chidananda, *An Instrument of Thy Peace*, p. 438.

9. Uri Shraga Fievel of Krisnapoli, *Or HaChokhmah*, Torah portion *Beha'alotkha*, quoted in Nachman Tsherin, *Derekh Chasidim, Shalom* and *Ahavat Rayim* 2.

Chapter 16: Individual and Collective Evolution

1. The *Dighanikaya*, 2:154/*sutta* 16.

2. Ya'acov Yosef of Polonnoye, *Toldot Ya'acov Yosef,* Torah portion *Shemini*, quoted in Shub, *Baal Shem Tov al haTorah*, Torah portion *Shemot* 5.

3. Yehudah Aryeh Leib Alter of Ger, *Sefat Emet*, end of Torah portion *Shemot*, quoted in Shub, *Baal Shem Tov al haTorah*, Torah portion *Shemot*, n. 4.

4. Godman, *The Power of the Presence*, vol. 3, p. 73.

5. "M," *The Gospel of Sri Ramakrishna*, trans. Nikhilananda, p. 142.

6. *Letters of Swami Vivekananda* (Calcutta: Advaita Ashram, 1946), p. 103, quoted in Chetanananda, *How to Live with God: In the Company of Rama-krishna* (St. Louis: Vedanta Society of St. Louis, 2008), p. 517.

7. Kalonymus Kalman of Krakow, *Maor vaShemesh*, first day of Sukkot, quoted in the name of Rebbe Mordekhai of Nesvizh, the Lechovitcher Rebbe.

8. Menachem Mendel of Kotsk, *Amud haEmet*: sichot, p. 94

9. Godman, *The Power of the Presence*, vol. 1, p. 231.

10. Rebbe Gedalyahu Rabinowitz of Linitz, *Tesuot Chen*, Torah portion *Va'era*, quoted in Shub, *Baal Shem Tov al haTorah*, Torah portion *Bereshit* 166.

11. Romain Rolland, *The Life of Ramakrishna*, pp. 250–51, quoted in Chetanan-anda, *God Lived with Them*, pp. 19–20.

12. "M," *The Gospel of Sri Ramakrishna*, trans. Nikhilananda, p. 934.

13. For example, in the *Shaar haGilgulim*, introduction 38, Chayim Vital tells the story of an outing with the Ari to the spot where the Idra Rabba was taught by Shimon bar Yochai. The Ari went to a spot where there was a large rock with

two deep clefts in it. The Ari sat down in a cleft on the north side of the rock where he said Rabbi Shimon sat, and he told Chayim to sit in the cleft on the south side, where Rabbi Abba, who wrote down the *Zohar*, sat. The Ari then proceeded to tell Chayim that Rabbi Abba was the *shoresh*, spiritual source, of Chayim's *nefesh*, or soul. Though the Ari does not expressly declare himself to be a spark of the soul of Rabbi Shimon, it is quite self-evident from his choice of place to sit.

14. *Baal Shem Tov al haTorah*, introduction, *Kuntris Meirat Eynayim* 4.

15. Ya'acov Yosef of Polonnoye, *Toldot Ya'acov Yosef*, Torah portion *Terumah*, on Exodus 25:8, "Build Me a sanctuary and I will dwell in your midst."

Bible Study / Midrash

Passing Life's Tests: Spiritual Reflections on the Trial of Abraham, the Binding of Isaac   *By Rabbi Bradley Shavit Artson, DHL*
Invites us to use this powerful tale as a tool for our own soul wrestling, to confront our existential sacrifices and enable us to face—and surmount—life's tests.
6 x 9, 176 pp, Quality PB, 978-1-58023-631-7 **$18.99**

The Messiah and the Jews: Three Thousand Years of Tradition, Belief and Hope   *By Rabbi Elaine Rose Glickman; Foreword by Rabbi Neil Gillman, PhD; Preface by Rabbi Judith Z. Abrams, PhD*
Explores and explains an astonishing range of primary and secondary sources, infusing them with new meaning for the modern reader.
6 x 9, 192 pp, Quality PB, 978-1-58023-690-4 **$16.99**

Speaking Torah: Spiritual Teachings from around the Maggid's Table—in Two Volumes   *By Arthur Green, with Ebn Leader, Ariel Evan Mayse and Or N. Rose*
The most powerful Hasidic teachings made accessible—from some of the world's preeminent authorities on Jewish thought and spirituality.
Volume 1—6 x 9, 512 pp, Hardcover, 978-1-58023-668-3 **$34.99**
Volume 2—6 x 9, 448 pp, Hardcover, 978-1-58023-694-2 **$34.99**

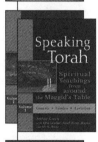

Masking and Unmasking Ourselves: Interpreting Biblical Texts on Clothing & Identity   *By Dr. Norman J. Cohen*
Presents ten Bible stories that involve clothing in an essential way, as a means of learning about the text, its characters and their interactions.
6 x 9, 224 pp, HC, 978-1-58023-461-0 **$24.99**

The Genesis of Leadership: What the Bible Teaches Us about Vision, Values and Leading Change   *By Rabbi Nathan Laufer; Foreword by Senator Joseph I. Lieberman*
6 x 9, 288 pp, Quality PB, 978-1-58023-352-1 **$18.99**

Hineini in Our Lives: Learning How to Respond to Others through 14 Biblical Texts and Personal Stories   *By Rabbi Norman J. Cohen, PhD*
6 x 9, 240 pp, Quality PB, 978-1-58023-274-6 **$18.99**

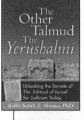

The Modern Men's Torah Commentary: New Insights from Jewish Men on the 54 Weekly Torah Portions   *Edited by Rabbi Jeffrey K. Salkin*
6 x 9, 368 pp, HC, 978-1-58023-395-8 **$24.99**

Moses and the Journey to Leadership: Timeless Lessons of Effective Management from the Bible and Today's Leaders   *By Rabbi Norman J. Cohen, PhD*
6 x 9, 240 pp, Quality PB, 978-1-58023-351-4 **$18.99**; HC, 978-1-58023-227-2 **$21.99**

The Other Talmud—The *Yerushalmi:* Unlocking the Secrets of *The Talmud of Israel* for Judaism Today   *By Rabbi Judith Z. Abrams, PhD*
6 x 9, 256 pp, HC, 978-1-58023-463-4 **$24.99**

Sage Tales: Wisdom and Wonder from the Rabbis of the Talmud
By Rabbi Burton L. Visotzky
6 x 9, 256 pp, Quality PB, 978-1-58023-791-8 **$19.99**; HC, 978-1-58023-456-6 **$24.99**

The Torah Revolution: Fourteen Truths That Changed the World
By Rabbi Reuven Hammer, PhD   6 x 9, 240 pp, HC, 978-1-58023-457-3 **$24.99**

The Wisdom of Judaism: An Introduction to the Values of the Talmud
By Rabbi Dov Peretz Elkins   6 x 9, 192 pp, Quality PB, 978-1-58023-327-9 **$16.99**

Or phone, fax, mail or email to: **JEWISH LIGHTS** Publishing
Sunset Farm Offices, Route 4 • P.O. Box 237 • Woodstock, Vermont 05091
Tel: (802) 457-4000 • Fax: (802) 457-4004 • www.jewishlights.com
Credit card orders: (800) 962-4544 (8:30AM–5:30PM EST Monday–Friday)
Generous discounts on quantity orders. SATISFACTION GUARANTEED. Prices subject to change.

Social Justice

Where Justice Dwells
A Hands-On Guide to Doing Social Justice in Your Jewish Community
By Rabbi Jill Jacobs; Foreword by Rabbi David Saperstein
Provides ways to envision and act on your own ideals of social justice.
7 x 9, 288 pp, Quality PB Original, 978-1-58023-453-5 **$24.99**

There Shall Be No Needy
Pursuing Social Justice through Jewish Law and Tradition
By Rabbi Jill Jacobs; Foreword by Rabbi Elliot N. Dorff, PhD; Preface by Simon Greer
Confronts the most pressing issues of twenty-first-century America from a deeply Jewish perspective. 6 x 9, 288 pp, Quality PB, 978-1-58023-425-2 **$16.99**
There Shall Be No Needy Teacher's Guide 8½ x 11, 56 pp, PB, 978-1-58023-429-0 **$8.99**

Conscience
The Duty to Obey and the Duty to Disobey
By Rabbi Harold M. Schulweis
Examines the idea of conscience and the role conscience plays in our relationships to government, law, ethics, religion, human nature, God—and to each other.
6 x 9, 160 pp, Quality PB, 978-1-58023-419-1 **$16.99**; HC, 978-1-58023-375-0 **$19.99**

Judaism and Justice
The Jewish Passion to Repair the World
By Rabbi Sidney Schwarz; Foreword by Ruth Messinger
Explores the relationship between Judaism, social justice and the Jewish identity of American Jews. 6 x 9, 352 pp, Quality PB, 978-1-58023-353-8 **$19.99**

Spirituality / Women's Interest

New Jewish Feminism
Probing the Past, Forging the Future
Edited by Rabbi Elyse Goldstein; Foreword by Anita Diamant
Looks at the growth and accomplishments of Jewish feminism and what they mean for Jewish women today and tomorrow.
6 x 9, 480 pp, HC, 978-1-58023-359-0 **$24.99**

The Divine Feminine in Biblical Wisdom Literature
Selections Annotated & Explained
Translation & Annotation by Rabbi Rami Shapiro
5½ x 8½, 240 pp, Quality PB, 978-1-59473-109-9 **$16.99***

The Quotable Jewish Woman
Wisdom, Inspiration & Humor from the Mind & Heart
Edited by Elaine Bernstein Partnow
6 x 9, 496 pp, Quality PB, 978-1-58023-236-4 **$19.99**

The Women's Haftarah Commentary
New Insights from Women Rabbis on the 54 Weekly Haftarah Portions, the 5 Megillot & Special Shabbatot
Edited by Rabbi Elyse Goldstein
Illuminates the historical significance of female portrayals in the Haftarah and the Five Megillot. 6 x 9, 560 pp, Quality PB, 978-1-58023-371-2 **$19.99**

The Women's Torah Commentary
New Insights from Women Rabbis on the 54 Weekly Torah Portions
Edited by Rabbi Elyse Goldstein
Over fifty women rabbis offer inspiring insights on the Torah, in a week-by-week format.
6 x 9, 496 pp, Quality PB, 978-1-58023-370-5 **$19.99**; HC, 978-1-58023-076-6 **$34.95**

*A book from SkyLight Paths, Jewish Lights' sister imprint

Theology / Philosophy / The Way Into... Series

The Way Into... series offers an accessible and highly usable "guided tour" of the Jewish faith, people, history and beliefs—in total, an introduction to Judaism that will enable you to understand and interact with the sacred texts of the Jewish tradition. Each volume is written by a leading contemporary scholar and teacher, and explores one key aspect of Judaism. The Way Into... series enables all readers to achieve a real sense of Jewish cultural literacy through guided study.

The Way Into Encountering God in Judaism
By Rabbi Neil Gillman, PhD
For everyone who wants to understand how Jews have encountered God throughout history and today.
6 x 9, 240 pp, Quality PB, 978-1-58023-199-2 **$18.99**; HC, 978-1-58023-025-4 **$21.95**
Also Available: **The Jewish Approach to God:** A Brief Introduction for Christians
By Rabbi Neil Gillman, PhD
5½ x 8½, 192 pp, Quality PB, 978-1-58023-190-9 **$16.95**

The Way Into Jewish Mystical Tradition
By Rabbi Lawrence Kushner
Allows readers to interact directly with the sacred mystical texts of the Jewish tradition. An accessible introduction to the concepts of Jewish mysticism, their religious and spiritual significance, and how they relate to life today.
6 x 9, 224 pp, Quality PB, 978-1-58023-200-5 **$18.99**

The Way Into Jewish Prayer
By Rabbi Lawrence A. Hoffman, PhD
Opens the door to 3,000 years of Jewish prayer, making anyone feel at home in the Jewish way of communicating with God.
6 x 9, 208 pp, Quality PB, 978-1-58023-201-2 **$18.99**

The Way Into Jewish Prayer Teacher's Guide
By Rabbi Jennifer Ossakow Goldsmith
8½ x 11, 42 pp, PB, 978-1-58023-345-3 **$8.99**
Download a free copy at www.jewishlights.com.

The Way Into Judaism and the Environment
By Jeremy Benstein, PhD
Explores the ways in which Judaism contributes to contemporary social-environmental issues, the extent to which Judaism is part of the problem and how it can be part of the solution.
6 x 9, 288 pp, Quality PB, 978-1-58023-368-2 **$18.99**; HC, 978-1-58023-268-5 **$24.99**

The Way Into Tikkun Olam (Repairing the World)
By Rabbi Elliot N. Dorff, PhD
An accessible introduction to the Jewish concept of the individual's responsibility to care for others and repair the world.
6 x 9, 304 pp, Quality PB, 978-1-58023-328-6 **$18.99**

The Way Into Torah
By Rabbi Norman J. Cohen, PhD
Helps guide you in the exploration of the origins and development of Torah, explains why it should be studied and how to do it.
6 x 9, 176 pp, Quality PB, 978-1-58023-198-5 **$16.99**

The Way Into the Varieties of Jewishness
By Sylvia Barack Fishman, PhD
Explores the religious and historical understanding of what it has meant to be Jewish from ancient times to the present controversy over "Who is a Jew?"
6 x 9, 288 pp, Quality PB, 978-1-58023-367-5 **$18.99**; HC, 978-1-58023-030-8 **$24.99**

Theology / Philosophy

Believing and Its Tensions: A Personal Conversation about God, Torah, Suffering and Death in Jewish Thought
By Rabbi Neil Gillman, PhD
Explores the changing nature of belief and the complexities of reconciling the intellectual, emotional and moral questions of Gillman's own searching mind and soul.
5½ x 8½, 144 pp, HC, 978-1-58023-669-0 **$19.99**

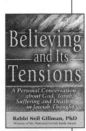

God of Becoming and Relationship: The Dynamic Nature of Process Theology   *By Rabbi Bradley Shavit Artson, DHL*
Explains how Process Theology breaks us free from the strictures of ancient Greek and medieval European philosophy, allowing us to see all creation as related patterns of energy through which we connect to everything.
6 x 9, 208 pp, HC, 978-1-58023-713-0 **$24.99**

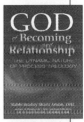

The Other Talmud—The Yerushalmi: Unlocking the Secrets of The Talmud of Israel for Judaism Today   *By Rabbi Judith Z. Abrams, PhD*
A fascinating—and stimulating—look at "the other Talmud" and the possibilities for Jewish life reflected there.   6 x 9, 256 pp, HC, 978-1-58023-463-4 **$24.99**

The Way of Man: According to Hasidic Teaching
By Martin Buber; New Translation and Introduction by Rabbi Bernard H. Mehlman and Dr. Gabriel E. Padawer; Foreword by Paul Mendes-Flohr
An accessible and engaging new translation of Buber's classic work—*available as an eBook only.*   eBook, 978-1-58023-601-0 Digital List Price **$14.99**

The Death of Death: Resurrection and Immortality in Jewish Thought
By Rabbi Neil Gillman, PhD   6 x 9, 336 pp, Quality PB, 978-1-58023-081-0 **$19.99**

Doing Jewish Theology: God, Torah & Israel in Modern Judaism   *By Rabbi Neil Gillman, PhD*
6 x 9, 304 pp, Quality PB, 978-1-58023-439-9 **$18.99**; HC, 978-1-58023-322-4 **$24.99**

From Defender to Critic: The Search for a New Jewish Self
By Dr. David Hartman   6 x 9, 336 pp, HC, 978-1-58023-515-0 **$35.00**

The God Who Hates Lies: Confronting & Rethinking Jewish Tradition
By Dr. David Hartman with Charlie Buckholtz   6 x 9, 200 pp, Quality PB, 978-1-58023-790-1 **$19.99**

A Heart of Many Rooms: Celebrating the Many Voices within Judaism
By Dr. David Hartman   6 x 9, 352 pp, Quality PB, 978-1-58023-156-5 **$19.95**

Jewish Theology in Our Time: A New Generation Explores the Foundations and Future of Jewish Belief   *Edited by Rabbi Elliot J. Cosgrove, PhD; Foreword by Rabbi David J. Wolpe; Preface by Rabbi Carole B. Balin, PhD*   6 x 9, 240 pp, Quality PB, 978-1-58023-630-0 **$19.99**; HC, 978-1-58023-413-9 **$24.99**

Maimonides—Essential Teachings on Jewish Faith & Ethics: The Book of Knowledge & the Thirteen Principles of Faith—Annotated & Explained
Translation and Annotation by Rabbi Marc D. Angel, PhD
5½ x 8½, 224 pp, Quality PB Original, 978-1-59473-311-6 **$18.99***

Maimonides, Spinoza and Us: Toward an Intellectually Vibrant Judaism
By Rabbi Marc D. Angel, PhD   6 x 9, 224 pp, HC, 978-1-58023-411-5 **$24.99**

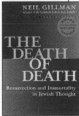

Our Religious Brains: What Cognitive Science Reveals about Belief, Morality, Community and Our Relationship with God
By Rabbi Ralph D. Mecklenburger; Foreword by Dr. Howard Kelfer; Preface by Dr. Neil Gillman
6 x 9, 224 pp, HC, 978-1-58023-508-2 **$24.99**

Your Word Is Fire: The Hasidic Masters on Contemplative Prayer
Edited and translated by Rabbi Arthur Green, PhD, and Barry W. Holtz
6 x 9, 160 pp, Quality PB, 978-1-879045-25-5 **$16.99**

I Am Jewish
Personal Reflections Inspired by the Last Words of Daniel Pearl
Almost 150 Jews—both famous and not—from all walks of life, from all around the world, write about many aspects of their Judaism.
Edited by Judea and Ruth Pearl   6 x 9, 304 pp, Deluxe PB w/ flaps, 978-1-58023-259-3 **$19.99**
Download a free copy of the *I Am Jewish Teacher's Guide* at www.jewishlights.com.

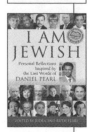

*A book from SkyLight Paths, Jewish Lights' sister imprint

Spirituality / Prayer

Davening: A Guide to Meaningful Jewish Prayer
By Rabbi Zalman Schachter-Shalomi with Joel Segel; Foreword by Rabbi Lawrence Kushner
A fresh approach to prayer for all who wish to appreciate the power of prayer's poetry, song and ritual, and to join the age-old conversation that Jews have had with God. 6 x 9, 240 pp, Quality PB, 978-1-58023-627-0 **$18.99**

Jewish Men Pray: Words of Yearning, Praise, Petition, Gratitude and Wonder from Traditional and Contemporary Sources
Edited by Rabbi Kerry M. Olitzky and Stuart M. Matlins; Foreword by Rabbi Bradley Shavit Artson, DHL
A celebration of Jewish men's voices in prayer—to strengthen, heal, comfort, and inspire—from the ancient world up to our own day.
5 x 7¼, 400 pp, HC, 978-1-58023-628-7 **$19.99**

Making Prayer Real: Leading Jewish Spiritual Voices on Why Prayer Is Difficult and What to Do about It *By Rabbi Mike Comins* 6 x 9, 320 pp, Quality PB, 978-1-58023-417-7 **$18.99**

Witnesses to the One: The Spiritual History of the *Sh'ma*
By Rabbi Joseph B. Meszler; Foreword by Rabbi Elyse Goldstein
6 x 9, 176 pp, Quality PB, 978-1-58023-400-9 **$16.99**; HC, 978-1-58023-309-5 **$19.99**

My People's Prayer Book Series: Traditional Prayers, Modern Commentaries *Edited by Rabbi Lawrence A. Hoffman, PhD*
Provides diverse and exciting commentary to the traditional liturgy. Will help you find new wisdom in Jewish prayer, and bring liturgy into your life. Each book includes Hebrew text, modern translations and commentaries from all perspectives of the Jewish world.

Vol. 1—The *Sh'ma* and Its Blessings
    7 x 10, 168 pp, HC, 978-1-879045-79-8 **$29.99**
Vol. 2—The *Amidah* 7 x 10, 240 pp, HC, 978-1-879045-80-4 **$29.99**
Vol. 3—*P'sukei D'zimrah* (Morning Psalms)
    7 x 10, 240 pp, HC, 978-1-879045-81-1 **$29.99**
Vol. 4—*Seder K'riat Hatorah* (The Torah Service)
    7 x 10, 264 pp, HC, 978-1-879045-82-8 **$29.99**
Vol. 5—*Birkhot Hashachar* (Morning Blessings)
    7 x 10, 240 pp, HC, 978-1-879045-83-5 **$24.95**
Vol. 6—*Tachanun* and Concluding Prayers
    7 x 10, 240 pp, HC, 978-1-879045-84-2 **$24.95**
Vol. 7—Shabbat at Home 7 x 10, 240 pp, HC, 978-1-879045-85-9 **$29.99**
Vol. 8—*Kabbalat Shabbat* (Welcoming Shabbat in the Synagogue)
    7 x 10, 240 pp, HC, 978-1-58023-121-3 **$24.99**
Vol. 9—Welcoming the Night: *Minchah* and *Ma'ariv* (Afternoon and
    Evening Prayer) 7 x 10, 272 pp, HC, 978-1-58023-262-3 **$24.99**
Vol. 10—Shabbat Morning: *Shacharit* and *Musaf* (Morning and
    Additional Services) 7 x 10, 240 pp, HC, 978-1-58023-240-1 **$29.99**

Spirituality / Lawrence Kushner

I'm God; You're Not: Observations on Organized Religion & Other Disguises of the Ego
6 x 9, 256 pp, Quality PB, 978-1-58023-513-6 **$18.99**; HC, 978-1-58023-441-2 **$21.99**

The Book of Letters: A Mystical Hebrew Alphabet
Popular HC Edition, 6 x 9, 80 pp, 2-color text, 978-1-879045-00-2 **$24.95**
Collector's Limited Edition, 9 x 12, 80 pp, gold-foil-embossed pages, w/ limited-edition silkscreened print, 978-1-879045-04-0 **$349.00**

The Book of Miracles: A Young Person's Guide to Jewish Spiritual Awareness
6 x 9, 96 pp, 2-color illus., HC, 978-1-879045-78-1 **$16.95** *For ages 9–13*

God Was in This Place & I, i Did Not Know: Finding Self, Spirituality and
Ultimate Meaning 6 x 9, 192 pp, Quality PB, 978-1-879045-33-0 **$16.95**

Honey from the Rock: An Introduction to Jewish Mysticism
6 x 9, 176 pp, Quality PB, 978-1-58023-073-5 **$18.99**

Invisible Lines of Connection: Sacred Stories of the Ordinary
5½ x 8½, 160 pp, Quality PB, 978-1-879045-98-9 **$16.99**

The Way Into Jewish Mystical Tradition
6 x 9, 224 pp, Quality PB, 978-1-58023-200-5 **$18.99**; HC, 978-1-58023-029-2 **$21.95**

Spirituality

Amazing Chesed: Living a Grace-Filled Judaism
By Rabbi Rami Shapiro Drawing from ancient and contemporary, traditional and non-traditional Jewish wisdom, reclaims the idea of grace in Judaism.
6 x 9, 176 pp, Quality PB, 978-1-58023-624-9 **$16.99**

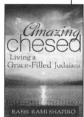

Jewish with Feeling: A Guide to Meaningful Jewish Practice
By Rabbi Zalman Schachter-Shalomi with Joel Segel
Takes off from basic questions like "Why be Jewish?" and whether the word God still speaks to us today and lays out a vision for a whole-person Judaism.
5½ x 8½, 288 pp, Quality PB, 978-1-58023-691-1 **$19.99**

Perennial Wisdom for the Spiritually Independent: Sacred Teachings— Annotated & Explained *Annotation by Rami Shapiro; Foreword by Richard Rohr*
Weaves sacred texts and teachings from the world's major religions into a coherent exploration of the five core questions at the heart of every religion's search.
5½ x 8½, 336 pp, Quality PB Original, 978-1-59473-515-8 **$16.99**

Aleph-Bet Yoga: Embodying the Hebrew Letters for Physical and Spiritual Well-Being
By Steven A. Rapp; Foreword by Tamar Frankiel, PhD, and Judy Greenfeld; Preface by Hart Lazer
7 x 10, 128 pp, b/w photos, Quality PB, Lay-flat binding, 978-1-58023-162-6 **$16.95**

A Book of Life: Embracing Judaism as a Spiritual Practice
By Rabbi Michael Strassfeld 6 x 9, 544 pp, Quality PB, 978-1-58023-247-0 **$24.99**

Bringing the Psalms to Life: How to Understand and Use the Book of Psalms
By Rabbi Daniel F. Polish, PhD 6 x 9, 208 pp, Quality PB, 978-1-58023-157-2 **$18.99**

Does the Soul Survive? A Jewish Journey to Belief in Afterlife, Past Lives & Living with Purpose *By Rabbi Elie Kaplan Spitz; Foreword by Brian L. Weiss, MD*
6 x 9, 288 pp, Quality PB, 978-1-58023-165-7 **$18.99**

Entering the Temple of Dreams: Jewish Prayers, Movements and Meditations for the End of the Day *By Tamar Frankiel, PhD, and Judy Greenfeld*
7 x 10, 192 pp, illus., Quality PB, 978-1-58023-079-7 **$16.95**

First Steps to a New Jewish Spirit: Reb Zalman's Guide to Recapturing the Intimacy & Ecstasy in Your Relationship with God *By Rabbi Zalman M. Schachter-Shalomi with Donald Gropman* 6 x 9, 144 pp, Quality PB, 978-1-58023-182-4 **$16.95**

Foundations of Sephardic Spirituality: The Inner Life of Jews of the Ottoman Empire
By Rabbi Marc D. Angel, PhD 6 x 9, 224 pp, Quality PB, 978-1-58023-341-5 **$18.99**

God & the Big Bang: Discovering Harmony between Science & Spirituality
By Dr. Daniel C. Matt 6 x 9, 216 pp, Quality PB, 978-1-879045-89-7 **$18.99**

God in Our Relationships: Spirituality between People from the Teachings of Martin Buber *By Rabbi Dennis S. Ross* 5½ x 8½, 160 pp, Quality PB, 978-1-58023-147-3 **$16.95**

The Jewish Lights Spirituality Handbook: A Guide to Understanding, Exploring & Living a Spiritual Life *Edited by Stuart M. Matlins*
6 x 9, 456 pp, Quality PB, 978-1-58023-093-3 **$19.99**

Judaism, Physics and God: Searching for Sacred Metaphors in a Post-Einstein World
By Rabbi David W. Nelson 6 x 9, 352 pp, Quality PB, inc. reader's discussion guide,
978-1-58023-306-4 **$18.99**; HC, 352 pp, 978-1-58023-252-4 **$24.99**

Meaning & Mitzvah: Daily Practices for Reclaiming Judaism through Prayer, God, Torah, Hebrew, Mitzvot and Peoplehood *By Rabbi Goldie Milgram*
7 x 9, 336 pp, Quality PB, 978-1-58023-256-2 **$19.99**

Repentance: The Meaning and Practice of Teshuvah
By Dr. Louis E. Newman; Foreword by Rabbi Harold M. Schulweis; Preface by Rabbi Karyn D. Kedar
6 x 9, 256 pp, HC, 978-1-58023-426-9 **$24.99** Quality PB, 978-1-58023-718-5 **$18.99**

The Sabbath Soul: Mystical Reflections on the Transformative Power of Holy Time
Selection, Translation and Commentary by Eitan Fishbane, PhD
6 x 9, 208 pp, Quality PB, 978-1-58023-459-7 **$18.99**

Tanya, the Masterpiece of Hasidic Wisdom: Selections Annotated & Explained
Translation & Annotation by Rabbi Rami Shapiro; Foreword by Rabbi Zalman M. Schachter-Shalomi
5½ x 8½, 240 pp, Quality PB, 978-1-59473-275-1 **$18.99**

These Are the Words, 2nd Edition: A Vocabulary of Jewish Spiritual Life
By Rabbi Arthur Green, PhD 6 x 9, 320 pp, Quality PB, 978-1-58023-494-8 **$19.99**

Inspiration

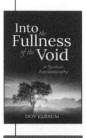

Into the Fullness of the Void: A Spiritual Autobiography *By Dov Elbaum*
The spiritual autobiography of one of Israel's leading cultural figures that provides insights and guidance for all of us. 6 x 9, 304 pp, Quality PB Original, 978-1-58023-715-4 **$18.99**

Saying No and Letting Go: Jewish Wisdom on Making Room for What Matters Most
By Rabbi Edwin Goldberg, DHL; Foreword by Rabbi Naomi Levy
Taps into timeless Jewish wisdom that teaches how to "hold on tightly" to the things that matter most while learning to "let go lightly" of the demands and worries that do not ultimately matter. 6 x 9, 192 pp, Quality PB, 978-1-58023-670-6 **$16.99**

The Bridge to Forgiveness: Stories and Prayers for Finding God and Restoring Wholeness *By Rabbi Karyn D. Kedar* 6 x 9, 176 pp, Quality PB, 978-1-58023-451-1 **$16.99**

The Empty Chair: Finding Hope and Joy—Timeless Wisdom from a Hasidic Master, Rebbe Nachman of Breslov *Adapted by Moshe Mykoff and the Breslov Research Institute*
4 x 6, 128 pp, Deluxe PB w/ flaps, 978-1-879045-67-5 **$9.99**

A Formula for Proper Living: Practical Lessons from Life and Torah
By Rabbi Abraham J. Twerski, MD 6 x 9, 144 pp, HC, 978-1-58023-402-3 **$19.99**

The Gentle Weapon: Prayers for Everyday and Not-So-Everyday Moments—Timeless Wisdom from the Teachings of the Hasidic Master, Rebbe Nachman of Breslov
Adapted by Moshe Mykoff and S. C. Mizrahi, together with the Breslov Research Institute
4 x 6, 144 pp, Deluxe PB w/ flaps, 978-1-58023-022-3 **$9.99**

The God Upgrade: Finding Your 21st-Century Spirituality in Judaism's 5,000-Year-Old Tradition *By Rabbi Jamie Korngold; Foreword by Rabbi Harold M. Schulweis*
6 x 9, 176 pp, Quality PB, 978-1-58023-443-6 **$15.99**

God Whispers: Stories of the Soul, Lessons of the Heart *By Rabbi Karyn D. Kedar*
6 x 9, 176 pp, Quality PB, 978-1-58023-088-9 **$16.99**

God's To-Do List: 103 Ways to Be an Angel and Do God's Work on Earth
By Dr. Ron Wolfson 6 x 9, 144 pp, Quality PB, 978-1-58023-301-9 **$16.99**

Happiness and the Human Spirit: The Spirituality of Becoming the Best You Can Be
By Rabbi Abraham J. Twerski, MD
6 x 9, 176 pp, Quality PB, 978-1-58023-404-7 **$16.99**; HC, 978-1-58023-343-9 **$19.99**

Life's Daily Blessings: Inspiring Reflections on Gratitude and Joy for Every Day, Based on Jewish Wisdom *By Rabbi Kerry M. Olitzky* 4½ x 6½, 368 pp, Quality PB, 978-1-58023-396-5 **$16.99**

The Magic of Hebrew Chant: Healing the Spirit, Transforming the Mind, Deepening Love *By Rabbi Shefa Gold; Foreword by Sylvia Boorstein*
6 x 9, 352 pp, Quality PB, 978-1-58023-671-3 **$24.99**

Restful Reflections: Nighttime Inspiration to Calm the Soul, Based on Jewish Wisdom
By Rabbi Kerry M. Olitzky and Rabbi Lori Forman-Jacobi 4½ x 6½, 448 pp, Quality PB, 978-1-58023-091-9 **$16.99**

Sacred Intentions: Morning Inspiration to Strengthen the Spirit, Based on Jewish Wisdom
By Rabbi Kerry M. Olitzky and Rabbi Lori Forman-Jacobi 4½ x 6½, 448 pp, Quality PB, 978-1-58023-061-2 **$16.99**

The Seven Questions You're Asked in Heaven: Reviewing and Renewing Your Life on Earth *By Dr. Ron Wolfson* 6 x 9, 176 pp, Quality PB, 978-1-58023-407-8 **$16.99**

Kabbalah / Mysticism

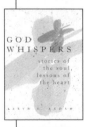

Ehyeh: A Kabbalah for Tomorrow
By Rabbi Arthur Green, PhD 6 x 9, 224 pp, Quality PB, 978-1-58023-213-5 **$18.99**

The Gift of Kabbalah: Discovering the Secrets of Heaven, Renewing Your Life on Earth
By Tamar Frankiel, PhD 6 x 9, 256 pp, Quality PB, 978-1-58023-141-1 **$18.99**

Jewish Mysticism and the Spiritual Life: Classical Texts, Contemporary Reflections *Edited by Dr. Lawrence Fine, Dr. Eitan Fishbane and Rabbi Or N. Rose*
6 x 9, 256 pp, HC, 978-1-58023-434-4 **$24.99**; Quality PB, 978-1-58023-719-2 **$18.99**

Seek My Face: A Jewish Mystical Theology *By Rabbi Arthur Green, PhD*
6 x 9, 304 pp, Quality PB, 978-1-58023-130-5 **$19.95**

Zohar: Annotated & Explained *Translation & Annotation by Dr. Daniel C. Matt; Foreword by Andrew Harvey* 5½ x 8½, 176 pp, Quality PB, 978-1-893361-51-5 **$18.99**
(A book from SkyLight Paths, Jewish Lights' sister imprint)

See also *The Way Into Jewish Mystical Tradition* in The Way Into... Series.

Meditation

The Magic of Hebrew Chant: Healing the Spirit, Transforming the Mind, Deepening Love
By Rabbi Shefa Gold; Foreword by Sylvia Boorstein
Introduces this transformative spiritual practice as a way to unlock the power of sacred texts and make prayer and meditation the delight of your life. Includes musical notations. 6 x 9, 352 pp, Quality PB, 978-1-58023-671-3 **$24.99**

The Magic of Hebrew Chant Companion—The Big Book of Musical Notations and Incantations
8½ x 11, 154 pp, PB, 978-1-58023-722-2 **$19.99**

Jewish Meditation Practices for Everyday Life: Awakening Your Heart, Connecting with God
By Rabbi Jeff Roth
Offers a fresh take on meditation that draws on life experience and living life with greater clarity as opposed to the traditional method of rigorous study.
6 x 9, 224 pp, Quality PB, 978-1-58023-397-2 **$18.99**

Discovering Jewish Meditation, 2nd Edition
Instruction & Guidance for Learning an Ancient Spiritual Practice
By Nan Fink Gefen, PhD 6 x 9, 208 pp, Quality PB, 978-1-58023-462-7 **$16.99**

The Handbook of Jewish Meditation Practices
A Guide for Enriching the Sabbath and Other Days of Your Life
By Rabbi David A. Cooper 6 x 9, 208 pp, Quality PB, 978-1-58023-102-2 **$16.95**

Meditation from the Heart of Judaism
Today's Teachers Share Their Practices, Techniques, and Faith
Edited by Avram Davis 6 x 9, 256 pp, Quality PB, 978-1-58023-049-0 **$18.99**

Ritual / Sacred Practices

God in Your Body: Kabbalah, Mindfulness and Embodied Spiritual Practice
By Jay Michaelson
The first comprehensive treatment of the body in Jewish spiritual practice and an essential guide to the sacred. 6 x 9, 272 pp, Quality PB, 978-1-58023-304-0 **$18.99**

The Book of Jewish Sacred Practices: CLAL's Guide to Everyday & Holiday Rituals & Blessings *Edited by Rabbi Irwin Kula and Vanessa L. Ochs, PhD*
6 x 9, 368 pp, Quality PB, 978-1-58023-152-7 **$18.95**

The Jewish Dream Book: The Key to Opening the Inner Meaning of Your Dreams
By Vanessa L. Ochs, PhD, with Elizabeth Ochs; Illus. by Kristina Swarner
8 x 8, 128 pp, Full-color illus., Deluxe PB w/ flaps, 978-1-58023-132-9 **$16.95**

Jewish Ritual: A Brief Introduction for Christians
By Rabbi Kerry M. Olitzky and Rabbi Daniel Judson
5½ x 8½, 144 pp, Quality PB, 978-1-58023-210-4 **$14.99**

The Rituals & Practices of a Jewish Life: A Handbook for Personal Spiritual Renewal *Edited by Rabbi Kerry M. Olitzky and Rabbi Daniel Judson*
6 x 9, 272 pp, Illus., Quality PB, 978-1-58023-169-5 **$18.95**

The Sacred Art of Lovingkindness: Preparing to Practice
By Rabbi Rami Shapiro 5½ x 8½, 176 pp, Quality PB, 978-1-59473-151-8 **$16.99***

Mystery & Detective Fiction

Criminal Kabbalah: An Intriguing Anthology of Jewish Mystery & Detective Fiction *Edited by Lawrence W. Raphael; Foreword by Laurie R. King*
All-new stories from twelve of today's masters of mystery and detective fiction—sure to delight mystery buffs of all faith traditions.
6 x 9, 256 pp, Quality PB, 978-1-58023-109-1 **$16.95**

Mystery Midrash: An Anthology of Jewish Mystery & Detective Fiction
Edited by Lawrence W. Raphael; Preface by Joel Siegel
6 x 9, 304 pp, Quality PB, 978-1-58023-055-1 **$16.95**

**A book from SkyLight Paths, Jewish Lights' sister imprint*

About Jewish Lights

People of all faiths and backgrounds yearn for books that attract, engage, educate, and spiritually inspire.

Our principal goal is to stimulate thought and help all people learn about who the Jewish People are, where they come from, and what the future can be made to hold. While people of our diverse Jewish heritage are the primary audience, our books speak to people in the Christian world as well and will broaden their understanding of Judaism and the roots of their own faith.

We bring to you authors who are at the forefront of spiritual thought and experience. While each has something different to say, they all say it in a voice that you can hear.

Our books are designed to welcome you and then to engage, stimulate, and inspire. We judge our success not only by whether or not our books are beautiful and commercially successful, but by whether or not they make a difference in your life.

For your information and convenience, at the back of this book we have provided a list of other Jewish Lights books you might find interesting and useful. They cover all the categories of your life:

Bar/Bat Mitzvah	Life Cycle
Bible Study / Midrash	Meditation
Children's Books	Men's Interest
Congregation Resources	Parenting
Current Events / History	Prayer / Ritual / Sacred Practice
Ecology / Environment	Social Justice
Fiction: Mystery, Science Fiction	Spirituality
Grief / Healing	Theology / Philosophy
Holidays / Holy Days	Travel
Inspiration	Twelve Steps
Kabbalah / Mysticism / Enneagram	Women's Interest

Stuart M. Matlins, Publisher

Or phone, fax, mail or email to: **JEWISH LIGHTS Publishing**
Sunset Farm Offices, Route 4 • P.O. Box 237 • Woodstock, Vermont 05091
Tel: (802) 457-4000 • Fax: (802) 457-4004 • www.jewishlights.com
Credit card orders: (800) 962-4544 (8:30AM–5:30PM EST Monday–Friday)
Generous discounts on quantity orders. SATISFACTION GUARANTEED. Prices subject to change.

For more information about each book, visit our website at www.jewishlights.com